Salesforce.com® For Dummies, 3rd Edition

Cheat Sheet

Navigating the Salesforce Home Page

- **Tabs:** Click the tabs to navigate Salesforce. When you click a tab, the tab's home page appears with sections for views, tools, and reports to help you manage your work.

- **AppExchange app menu:** Use the AppExchange app drop-down menu to switch between sets of tabs most used by different types of Salesforce users.

- **Create New drop-down list:** Select an item on the Create New drop-down list to create new records in Salesforce such as accounts, contacts, and opportunities.

- **Recycle Bin:** Click the Recycle Bin link on the sidebar if you've deleted a record(s) in the last thirty days that you want to restore to keep your job.

- **Calendar:** Use the home page calendar to keep track of your schedule in Salesforce. With the calendar view icons, you can jump to different time periods and view the calendars of other users or resources.

- **My Tasks:** Use the My Tasks section to stay up to speed on your to-do items.

- **Search:** Find information fast in Salesforce by entering keywords and clicking Search. A search results page appears with lists of records that matched your search.

- **Recent Items:** Use Recent Items to open records that you recently visited.

- **Messages and Alerts:** View Messages and Alerts for important communications from your Salesforce project team or managers.

- **Custom Links:** Click links in the Custom Links section on the sidebar to quickly access important Web sites or corporate applications.

- **Personal Setup:** Click the Setup link in the top-right corner to go to the Personal Setup page and modify your personal settings. If you're an administrator, use Personal Setup to customize, configure, and administer Salesforce.

- **Help and Training:** If you need help, click the Help and Training link in the top-right corner to see the tips in the following section.

W9-CPE-782

Getting Help Fast

- Contact your system administrator. If you're the administrator, proceed to the next bullet.

- For reinforcement training, click the Help and Training link in the top-right corner, and then click the Training tab in the window that appears.

- For help documentation, click the Help link on most pages of Salesforce page or the Help and Training link to access the help guide.

- For general support, click the Help and Training link, and type in some keywords related to your question into the Search bar. You'll get a list comprised of suggested solutions that include Help topics.

- If all else fails, click the Help and Training link, then click the Support tab. On the Support tab, click the Find Solution button to search the knowledge base or click the Log a Case button to initiate a formal inquiry.

For Dummies: Bestselling Book Series for Beginners

Salesforce.com® For Dummies,® 3rd Edition

Cheat Sheet

Quick Answers on Common Everyday Operations

How do I . . .

- **Track a suspect?** Select the Create New Lead item on the sidebar, fill in the record, and click Save.

- **Track a company?** Select the Create New Account item on the sidebar, complete the record, and click Save.

- **Set up parent/child relationships?** Create records for parent and child accounts. Click the Edit button on a child account and use the Lookup icon next to the Parent Account field to associate the parent. Click Save to reunite the family.

- **Track a person?** Go to an Account detail page where the person is employed, and then select the Create New Contact item on the sidebar. Fill in the record and click Save.

- **Establish org hierarchies?** Create records for contacts of an account. Click the Edit button on a contact record and use the Lookup icon next to the Reports To field to associate the manager. Click Save.

- **Add a deal?** Go to an Account detail page for the related customer, and then select the Create New Opportunity item on the sidebar. Complete the fields including the Stage and Close Date fields, and then click Save.

- **Schedule a meeting?** Click the New Event button on your home page, complete the record, and click Save.

- **Look at my calendar?** From the home page, click the calendar view icons to find your desired view.

- **Set up a to-do?** Go to a related record detail page (such as a contact or account) and select the Create New Task item on the sidebar. Complete the fields and click Save.

- **Log a call?** Go to a related record detail page and click the Log A Call button on the Activity History related list. Complete the fields and click Save.

- **Send an e-mail?** Go to a related record detail page (such as a contact or lead) and click the Send An Email button on the Activity History related list. Complete the fields and click Save.

- **Access sales collateral?** Click the Documents tab and in the Find Documents section, enter keywords to search for sales collateral.

- **Manage a campaign?** If you have campaigns and the proper permissions, click the New Campaign button on the taskbar. Fill in the fields and click Save.

- **Initiate a customer service inquiry?** Go to a related record detail page (such as an account or contact) and select the Create New Case item on the sidebar.

- **Create a reusable focus list?** Click a relevant record tab and click the Create New View link in the corresponding Views section. Complete the settings for the view and click Save.

- **Create a report?** Click the Reports tab and then click the Create New Custom Report button. Follow the steps through the wizard and click the Run Report button when ready.

- **Export a report?** Go to a report and click the Export to Excel button. Follow the steps to export the report.

- **Merge duplicate records?** On a Lead detail page, click the Find Duplicates button. For merging accounts, click the Merge Accounts link in the Tools section on the Accounts home page. For merging contacts, go to an Account detail page and click the Merge Contacts button on the Contacts related list. In each situation, follow the steps in the merge wizard to complete the operation.

- **Transfer a record?** Assuming you have transfer rights, go to a record detail page and click the Change link in brackets next to the Owner field. Complete the fields and click Save.

Salesforce.com®

FOR

DUMMIES®

3RD EDITION

by Tom Wong and Liz Kao

Wiley Publishing, Inc.

Salesforce.com® For Dummies®, 3rd Edition
Published by
Wiley Publishing, Inc.
111 River Street
Hoboken, NJ 07030-5774

www.wiley.com

WILEY

About the Authors

Tom Wong claims he is the number one fan of Salesforce. He keeps a picture of the Web site on his desktop and a Team Edition football in his car. He sends his wife Salesforce meeting invitations. His friends say he can't talk about anything else.

Prior to writing the first edition, Tom was vice president in charge of CRM solutions for Theikos, a leading salesforce.com partner. And before then, he held several senior management positions at Gomez, another satisfied salesforce.com customer. He is a certified salesforce.com partner and has been involved in over thirty implementations impacting thousand of users.

Tom currently works for salesforce.com as Vice President, Dreamforce, where he gets to travel the world to bring together Salesforce customers, partners, employees, and other fans, to learn about the amazing new Saleforce features popping up to help you be successful with your business. He has an amazing and highly patient wife; a son who is a talented drummer; and a daughter aspiring to be a ballerina. They try not to discuss salesforce.com.

Liz Kao was an enthusiastic early adopter of the software-as-service (SaaS) model and has been a Salesforce user since 1999. Through the years, she has played both in-house and consultant roles at salesforce.com.

As a salesforce.com consultant and a member of salesforce.com's Professional Services team, Liz implemented dozens of CRM solutions for companies of all sizes across a variety of industries, including a Salesforce-native purchase requisition system used by salesforce.com's own Global Marketing division. She developed more than a third of the applications created by salesforce.com for the debut of its AppExchange directory, the first online service for sharing on-demand applications. Her insights for new administrators are shared with thousands of visitors to salesforce.com's best practices Web site, successforce.com. She also offers general Salesforce tips on her Kao Consulting site (`http://www.kao consulting.com/salesforcecom-tips/`)

A veteran of the enterprise software industry, Liz lives in San Francisco and has worked at Oracle, NetSuite, and salesforce.com in marketing, product marketing, product management, sales, and professional services. In addition to writing about Salesforce and the AppExchange, she advises non-profits and SaaS startups on a variety of product needs. In her spare time, she searches for undiscovered culinary delights, and enjoys the natural surroundings of the Bay Area.

Dedications

To my wife and family. I asked Lorraine to believe in me, and she has always been there for me. She has been my emotional support throughout the entire process. She, JT, Phoebe, and the rest of the Wong clan have been a constant source of inspiration. Tom

To my friends and family. Without their support, encouragement, sense of humor, late night snacks, and patience in hearing me talk about "the Dummies project", I wouldn't be writing this sentence today. Liz

Authors' Acknowledgments

Thanks to the many individuals that came together to make this third edition a reality. Some people think it's a cinch writing a book, but they're wrong, especially when it comes to writing about an on-demand application. It takes a team of official and unofficial participants, some of whom we'd like to thank below.

First and foremost, thanks to our editors at Wiley: Bob Woerner for being the shining example of one who always see the glass as half full; Pat O'Brien for his quiet fortitude in making this book a reality; Matt Kaufman for his eagle eyes and keeping us on our toes, and Kevin Broccoli for proofing.

We'd be telling a bald-faced lie if we said we could write this without any help from our friends at salesforce.com. Behind the application and the company is a set of incredibly intelligent and dedicated people who have provided us with both knowledge and support prior to and during this book. Elay Cohen, Carolyn Dismuke, Jessica Held, Jane Hynes, Elizabeth Pinkham, Jeanine Thorpe, and Andrea Wildt are just a few of the many individuals who went above and beyond the call of duty to provide additional customer and product insights and help break logjams along the way.

Finally, we'd like to thank our various friends for their feedback and support this third time around. Your willing ear, sense of humor, and overall wit inspired our occasional forays into standup comedy in the book. VP, VC, TBJ, MK, and salesforce.com friends and alumni (you know who you are) thanks for keeping the spirit alive. High fives all around to the Krafts, Finellis, and "friends of Gomez" as always.

Publisher's Acknowledgments

We're proud of this book; please send us your comments through our online registration form located at `www.dummies.com/register/`.

Some of the people who helped bring this book to market include the following:

Acquisitions, Editorial, and Media Development

Project Editor: Pat O'Brien

Acquisitions Editor: Bob Woerner

Copy Editor: Laura K. Miller

Technical Reviewer: Matt Kaufman
`www.mkpartners.com`

Editorial Manager: Kevin Kirschner

Media Development Manager:
Laura VanWinkle

Editorial Assistant: Amanda Foxworth

Sr. Editorial Assistant: Cherie Case

Cartoons: Rich Tennant
(`www.the5thwave.com`)

Composition Services

Project Coordinator: Katherine Key

Layout and Graphics: Stacie Brooks, Reuben W. Davis, Melissa K. Jester, Tobin Wilkerson, Christine Williams

Proofreaders: Melissa Bronnenberg, John Greenough, Christine Sabooni

Indexer: Potomac Indexing, LLC

Publishing and Editorial for Technology Dummies

Richard Swadley, Vice President and Executive Group Publisher

Andy Cummings, Vice President and Publisher

Mary Bednarek, Executive Acquisitions Director

Mary C. Corder, Editorial Director

Publishing for Consumer Dummies

Diane Graves Steele, Vice President and Publisher

Joyce Pepple, Acquisitions Director

Composition Services

Gerry Fahey, Vice President of Production Services

Debbie Stailey, Director of Composition Services

Contents at a Glance

Table of Contents

Introduction

This book is for users of Salesforce, including those users who have Unlimited, Enterprise, Professional, Team, or Personal Edition. It's for Salesforce users who want to quickly know how to use this browser-based software-as-a-service (SaaS). Don't look in this book to find out how Salesforce works. Use this book to find out how you can manage your customers and your teams and close more business by using Salesforce.

- ✔ **If you're a sales rep,** this book can help you use Salesforce to manage your leads, accounts, contacts, and opportunities. Spend less time doing administrative work and more time focused on making money.

- ✔ **If you're a sales manager,** find out how to use Salesforce to track team activities, shorten the ramp-up time on new hires, and pinpoint key deals that require your involvement.

- ✔ **If you're in channel sales,** we teach you how to track your relationships with companies that are or will be your partners, and all the deals they work for you.

- ✔ **If you're a partner**, we show you the world of Salesforce and how you can improve your deal pipeline and win rate with your vendor.

- ✔ **If you're in marketing,** you learn how to use Salesforce to make an imm-ediate and measurable impact on your sales organization. We cover how to manage campaigns, track leads, measure return on investment (ROI), and create some Internet marketing campaigns with Google AdWords, too.

- ✔ **If you're in customer service,** we show you how to manage customer issues, from creation to resolution. Support managers will learn how to improve team productivity and customer self-sufficiency.

- ✔ **If you sit on the executive team,** this book shows you how to use Salesforce to measure your overall business.

- ✔ **If you're an administrator or involved in your company's customer relationship management (CRM) initiative,** this book gives you practical knowledge for customizing, configuring, maintaining, and successfully implementing your solution. To start, we suggest you flip through the sales, marketing, and support chapters in Parts II, III, and IV to understand how Salesforce is commonly used by end users. Then use that to guide you in administering Salesforce in Parts V and VI.

Although this book applies to users of all Salesforce editions, be aware that not all portions of this book necessarily apply to your edition. Different editions have varying degrees of feature and functionality. We make sure to point this out where it's relevant.

Updates to the Third Edition

The third edition of this book has been revised to reflect Salesforce.com's latest product and feature offerings as of the Summer '08 release. Salesforce is an Internet-based service where new releases occur simultaneously for all customers, without your having to lift a finger (ok, except to just log in). Because of this model, salesforce.com can more quickly release several versions of its product than many traditional software vendors . . . and us! We've done our best to update this book to the current version of the product, but please bear in mind that new versions of Salesforce are always in the works.

References to the product use the word "Salesforce," while references to the company that makes the family of products, or the family of products as a whole, use the phrase "salesforce.com." That's a little detail but we didn't want you to think our eagle eyes had glossed over that.

Here's a bare outline of the parts of this book:

✔ **Part I: Salesforce Basics** — Part I gives you the big picture on Salesforce. We show you the best ways to navigate the system, where to go for help, and how to personalize Salesforce.

✔ **Part II: Tracking Sales** — Part II shows you how to use Salesforce for the most common facets of your sales process. We explain how you can use Salesforce for managing your existing business relationships, as well as those with key prospects.

✔ **Part III: Driving Sales** — Part III shows sales organizations how to use Salesforce to track sales, from lead to close, and everything in between. We also discuss specifying which products you're selling in a deal, and applying price books to address more complex sales models. We also explain how channel reps, channel managers, and partners can use Salesforce to work together to bring in more channel revenue.

✔ **Part IV: Optimizing Marketing** — If you're in marketing, Part IV is your friend. Marketing in Salesforce and your business is much more than campaign management. You discover how to use Salesforce with Google AdWords to manage your Internet marketing campaigns, and we also discuss how to control your sales collateral.

✔ **Part V: Delivering Excellent Customer Service** — Part V shows customer service agents and managers how to use Salesforce Service & Support to more efficiently manage the customer issue lifecycle. Agents learn how to create, track, and resolve cases in Salesforce. Customer service managers will learn ways to increase their team's efficiencies by increasing the quality of service while decreasing case resolution time.

✔ **Part VI: Measuring Overall Business Performance** — Part VI shows every rep, manager, and senior executive how to use Salesforce to measure and analyze their business. This book doesn't tell you how to improve your business (that's largely up to you), but Part VI helps you place the data at your fingertips.

✔ **Part VII: Designing the Salesforce Solution** — Salesforce is great out of the box, but you can get more out of it when you customize it to meet your corporate objectives. Part VII is for system administrators and the CRM project team. You get to know the important steps for configuring, customizing, and maintaining your system. We also discuss custom objects and the AppExchange.

✔ **Part VIII: The Part of Tens** — In Part VIII, you get lists that are guaranteed to catch your attention. Here, we show you the best resources for finding information after becoming *Salesforce.com For Dummies* graduates. Plus we review the best-but-sometimes-overlooked productivity tools. We also summarize some best practices for successfully implementing Salesforce.

We show you everything you need to know to manage the lifecycle of your customer relationships in Salesforce from qualifying leads to closing opportunities to handling customer service inquiries. Even the channel sales team and partners can join the party. Along the way, you have a laugh or two. And this book can expose you to useful features and functionality that you might not have even known existed.

How to Use This Book

This book is divided into parts and then chapters based loosely on three widely accepted pillars of customer relationship management: sales, marketing, and customer service. We've organized the sections based on your function in the company and what you might want to know about Salesforce based on your role.

You can choose to read this book from front to back (although there's no surprise ending in the last chapter). Or, you can use this book as a reference, similar to other *For Dummies* books. You can go to any topic in this book and know what to do with minimal leafing to other sections.

You can get the most out of this book if you're using it while you're logged in to Salesforce (and sitting on your favorite chair). The best way to know what to do, in my experience, is by doing it, and for that you need the salesforce.com Web site open, revved, and raring to go.

In this book, we provide you the easiest or best way to perform a task in Salesforce. Like other easy-to-use applications, the method shown might not be the only way, and sometimes you might find another method that works better for you. That's okay, we promise it won't hurt our feelings.

Foolish Assumptions

Please forgive us, but we make one or two foolish assumptions about you, the reader. We assume these things:

- ✔ You have access to an Internet connection and you've used a browser before. If we've assumed incorrectly, you have much more pressing problems than understanding the effective use of Salesforce.

- ✔ You have a Salesforce account and some interest in knowing how to use it beyond the mere curiosity of reading our riveting prose.

- ✔ You have some business experience — at least enough to understand that winning deals is good and losing deals is bad.

- ✔ You have at least a vague idea of what a database is, including basic concepts such as fields, records, files, and folders.

Icons Used in This Book

To help you get the most out of this book, we place icons here and there that highlight important points. Here's what the icons mean:

Next to the Tip icon, you can find shortcuts, tricks, and best practices to use Salesforce more effectively or productively.

Pay extra attention where you see a Warning icon. It means that you might be about to do something that you'll regret later.

When we explain a juicy little fact that bears remembering, we mark it with a Remember icon. When you see this icon, prick up your ears. You can pick up something that could be of wide or frequent use as you work with Salesforce.

When we're forced to describe something geeky, a Technical Stuff icon appears in the margin. You don't have to read what's beside this icon if you don't want to, although some readers might find the technical detail helpful.

Part I
Salesforce Basics

The 5th Wave   By Rich Tennant

In this part . . .

Salesforce is a customer relationship management (CRM) system, but it's different from just about any other software solution you've ever used. Maybe that's because unlike traditional software, Salesforce is an Internet-based service that requires no software installation on your part; you simply log in as you would any other secure Web site, and you and your company can begin managing your partners and customers.

But that's an oversimplification. Salesforce is different from most other CRM systems. By placing the technology burden on itself, Salesforce allows you to concentrate directly on your business challenges. Its navigation is so simple that you'll actually enjoy using it. Salesforce focuses squarely on you, the user, so you can personalize your CRM system to suit your individual habits and preferences.

In this part, you find details and tips on each of these critical promises. We discuss high-level features of Salesforce and how those features can be applied to typical business challenges. You discover just how easily you can navigate Salesforce and how to personalize Salesforce to manage your business.

Chapter 1

Looking Over Salesforce

In This Chapter

▶ Solving business challenges

▶ Extending the value of what you have

▶ Deciding what Salesforce size fits you

*Y*ou might not realize it yet, but every time you log in to Salesforce, you're accessing an extremely powerful lever of change for you, your group, and your company.

Sounds like a tall order, but consider this: What value do you put on your customer relationships? Your partner relationships? If you're a sales rep, it's your livelihood. And if you're in management, you have fewer assets more valuable than your existing partner and customer base. What if you had a tool that could truly help you manage your partners and customers?

Salesforce isn't the first customer relationship management (CRM) system to hit the market, but it's dramatically different than the other CRM systems you might have used (spreadsheets and sticky notes count as a system, too!). Unlike traditional CRM software, Salesforce is an Internet service. You sign up and log in through a browser, and it's immediately available. Salesforce customers typically say that it's unique for three major reasons:

- ✔ **Fast:** When you sign on the dotted line, you want your CRM system up yesterday. Traditional CRM software can take more than a year to deploy; compare that to months or even weeks with Salesforce.

- ✔ **Easy:** End user adoption is critical to any application, and Salesforce wins the ease-of-use category hands down. You can spend more time putting it to use and less time figuring it out.

- ✔ **Effective:** Because it's easy to use and can be customized quickly to meet business needs, customers have proven that it has improved their bottom lines.

With Salesforce, you now have a full suite of services to manage the customer lifecycle. These services include tools to pursue leads, manage accounts, track opportunities, resolve cases, and more. Depending on your team's objectives, you might use all Salesforce's tools from day one, or you might focus on just the functionality to address the priorities at hand.

The more you and your team adopt Salesforce into your work, the more information you have at your fingertips to deepen customer relationships and improve your overall business.

In this chapter, we reveal the many great things that you can do with Salesforce. Then we describe how you can extend Salesforce to work with many of the common applications that you already use. Finally, we help you decide which Salesforce edition is right for you, just in case you're still evaluating your options.

Using Salesforce to Solve Critical Business Challenges

We could write another book telling you all the great things you can do with Salesforce, but you can get the big picture from this chapter. We focus here on the most common business challenges that we hear from sales, marketing, and support executives — and how Salesforce can overcome them.

Understanding your customer

How can you sell to and retain customers if you don't understand their needs, people, and what account activities and transactions have taken place? With Salesforce, you can track all your important customer data in one place so that you can develop solutions that deliver real value to your customers.

Centralizing contacts under one roof

How much time have you ever wasted tracking down a customer contact or an address that you know exists within the walls of your company? With Salesforce, you can quickly centralize and organize your accounts and contacts so that you can capitalize on that information when you need to.

Expanding the funnel

Inputs and outputs, right? The more leads you generate and pursue, the greater the chance that your revenue will grow. So the big question is, "How do I make the machine work?" With Salesforce, you can plan, manage, measure, and improve lead generation, qualification, and conversion. You can see how much business you or your team generates, the sources of that business, and who in your team is making it happen.

Consolidating your pipeline

Pipeline reports give companies insight into future sales. Yet we've worked with companies in which generating the weekly pipeline could take a day of cat herding and guesswork. Reps waste time updating spreadsheets. Managers waste time chasing reps and scrubbing data. Bosses waste time tearing their hair out because the information is old by the time they get it. With Salesforce, you can shorten or eliminate all that. As long as reps manage all their opportunities in Salesforce, managers can generate updated pipeline reports with the click of a button.

Working as a team

How many times have you thought that your own co-workers got in the way of selling? Nine out of ten times, the challenge isn't people, but standardizing processes and clarifying roles and responsibilities. With Salesforce, you can define teams and processes for sales, marketing, and customer service, so the left hand knows what the right hand is doing. Although Salesforce doesn't solve corporate alignment issues, you now have the tool that can drive and manage better team collaboration.

Collaborating with your partners

In many industries, selling directly is a thing of the past. To gain leverage and cover more territory, many companies work through partners. By using Salesforce, your channel reps can track and associate partners' deals and get better insight on who their top partners are. Partners now can strengthen their relationships with their vendors by getting more visibility into their joint sales and marketing efforts.

Beating the competition

How much money have you lost to competitors? How many times did you lose a deal only to discover, after the fact, that it went to your arch nemesis? If you know who you're up against, you can probably better position yourself to win the opportunity. With Salesforce, you and your teams can track competition on deals, collect competitive intelligence, and develop action plans to wear down your foes.

Improving customer service

As a sales person, have you ever walked into a customer's office expecting a renewal only to be hit with a landmine because of an unresolved customer issue? And if you work in customer support, how much time do you waste on trying to identify the customers and their entitlements? With Salesforce, you can efficiently capture, manage, and resolve customer issues. By managing cases in Salesforce, sales reps get visibility into the health of their accounts, and service can stay well informed of sales and account activity.

Accessing anytime, anywhere

Companies are more mobile than ever before. People work from home or on the road. Offices are spread out. You expect to get access to information from multiple devices, easily and reliably. With Salesforce, you can access and manage your critical customer information, at 3 p.m. or 3 a.m., online or offline, in multiple languages, and from multiple devices.

Measuring the business

How can you improve what you can't measure? Simple, huh? — and yet how many companies have you worked for that couldn't accurately or reliably measure the business? If you use Salesforce correctly and regularly to manage customers, you have data to make informed decisions. That benefits everyone. If you're a rep, you know what you need to do to get the rewards you want. If you're a manager, you can pinpoint where to get involved to drive your numbers. And Salesforce's reporting and dashboards give you easy-to-use tools to measure and analyze your business.

Extending the Value Chain

Salesforce.com understands that most companies already rely on existing tools for parts of their businesses. Such tools might include your e-mail, Office tools, your public Web site, and your intranet. Salesforce.com isn't naïve enough to think people will stop using these tools. In fact, you can readily integrate Salesforce with many of the tools you use today to interact with your customers.

Synchronizing with Outlook

If you work for a company, you probably use Microsoft Outlook every day for common tasks, such as sending e-mails, maintaining your address book, managing your calendar, and jotting down your to-do list. With the latest version of Connect for Microsoft Outlook, you can easily capture this information on your Salesforce records (including cases) and synchronize your addresses, contacts, calendar, and to-do list bi-directionally at your discretion.

You don't need to archive every e-mail you send or receive, or every appointment you make, in Salesforce, but you might want to track the important customer ones. By noting the relevant milestones, you and your team can stay up-to-date on e-mail discussions and related activities.

If you use Lotus Notes, you have an e-mail synchronization solution, too. Like Connect for Outlook, Connect for Lotus Notes allows you to work more efficiently within Salesforce and your e-mail system.

Integrating with your Web site

For many companies, the public Web site is a primary way to communicate information to their customers. You might use your Web site as a channel for visitors to request information or log customer service issues. When you use Salesforce, you can capture leads and cases directly from your Web site, route them directly into Salesforce, and assign them to the right reps. And Salesforce's assignment rules can make sure that incoming leads or cases get to the right reps in a timely manner. With minimal effort, you can even offer self-service options in the form of a public knowledge base or a private portal, enabling customers to help themselves.

Connecting to other Web sites

As part of your job, you might regularly use Web sites for tasks such as researching potential customers, getting driving directions, and getting the inside scoop on your competition. With the help of your system administrator, your company can build custom links in Salesforce that can connect you directly with the relevant pages of important sites. Accessing your intranet, populating a Web form to provision a demo, creating and propagating a Salesforce record — all these tasks are within reach. And all this means time saved for you.

Integrating with other applications

Your company might have other applications that contain critical customer data — financial and enterprise resource planning (ERP) applications are just a few examples. Many applications provide unique and indispensable value to your organization. Your company isn't going to retire them just because you're using Salesforce. But, based on company objectives, those applications might need to integrate with Salesforce. Because of Salesforce's open architecture, your company can integrate applications if you have the right technical assistance.

Managing other business processes

When you log in to Salesforce, you see several tabs, grouped into tabsets called *apps*. Salesforce.com prioritized the development of each of those tabs based on core CRM functions. But, depending on your business needs, you might require apps that have different functionality for teams that may or may not have anything related to sales, marketing, or service and support. Submitting expenses and requesting vacation time are just a few examples of what any employee might need. With salesforce.com's Force.com platform, your company can now easily build or download these custom apps to fit your specific business needs. A company can now use Salesforce for more than CRM and ultimately manage a significant, if not complete, portion of its business online.

Deciding Which Edition Is Best for You

If you already use Salesforce, this topic might be a moot point. At the very least, you know which version of Salesforce you have.

Salesforce.com has five versions of its service. All versions have the same consistent look and feel, but each varies by feature, functionality, and pricing (if you're considering using Salesforce, consult with an account executive for more details about edition differences, pricing, and upgrade paths):

- **Personal Edition:** Basic account, contact, and opportunity management for one person.

- **Group Edition:** Basic CRM for teams of up to five users.

- **Professional Edition:** Thorough CRM for any size organization that's starting to nail down processes. Some optional features come at extra cost.

- **Enterprise Edition:** More functionality for more complex organizations. This edition provides more value than if you pay extra for certain features in more basic editions.

- **Unlimited Edition:** A lot more customization capabilities for extending Salesforce to other business uses. You need a dedicated (and usually technical) administrator to take advantage of all the options that this edition delivers.

Professional or Enterprise Edition?

Most companies tend to make a decision between Professional and Enterprise Edition. Budget might be an issue, but the decision usually boils down to core business needs. Consider these questions.

Does your company . . .

- Have different groups with distinct sales processes, customers, and products?

- Sell multiple products and need visibility into them?

- Need scheduling on opportunities to estimate revenue recognition?

- Plan to integrate Salesforce with other applications?

- Require complex data migration into Salesforce?

- Need greater control over user profiles and their permissions?

- Sell in defined teams with specific roles?

- Require workflow to further automate processes?

If the answer to any of these questions is a definitive "Yes," your company should probably evaluate Enterprise Edition. The extent of your company's needs in the preceding list determines whether Unlimited Edition is the optimal choice. Be sure to prioritize what you need today and figure out what can wait.

Whichever edition you choose, the good news is that every edition of Salesforce is rich with features that can help companies of every size address their business challenges. You can choose a more basic edition today and upgrade later, as needed. Because Salesforce is an Internet-based service, upgrading is handled immediately and behind the scenes, so you can focus on the business processes that drive the need for new functionality. And when salesforce.com rolls out new releases of its service, it provides product enhancements for the different editions wherever relevant.

Chapter 2

Navigating Salesforce

. . . .

. . . .

*I*f an application isn't easy to use, you won't use it. Period. Salesforce succeeds not only because it offers a universe of integrated tools, but also because users can pick it up within minutes. You navigate it much the same way you do other Web sites: by pointing and clicking over text links and buttons.

Still, you have so many ways to navigate Salesforce that it makes sense to lay down the obvious (and not-so-obvious) best practices for getting around the application.

Even if you're familiar with Salesforce, you might want to skim this chapter because we cover terms that we use repeatedly throughout this book.

In this chapter, you can find out how to log in to the Salesforce site and use the home page to manage your activities, create records, and jump to other tabs. We briefly review the major tabs and how to use the interior home pages, list pages, detail pages, and related lists. Finally, we cover where you can go for help.

Getting Familiar with Basic Terms

Before we delve into the mechanics of navigating Salesforce, familiarize yourself with these basic terms:

✔ **Salesforce:** When we use the term Salesforce, we mean the secure Web site that your users log in to that contains your customer information. Salesforce.com, Inc., offers a family of products and has thousands of clients who use its service, but each company's secure Web site is separate from the other Web sites and might look different to suit that company's unique needs.

✔ **Home page:** The main page that appears when you log in to Salesforce or click the Home tab.

✔ **Tabs:** Clickable tabs appear at the top of any Salesforce page. Each tab represents a major module in which your company needs to know some information. By clicking a tab, you go to a tab-specific home page. For example, if you click the Accounts tab, the Accounts home page appears.

✔ **Apps:** Apps are tabs that have been grouped together and given a name, so certain users get the convenience of seeing only those tabs most relevant to them.

✔ **Tab home pages:** Where you go to find, organize, and manage specific information related to a particular tab. For example, to access your opportunity records, you could go to the Opportunities home page.

✔ **Record:** A bunch of fields that hold information to describe a specific item. For example, a contact record typically contains fields pertinent to a person, including name, title, phone number, and e-mail address. A record is displayed on a detail page.

✔ **Detail page:** A Web page that shows both the saved record and a set of related lists pertinent to the record.

We often use the terms *record* and *detail page* interchangeably. From a detail page, you can perform and track a variety of tasks related to the specific record. For example, if you have and are looking at an Account detail page for Cisco, you see fields about the company and lists of other records related to Cisco.

✔ **Related lists:** Lists of other records linked to the record that you're looking at. For example, the Account detail page for Cisco might display related lists of contacts, opportunities, activities, and so on associated with that company.

✔ **Sidebar:** The left margin of a Salesforce page. The sidebar displays a search tool, recent items, and a drop-down list that you can use to create new records.

Accessing Salesforce

You need to log in to your account to access your company's instance of Salesforce, because every company's Salesforce Web site is different, and salesforce.com goes to great lengths to protect your information.

Setting up a password

The first time you log in to the Salesforce service, you receive an e-mail entitled "Salesforce password confirmation." To log in the first time and reset your password, follow these steps:

1. **Open the e-mail and click the first link, which contains both your user name and temporary password.**

   A page appears, prompting you to set a new password, and select and answer a question that can verify your identity if you forget your password.

2. **Complete the fields.**

   Use this password from now on unless your administrator resets the passwords.

3. **When you're done, click Save.**

   The home page of Salesforce appears.

Logging in

You log in to Salesforce just as you would any other secure Web site.

To log in, open a browser and follow these steps:

1. **In your browser's address bar, type** www.salesforce.com **and press Enter.**

   The salesforce.com public Web site appears.

2. **Click the Customer Login tab highlighted in black.**

   The login page appears.

3. **Enter your user name and password, then click the Login button, as shown in Figure 2-1.**

   Your user name is typically your corporate e-mail address. Select the Remember User Name check box if you want your computer to remember it. After you click the Login button, your main home page appears.

To save yourself steps when logging in, use your browser tools to bookmark the login page.

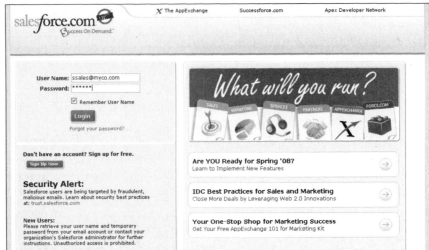

Figure 2-1:
Logging in to
Salesforce.

Navigating the Home Page

Every time you log in to Salesforce, you begin at your home page. The look and feel of the elements on your home page are similar to other users' home pages, but the tasks and events that appear in the body of the page are specific to you.

Use the home page to manage your calendar and tasks, jump to other areas by clicking tabs, or search and access specific information by using the sidebar. If your company uses the customizable home page feature, you might also see key charts or graphs from your company's dashboards. (*Dashboards* are visual snapshots of key performance metrics based on your custom report data.)

Managing your calendar

The calendar section of the home page defaults to a calendar of the current month and your scheduled events for the next seven days. Like other calendar tools, the calendar allows you to drill down. Your scheduled events are based on events that you or other users have assigned to you.

From this calendar section (shown in Figure 2-2), you can do the following:

Figure 2-2:
Looking
over your
calendar
options.

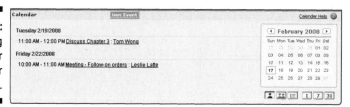

✔ Click the New Event button if you want to schedule a new activity. A New Event page appears in Edit mode.

✔ If you see a listed event, click the link to view the event record. A page appears with details on the activity.

✔ Click a date link on the calendar to drill into your schedule for a specific day. The Day View page appears.

✔ Click one of the six calendar icons (as shown below the calendar in Figure 2-2) to manage your calendar by Day, Week, Month, Single User (selected by default), Multi User, or Activity List View.

✔ If you want to schedule a group activity, click the Multi User View icon (which looks like two little people). A page appears for the selected day that displays the availability of multiple users.

To view other user or public calendars, click the Day, Week, or Month View calendar icon, and then click the Change link in brackets at the top of the view. In the pop-up window that appears, you can choose from the options to see another calendar.

Tracking your tasks

On the home page, you see a section entitled My Tasks, which displays tasks that you've created for yourself or that have been assigned to you. The My Tasks section also appears on the Day View and Week View of the calendar.

A *task* is an activity that you need to do, and it can have a due date. But — unlike an event — a task doesn't have a specific time and duration. For example, if you want to remind yourself to send a proposal, you typically create a task, instead of scheduling an event. (See Chapter 6 if you want additional tips on managing tasks.)

From the My Tasks section (as shown in Figure 2-3), you can do the following:

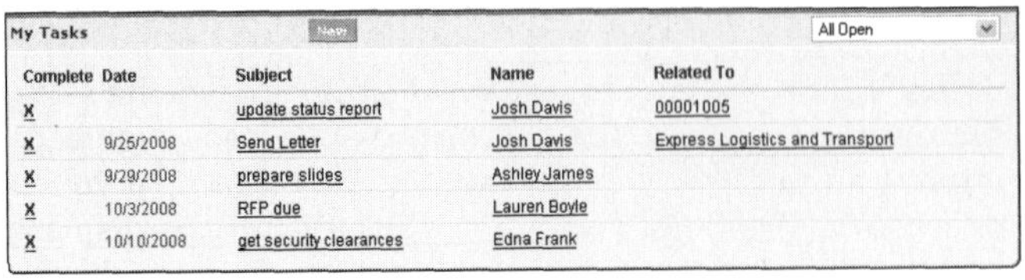

Figure 2-3:
Reviewing
the My
Tasks sec-
tion from the
home page.

My Tasks		New			All Open ▼
Complete	**Date**	**Subject**		**Name**	**Related To**
X		update status report		Josh Davis	00001005
X	9/25/2008	Send Letter		Josh Davis	Express Logistics and Transport
X	9/29/2008	prepare slides		Ashley James	
X	10/3/2008	RFP due		Lauren Boyle	
X	10/10/2008	get security clearances		Edna Frank	

✔ Click the New button if you want to add a new task. A New Task page appears in Edit mode.

✔ Use the drop-down list at the top of the My Tasks section to select from a list of common task views. For example, select Overdue if you want to see your open tasks that are past their respective due dates.

✔ Click a link in the Subject column to review a task. A task record appears with details.

✔ Click links in the Name or Related To columns to go to associated records.

✔ Click an X link in the Complete column to complete the task and enter any details before saving. (You can also use this link to update a task, but if you haven't completed the task, remember to adjust the Status field before you save it.)

✔ If you have several tasks in your list, the View More link appears at the bottom of the My Tasks section on the home page. Click it to see more tasks on the list. The Day View appears, and the My Tasks section appears in the right column.

Using dashboard snapshots from the home page

If your company has customized your home page, you might also see and select up to three key charts and tables from your dashboards. *Dashboards* display important information from reports in Salesforce that can provide key performance indicators on the health of your business. Each dashboard chart or table is called a *component*. See Chapter 18 for details on building dashboards that can measure and analyze your business. Dashboards are currently available in the Professional, Enterprise, and Unlimited Editions.

If you see a chart or table on your home page, you can also perform these actions from the Dashboard section:

✔ Click a chart or table to drill into the detail. A report page appears with the data that supports the graphic.

✔ Click the Customize Page button at the top-right of the section to choose a different dashboard. The Customize Your Home Page page appears, and here you can select from available dashboards, if you have the proper administrator permissions. Your home page displays a snapshot of only the three components along the top of any dashboard.

✔ Click the Refresh button in the top of the section to refresh the dashboard snapshot. In the left of the section, a date and timestamp of when your dashboard was last refreshed appears.

Accessing information with the sidebar

The sidebar is the column on the left that appears on just about every page of Salesforce, except dashboards and reports. On the home page, use the sidebar to search for records, quickly go back to pages you recently clicked, stay informed about important company messages or Web sites, and create new records.

Finding items with Search

You can find a majority of the information that you want by using Search. Depending on your company's sharing rules, your results might vary. To search for information, follow these steps:

1. **In the sidebar, enter keywords into the Search field and click the Go! button.**

   A Search Results page appears, as shown in Figure 2-4. Salesforce organizes the search results in lists according to the major types of records, including accounts, contacts, opportunities, and leads.

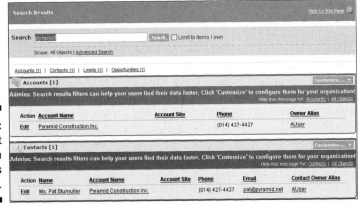

Figure 2-4: Looking at a Search Results page.

2. **Scroll down the page and, if you find a record that you want to look at, click a link in the Name column for that record grouping.**

   The detail page appears, allowing you to review the record and its related lists.

3. **If you don't find what you want, click the Advanced Search link on the Search Results page.**

   The Advanced Search page appears.

   If you're focusing on a page (such as a list of search results or a report) but need to jump to a record, instead of clicking the Advanced Search link, right-click that link and choose Open Link in New Window from the pop-up menu that appears. This approach can save you a lot of time.

Creating new records

Use the compact Create New picklist on the sidebar to go to one place where you can quickly create any new record.

Revisiting recent items

The Recent Items section displays up to ten records that you most recently clicked. Use the list to quickly get back to records that you've been working on, even if you logged out and logged back in. The recent items show an icon and the name or number of the record. These items include mostly the records that are organized under a tab heading, such as Accounts, Contacts, and so on. To visit the detail record of a recent item, simply click a listed link.

Getting more out of your home page sidebar

With the help of your administrator, you can offer other tools and information from the sidebar on the home page to improve productivity and drive overall adoption. Review the following tips, see Chapter 21 on customizing Salesforce, and consult with your administrator if some of these features could help your organization:

- **Add new search tools.** The Search and Advanced Search tools can't find product, document, and solution records in Salesforce. Your company can customize home page layouts with any or all of these specific search tools. Depending on your profile, some or all of these tools might help you do your job better. For example, if you're in customer service, you might need a search tool on your home page to help you quickly search for solutions to common inquiries.

- **Update company messages.** Your administrator can add messages to the home page to keep users informed of important announcements. For example, if you're in sales management, you might want to use the home page to alert reps to end-of-quarter goals or bonus incentives.

✔ **Emphasize important custom links.** If you rely on other Web sites to do your jobs, your administrator can help you post them for all your users or just ones that fit certain profiles. For example, if you have a company intranet, your company can add useful links to the home page sidebar so that you can quickly access information outside of Salesforce without ever leaving Salesforce.

If you'd rather not have the sidebar take up some of your browser window's real estate, Salesforce allows you to hide and expand the sidebar when you want. Your administrator can set up this option for users by going to Setup⇨ App Setup⇨User Interface and checking the Enable Collapsible Sidebar box.

Navigating the Apps

Salesforce.com allows you to organize tabs into groups. These groups, also known as *apps,* help reduce screen clutter and give different types of users quicker access to the tabs that they use the most. For example, a marketing manager may rarely use the Cases or Solutions tabs, but spend most of her time looking at Campaigns and Leads.

With salesforce.com's Force.com platform, companies can now create their own custom apps for more specific uses within CRM — or for anything else, for that matter. Sales reps can use an expense reporting app, and product managers can use a product release app to manage their product requirements. The mind-blowing part of all this is that apps can be comprised of standard tabs or *ones that don't even exist yet.* Anyone in your company can benefit from sharing one set of data. And don't worry if you're not the most creative type. Salesforce.com has a bunch of prebuilt apps available (for free or an additional charge), which we discuss in more detail in Chapter 22.

Discovering the AppExchange app menu

In the upper-right corner of any Salesforce page, you can find the AppExchange app menu (see Figure 2-5). The picklist allows you to switch between apps. You find some standard tab groupings, such as Sales and Call Center. Administrators can also add or create new apps to address what their specific users need to see. Don't worry if you choose an app and see new tabs. You can always go back to the picklist, select your previous app, and have your familiar tabs return.

Finding out about the tabs

If the tabs in Salesforce look strangely familiar, they should. When the founders of salesforce.com designed it, they patterned the site after popular Web sites such as Amazon, where you click a tab to jump to an area.

In this section, we describe the major tabs in Salesforce and how to use the tab home pages to quickly access, manage, or organize information.

Each of the tabs within Salesforce represents a major module or data element in an interconnected database. That's as technical as we get.

Figure 2-5:
Choosing apps by using the App Exchange app menu.

In the following list, we briefly describe each of the standard tabs (as shown in Figure 2-6). We devote a chapter to each of the tabs mentioned here:

Figure 2-6:
Navigating through the tabs.

- ✔ **Leads:** *Suspects* (that is, people and companies with whom you want to do business). But don't start grilling your lead about where she was on the morning of June 23 because the only clue you'll gather is the sound of a dial tone.

- ✔ **Accounts:** Companies with whom you do business. You can track all types of accounts, including customers, prospects, partners, and competitors.

- ✔ **Contacts:** Individuals associated with your accounts.

- ✔ **Opportunities:** The deals that you pursue to drive revenue for your company. Your open opportunities constitute your pipeline, and opportunities can contribute to your forecast.

✔ **Cases:** Customer inquiries that your support teams work to manage and resolve.

✔ **Solutions:** Answers to cases and other frequently asked questions.

✔ **Documents:** The sales and marketing collateral and documents that you use as part of your selling or service processes.

✔ **Reports:** Data analyses for you and your entire organization. Salesforce provides a variety of best practices reports, and you can build custom reports on the fly to better measure your business.

✔ **Dashboards:** Graphs, charts, and tables based on your custom reports. You can use dashboards to visually measure and analyze key elements of your business.

✔ **Products:** Your company's products and services, associated with the prices for which you offer them. You can link products and their prices to your opportunities.

✔ **Campaigns:** Specific marketing activities that you manage to drive leads, build a brand, or stimulate demand.

Discovering a tab home page

When you click a tab, the tab's interior home page appears. For example, if you click the Accounts tab, the Accounts home page appears. The tab's home page is where you can view, organize, track, and maintain all the records within that tab.

Do this right now: Click every tab visible to you.

The look and feel of the interior home pages never change, regardless of which tab you click (except for the Home, Reports, and Dashboards tabs). On the left, you have the sidebar with Search, the Create picklist, Recent Items, and (depending on your company and the tab) a Quick Create tool. In the body of the page, you have a Views menu, a Recent Items section, and sections for popular Reports and Tools (see Figure 2-7).

Using the Views menu

Strategy and execution are all about focus. With views, you can see and use lists to better focus on your business. A *view* is a segment of the tab's records based on defined criteria. When you select a view, a list of records appears based on your criteria.

On each tab, Salesforce provides a selection of popular default views to get you started. To try a view (using Accounts as the example), follow these steps (which apply to all tabs):

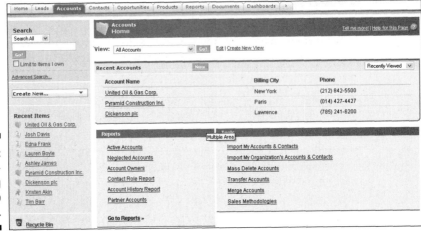

Figure 2-7:
Decon-
structing
the tab
home page.

1. **Click the Accounts tab.**

   The Accounts home page appears.

2. **Select My Accounts from the Account Views drop-down list.**

   A list page appears that displays a set of columns representing certain standard account fields and a list of your account records. If no account records appear, you currently don't own any in Salesforce.

3. **From the list page, you can perform a variety of functions:**

   • Click a column header if you want to re-sort the list, as shown in Figure 2-8. For example, if you click the Account Name header, the list sorts alphabetically.

Action	Account Name	Account Site	Billing State/Province	Phone	Type	Owner Alias
Edit | Del	Burlington Textiles Corp of America		NC	(336) 222-7000	Customer - Direct	AUser
Edit | Del	Dickenson plc		KS	(785) 241-6200	Customer - Channel	AUser
Edit | Del	Edge Communications		TX	(512) 757-6000	Customer - Direct	AUser
Edit | Del	Express Logistics and Transport		OR	(503) 421-7800	Customer - Channel	AUser
Edit | Del	GenePoint		CA	(650) 867-3450	Customer - Channel	AUser
Edit | Del	Grand Hotels & Resorts Ltd		IL	(312) 596-1000	Customer - Direct	AUser
Edit | Del	Pyramid Construction Inc.			(014) 427-4427	Customer - Channel	AUser
Edit | Del	sForce		CA	(415) 901-7000		AUser
Edit | Del	United Oil & Gas Corp.		NY	(212) 842-5500	Customer - Direct	AUser

Figure 2-8:
Re-sorting
a list.

- Click a letter link above the list to view records beginning with that letter.

- If you have a long list, click the up or down button at the bottom of the page to display fewer or more records on the page, or click the Next Page link to see the next set of records.

- To view a specific record, click the link for that record in the Account Name column. The Account detail page appears, displaying the record and its related lists.

- To update a specific record, click the Edit link at the beginning of its row. The account record appears in Edit mode.

- To delete a record, click the Del link near the beginning of that record's row. A pop-up window appears, prompting you to click OK to accept the deletion. If you click OK, the list page reappears, minus the account that you just wiped out. Don't worry: Later in this chapter, in the section "Resurrecting from the Recycle Bin," we show you how to bring deleted records back to life.

Building a custom view

If you have a particular way in which you like to look at records, you can build a custom view. If you have the right permissions, you can share this view with other groups or your entire organization. (Or maybe you should just keep your views to yourself.)

To create a custom view (using Contacts as the example), follow these steps (which apply to all tabs):

1. **Click the Contacts tab.**

   The Contacts home page appears.

2. **To the right of the Views menu, click the Create New View link.**

   A Create New View page appears.

3. **Name the view by typing a title in the Name field.**

   For example, if you want to create a list of your contacts that are senior executives, use a title like My Senior Execs.

4. **Select whether you want to search All Contacts or just My Contacts by clicking one of the two radio buttons.**

   In this example, select the My Contacts radio button.

5. **If your marketing manager has created campaigns, then you may tie a campaign to filter your list view after identifying which Contacts you want the view to search.**

Type the Campaign Name into the campaign name field.

Tying a campaign to your list view filters your results to those related to a specific marketing campaign. Users with the right permissions in the Professional, Enterprise, and Unlimited Editions have this capability.

6. **Below the Filter by Additional Fields area, enter optional search criteria.**

   A basic criteria query is made up of three elements:

   - **Field:** The leftmost box is a drop-down list of all the fields on the contact record. In this example, you'd choose Title.

   - **Operator:** The middle box is a drop-down list of operators for your search. That sounds complicated, but it's easier than you think. For this example, you'd select the Contains option.

   - **Value:** In the rightmost box, you type the value that you want in the search. In this example, you might type **vp, vice president, ceo, cio, cto.**

7. **Select the columns that you want displayed by selecting a value from the drop-down lists in some or all of the fields provided.**

   Although Salesforce's preset views take common fields, such as Phone and Email, you can select any of up to 11 fields to display on your custom view page.

8. **Decide whether you want others to see your custom view.**

   Administrators and certain users have this permission. Your decision is made simple if the step doesn't appear. Otherwise, select one of the three options. (Basically, the three radio buttons translate to all, none, or selective.) If you choose the third option, use the drop-down list to select a group and then click the arrows to move that group into the Shared To column.

9. **When you're done, click Save.**

   A new view appears based on your custom view criteria. If you don't get all the results that you anticipate, you might want to double-check and refine the search criteria. For example, if your list should include directors but doesn't, click the Edit link and update the view.

Reviewing the Recent Items section

On a tab's home page, just below the views, you see a Recent Items section. This section comes with three or four relevant columns that you can modify. You can see as few as 10 items and as many as 25 items at a time by clicking the link at the bottom of the table.

To test the Recent Items section (by using Leads as the example), go to the Leads home page and follow these steps (which you can apply to all tabs):

1. **In the Recent Leads section, select an option from the drop-down list at the top-right corner of the table.**

   The table reappears with changes based on what you select.

2. **Click a link in the table to go to a record.**

   The detail page appears, displaying the record and related lists.

3. **Click the New button in the top-middle of the table to create a new lead record.**

   A New Lead page appears in Edit mode, ready and waiting.

Reviewing common reports

In the bottom-left corner of a tab's home page, Salesforce displays a small selection of commonly used reports associated with that tab. You can click a link to go directly to the report or click the Go to Reports link, which takes you to the Reports home page.

Tooling through the Tools section

In the bottom-right corner of a tab's home page, Salesforce provides a set of unique tools associated with a particular tab. Depending on which tab you're viewing, use these tools to help you manage and maintain records within that tab. For example, on the Accounts home page, in the Tools section, you can click the Merge Accounts link to merge duplicate accounts. See the related chapters later in this book for details on using specific tools.

Using the Create New Drop-Down List

By using the Create New drop-down list, you can easily add new records into Salesforce.

Creating records

To create a record (by using Contacts as the example), follow these steps (which can be applied to all Create New *Items* on the picklist):

1. **On the home page, select the Contact option on the Create picklist, as shown in Figure 2-9.**

   A New Contact page appears in Edit mode.

Figure 2-9: Creating records by using the Create New drop-down list.

2. **Complete the fields, as necessary.**

   Even while you're in Edit mode, the picklist is available.

3. **When you're done, click Save.**

   The Contact detail page appears, and here you can begin tracking information.

Resurrecting from the Recycle Bin

Occasionally, you delete a record and regret it. Don't panic — the Salesforce Recycle Bin gives you 30 days to restore up to 5,000 recently deleted records, including any associated records (such as activities deleted in the process), and your credibility.

To restore a deleted record, follow these steps:

1. **On your sidebar, click the Recycle Bin link.**

   The Recycle Bin page appears. If you're an administrator, use the View picklist to view and restore records deleted within the last 30 days by other users.

2. **Navigate the list as you would a normal list page until you find the desired record or records.**

3. **Select the check box(es) in the Action column corresponding to the record(s) that you want to restore.**

   You can click the Select All link to select all the records on the page.

4. **When you're done, click the Undelete button.**

   The Recycle Bin page reappears, and a link to your restored record appears in the sidebar below Recent Items.

Detailing the Record

After you create a record, the record appears on its own detail page (see Figure 2-10). You can use the detail page to update the record fields or manage and track activities and common operations on the related lists displayed below the record. In this section, we show you how to navigate the detail page. The other chapters in this book give you specific details about managing particular related lists.

Many of the features that we describe in the following sections aren't enabled by default. Have your administrator go to Setup⇨App Setup⇨User Interface to turn on many of these capabilities.

Tagging records

You can assign your own words or phrases (called *tags*) to each record so that you can organize them according to your personal style. If your administrator has enabled this feature, a Personal Tags list and the Add Personal Tags tab appear in the top-right of the record. To start tagging your records, perform the following on a record that you own:

✔ Click the Add Personal Tags tab to reveal the Personal Tags field.

✔ Type in keywords or phrases into the Personal Tags field that appears (such as 2008 Hot Lead or Berkeley) and hit Save when you finish to associate these tags with this record. In Figure 2-11, we show some keywords we use to associate with a fictitious company.

✔ If you click the keyword or phrase that appear to the right of the Personal Tags fieldname, all other records tagged with the same keyword or phrase appear on a new Personal Tags page.

✔ Clicking the Personal Tags link also takes you to the Personal Tags page, where you can access all the tags you've ever used to describe a record. You can sort the list alphabetically, by frequency, or by most recent use.

Make sure you use phrases that are specific enough to have meaning for you. Tagging something with a generic word, such as Customer, doesn't help you efficiently differentiate your records.

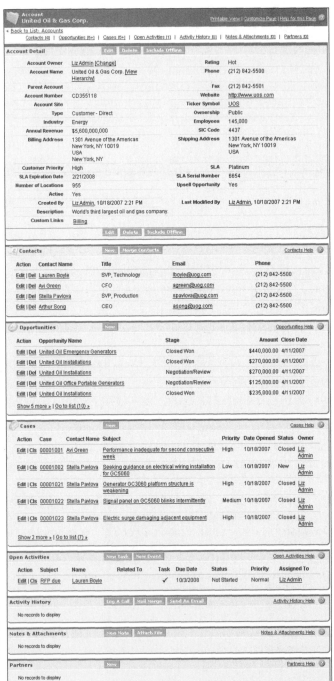

Figure 2-10:
Looking
over the
detail page.

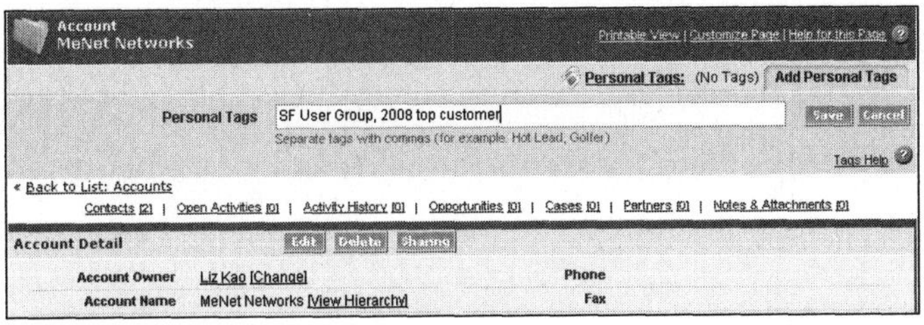

Figure 2-11:
Adding
personal
tags to an
Account
record.

Using links and buttons on the detail page

At the top of any record's detail page, you can use several links and buttons to perform different actions. Go to any detail page and try these out:

- ✔ At the top of the page, below the folder icon, click the Back to List link. If you've been working from a list, that list page appears. Click the Back button on your browser to return to the detail page.

- ✔ Click the Edit button to edit the record. The record appears in Edit mode. Click the Back button.

- ✔ Click the Delete button to delete it. Click the Cancel button in the pop-up window.

- ✔ Click the Sharing button to share the record with other users. (This button doesn't appear on all records.) Click the Back button.

- ✔ Click the Printable View button to view a printable version of the page in a new window. Then click the Print This Page link in the top-right corner of the window to print out a copy of the entire page. Many users like to print hard copies that they can review while traveling.

Modifying records with inline editing

To cut down on the number of steps you have to take when you update records in Salesforce, you can edit fields directly in detail pages.

Make sure your administrator has enabled this feature.

Follow these steps to edit a field inline:

1. **Hover your mouse over any field on a record that you own (and thus have permissions to edit).**

Figure 2-12 shows a person updating the e-mail address of a contact within a company.

An icon appears to the right of a field, telling you whether you can edit that field:

- **Pencil icon:** Appears to the right of editable fields, which become highlighted in white.

- **Padlock icon:** Appears to the right of fields that you can't edit.

- **No icon:** You can edit a field that doesn't have an icon, but not with the inline editing feature. You'll have to edit the record the old-fashioned way, using the Edit button.

2. **Double-click an editable field and update the information in that field.**

3. **Press Enter to complete the editing of that field.**

4. **After you finish editing all the fields you want for that record, remember to click the Save button for the record.**

If you happen to delete information in a field that requires something in it, don't worry. Salesforce is smart enough to remind you about required fields before letting you save your changes.

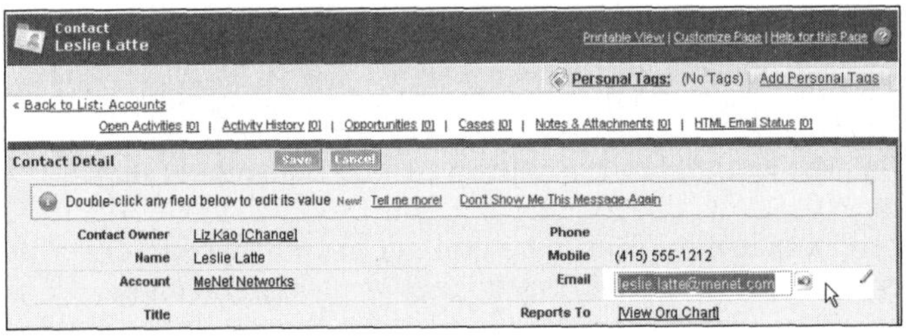

Figure 2-12:
Editing a
field inline.

Capitalizing on related lists

Related lists: Say it three times so you don't forget the term. By designing the page with related lists, Salesforce enables you to gain 360-degree customer visibility and ensure that more detailed information is only a click away. For example, if you open an account detail page for one of your major customers and scroll down below the record fields, you can see multiple contacts, activities, opportunities, cases, notes, attachments, and so on listed as links from organized related lists. And if you don't see these links, you have work to do.

Looking things up with lookup hovers

On any detail page, you can hover your mouse over a lookup field to get a pop-up preview of that other record's contents. Figure 2-13 shows us on a contact record, hovering over the contact's company name to get a preview of the account record.

The lookup hover feature isn't enabled by default, so if you want it, ask your administrator to set it up for you.

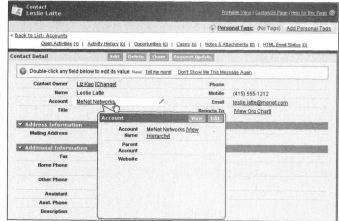

Figure 2-13: Hovering over a lookup field provides a preview of that record.

A *lookup field* is any field that actually links to another record. A lookup field's content is underlined to show that it acts as a link to another record. (But don't confuse lookup fields with the set of related lists that appears below the main body of a record's detail page.)

Getting Help and Setting Up

In the top-right corner of any Salesforce page, to the left of the AppExchange app menu, you can find three links that can help you get more out of Salesforce:

✔ **Setup:** Click this link to open a page containing the Personal Setup menu. Modify your personal setup, or if you're an administrator, administer and customize Salesforce for your company.

✔ **Help and Training:** Click this link to open a window that contains the Salesforce Help & Training home page and additional tabs for help, support, and training.

✔ **Logout:** Clicking this link logs you out of Salesforce. Alternatively, you can just close your browser to log out of your session.

If the System Log link appears in between the Setup and Help links, ignore it for now. This link is for technical administrators, who use it to analyze or troubleshoot automated processes and the use of Apex code.

Chapter 3

Personalizing Your System

. . . .

. . . .

Salesforce was built by salespeople for salespeople. The tool had to be simple to use, relevant to the business of selling, and personally customizable so that you could use it to do your job more effectively.

From the Personal Setup page, you can personalize your application to better suit the way you look at and manage your business. And if you capitalize on the tools available to you in Salesforce, you can give yourself an edge against the competition and your peers.

In this chapter, we describe how to modify your settings by using Personal Setup, change your display, and access Salesforce anytime, anywhere.

Using the Personal Setup Menu

Personal Setup, which you can access by clicking the Setup link when you log in to Salesforce, is a set of tools and options that you can use to set up and customize Salesforce according to your individual preferences. You can decide to show only certain tabs, synchronize your Salesforce data with Outlook, and work with Salesforce while you're not connected to the Internet.

Salesforce makes it easy for you to better personalize your system by providing all your setup tools in one area.

To locate and navigate your Personal Setup area, follow these steps:

1. **Click the Setup link in the top-right corner of any page.**

   The Personal Setup page appears with an expandable sidebar, as shown on the left in Figure 3-1. The body of the page and the sidebar work hand in hand, but we like to use the sidebar so we don't get lost.

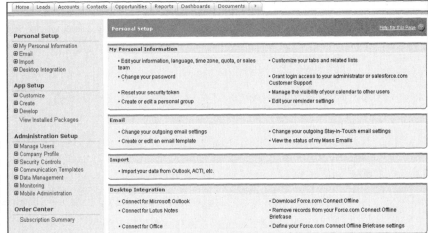

Figure 3-1:
Looking over the Personal Setup page.

2. **Click all the small + icons below the Personal Setup heading on the sidebar so you can see the full range of options (shown in Figure 3-2).**

   Menus appear. The body of the page doesn't change if you simply expand the heading within the sidebar.

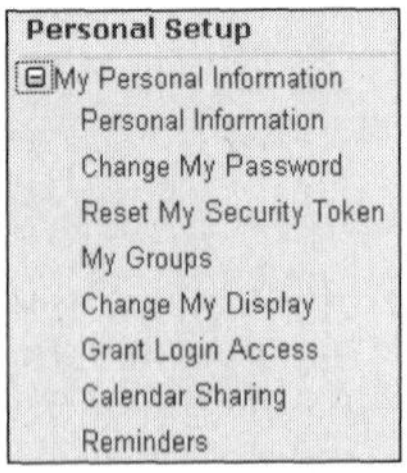

Figure 3-2:
Expanding the menu.

3. **Click any heading.**

   The page for that heading appears.

4. **Click the Back button on your browser to return to the previous page or click another heading to open that heading's page.**

   You've now mastered basic navigation in the Personal Setup menu.

Modifying Your Personal Information

By using your personal information folder, you can keep your user record current, expand sharing privileges to other users and groups, and customize your personal display to suit your tastes.

Updating your user information

In Salesforce, you have a user record that corresponds to you. You can use that record to keep other users up to date on your contact information. You can also update your user record to associate quotas, share information, and more.

To find out how to navigate to the Personal Setup area, see the preceding section.

To modify your user record, follow these steps:

1. **Click the My Personal Information link or the small + to the left of that link on the sidebar (refer to Figure 3-1).**

   A series of options appears below the link.

2. **Click the Personal Information link.**

   Your User page appears.

3. **Click Edit.**

   The page appears in Edit mode. Review the accuracy of and update your information.

Especially if you travel frequently, make sure that you update your time zone both in Salesforce and on your laptop, reflecting your current location. This is particularly important if you're managing your schedule and synchronizing with offline tools, such as Outlook.

4. **When you're done, click Save.**

   The User page appears again with the updated information.

Changing your display

If you log in and feel as if you really need only a fraction of the tabs or a select number of related lists, you can customize your personal display. Your administrator can still override your personal setup, if necessary. For example, if you sell but don't want to see or use the Opportunities tab, something would have to change (probably your job).

Modifying your tabs

Salesforce already provides many standard tabs and groups some of them into apps that you choose from the AppExchange app menu. Companies can also create their own tabs. For most users, you just don't need to see all those tabs at the same time.

To customize your tabs, follow these steps:

1. **Click the Change My Display link on the sidebar (refer to Figure 3-2).**

   The Change My Display page appears.

2. **Click the Customize My Tabs button if you want to add, remove, or change the order of your tabs within an app.**

   The Customize My Tabs page appears.

3. **Select which app's tab set you want to customize from the Custom App drop-down list.**

   The default Selected Tabs list changes when you change the Custom App selection. Salesforce has pre-grouped its tabs into three standard apps called Sales, Marketing, and Call Center. Depending on your business, having these tabs visible may be perfect, or you may want to see more or less tabs.

4. **Use the two list boxes to highlight a tab and either remove it from or add it to your display, as shown in Figure 3-3.**

   For example, if you're in marketing and spend most of your time with leads, you might decide to add the Campaigns tab and remove the Opportunities tab from your sales custom app.

5. **Use the up and down arrows to change the order of the tabs.**

   The only exception is that you can't move or remove the Home tab.

6. **When you're done, click Save.**

   The Change My Display page reappears, and your tabs reflect your changes.

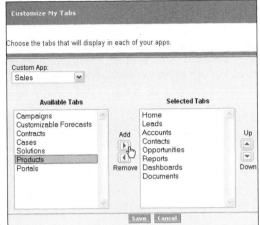

Figure 3-3:
Modifying
your tabs.

Customizing pages

You can also personalize your display by changing the layout on a record page. Doing so enables you to see the most relevant sections first. For example, if you work in a call center, you may want to see cases at the top of your related lists on an account page.

To customize the display of a page, follow these steps:

1. **Click the Change My Display link on the sidebar (refer to Figure 3-2).**

   The Change My Display page appears.

2. **Go to the picklist below the Customize My Pages section and select an option to the page of a specific tab that you want to modify (the Accounts tab, for instance) and click the Customize My Pages button.**

   The Customize My Page page appears.

3. **Select lists from the two list boxes and then add or remove them from your page.**

   For example, if you sell directly to customers, you might want to remove the Partners related list from the Account detail page.

4. **Use the up and down arrows to change the order of the lists on your page layout.**

5. **When you're done, click Save.**

   The Change My Display page reappears.

Granting login access

When you need help from your administrator or salesforce.com customer support, you can grant either or both temporary login access to your account. By gaining access to your account, the person helping you can provide better assistance because she can view your pages.

To grant login access, follow these steps:

1. **Click the Grant Login Access link on the sidebar (refer to Figure 3-2).**

   The Grant Login Access page appears.

2. **Grant *support* and/or *administrator* access by clicking the relevant calendar icon to select an expiration date, and then click the Save button.**

   The My Personal Information page appears.

If you're an administrator and a user has granted you access, you can log in to the user's account as follows: Below the Manage Users heading on the sidebar, click the Users link and then select the Active Users list. On the list, click the Login link to the left of the user's name.

If you use a web-based e-mail system like Google's GMail or Yahoo! Mail, you can save specific e-mails that you send to your customers, right into Salesforce without having to manually copy and paste that activity. This integration is very encouraging for businesses that are increasingly running all their business applications online. Click the My Email to Salesforce link that's in the Setup ➪ Personal Setup ➪ Email section (which you'll see only if your administrator has enabled the Email to Salesforce feature)Clicking on the My Email to Salesforce link takes you to the My Email to Salesforce page. A highlighted "Your Email to Salesforce address is:" field in the middle of the page provides a long e-mail address comprised of random alphanumeric characters for you to add into the BCC: field of the e-mail you're composing that you want automatically saved in Salesforce. Salesforce looks at the recipient's e-mail address and looks for a matching Lead or Contact within Salesforce to associate the e-mail activity with.

We discuss more specifics about saving e-mails to Salesforce in Chapter 7.

Working with Salesforce Remotely

If travel is part of your job, you might not always be connected to the Internet, let alone to your laptop. In spite of this, you still have many options for accessing your customer information from Salesforce, including synchronizing with Outlook and working with Force.com Connect Offline.

Synchronizing with Outlook

Connect for Microsoft Outlook lets you record Microsoft Outlook e-mails into Salesforce via a plug-in that synchronizes your Outlook's contacts, meetings, and tasks. In the following sections, we show you how to install and configure Outlook Edition and then back up your data prior to your first synchronization.

If you're the administrator responsible for maintaining accurate data in Salesforce, encourage your company to adopt Salesforce as the system of record or "the single source of truth." For example, tell users to make updates to accounts and contacts in Salesforce, rather than in Outlook. Then, have them configure Connect for Microsoft Outlook to allow Salesforce to win if a conflict resolution occurs between Salesforce and Outlook. By doing this, you can reduce common synchronization issues and influence greater Salesforce adoption.

Installing and configuring Connect for Microsoft Outlook

In most cases, installing Connect for Microsoft Outlook is a simple process. If you connect to the Internet via a proxy server or your company has a firewall, you might want to consult with your IT department.

To download and install Connect for Microsoft Outlook, follow these steps:

1. **Click the Connect for Microsoft Outlook link below My Personal Information⇨Desktop Integration on the sidebar.**

   The Connect for Microsoft Outlook page appears.

2. **Click the Install Now button.**

   The installation process begins. In the upper-left of the section, a subtle status line appears after your installation starts.

   A new InstallShield Wizard window appears.

3. **Follow the appropriate steps in the InstallShield Wizard, as shown in Figure 3-4.**

   After your installation is complete, the Connect for Microsoft Outlook page reappears.

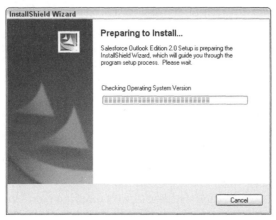

4. **Open Microsoft Outlook to configure your Connect for Microsoft Outlook settings.**

    A Connect for Microsoft Outlook screen appears to show you that it's been successfully installed in Outlook. The setup wizard appears. If you want to return to this setup wizard another time, remember to check the box marked Show This Wizard Again Next Time Outlook Starts.

5. **Click Next after reading the brief welcome message.**

6. **Enter your Salesforce user name and password in the appropriate boxes and click Next.**

7. **Using the check boxes, set your synchronization options to sync contacts, events, and tasks.**

    You may also select the direction in which you want data to flow.

8. **Click Next.**

    In addition to optionally associating your e-mails in Outlook to contacts and leads, you may also select another object to tie with your e-mail, such as Accounts or Opportunities.

9. **For this example, check the Accounts check box in the Email Options screen and then click Next.**

    If you want to set more advanced options, the screen that appears tells you where to go.

10. **Click Next.**

    Now it's time to start using Connect for Microsoft Outlook. Of all the
    screens, make sure you read the one that appears now so that you can
    understand how you choose which items you want to sync.

11. **Click Finish.**

Backing up your data

Synchronizing is tricky, especially if you're in a large organization with potentially complex sharing rules or if the system has a lot of old data (more on
that in Chapter 22). We always recommend backing up the data from your
offline tool before your initial synchronization.

Use the menu bar in Outlook (Outlook 2003, in this case) to back up your
data prior to synchronizing for the first time.

To back up your data, follow these steps:

1. **Open Microsoft Outlook.**

2. **Choose File⇨Import and Export.**

    The Import and Export Wizard opens in a dialog box.

3. **Select the Export to a File option in the list box and click Next.**

4. **Select the Personal File Folder (.pst) option in the list box and click
   Next.**

5. **Select a folder to export (Calendar, Contacts, or Tasks) from the
   Personal Folders list that appears and click Next.**

6. **In the Save the File As field, enter a new location and filename, and
   then click Finish.**

7. **Repeat Steps 2 through 6 for each folder (Calendar, Contacts, and
   Tasks).**

If your company plans to synchronize your calendars with Outlook, make a
habit of synchronizing daily to keep your activities up to date.

If you discover that you accidentally deleted records in Salesforce while synchronizing, you can go to your Recycle Bin and restore those records within
30 days from the date you deleted the records.

Working offline

In today's world of hotspots and Wi-Fi, it's hard to imagine ever being untethered from the Internet. Still, on those occasions when you can't get connected, you can use Force.com Connect Offline and hardly notice the difference. Force.com Connect Offline is a downloadable application that you access through a browser, and it has the same look and feel as its online big brother. Like a briefcase, Force.com Connect Offline lets you carry a set of your Salesforce information, and it allows you to synchronize your various records. Before you can run Force.com Connect Offline, you need to install the application, configure the Briefcase, and then update it when you run it the first time. Go to Setup⇨Personal Setup⇨Desktop Integration⇨Force.com Connect Offline to install the application and then configure the Briefcase.

Force.com Connect Offline is included in the Salesforce Enterprise and Unlimited Editions, and it's available at an additional charge for Professional Edition.

Importing Your Contacts

One of the keys to making Salesforce productive for you from day one is to get your contacts into the system. If your contacts exist primarily in Microsoft Outlook, you might be better off synchronizing your data. Otherwise, Salesforce provides easy-to-use wizards that help you import contacts and accounts. See Chapter 5 for the details on importing, and see your administrator if your data goes beyond the limits of the import wizard. (For example, if you have historical activity linked to contacts, you can't import those records by using standard wizards.)

Part II
Tracking Sales

The 5th Wave   By Rich Tennant

"Well, here's what happened—I forgot to put 'dressing' on my 'To Do' list."

In this part . . .

Sales are the lifeblood of any organization. When sales are growing, life is good. Employees are energized, groups are happy to work together, and the company has money to innovate and stay ahead of the competition. When sales are down, life gets rough. Everyone feels more pressure to perform, the company tightens its belt, and you start receiving lectures on how coffee is for closers. So how can you and your sales teams consistently perform so that you have enough leads at the top of the funnel to ensure a consistent flow of sales at the bottom of the funnel?

Salesforce, a tool built by sales people for sales people, is designed to do just that. With the core sales tabs in Salesforce, you can effectively manage both existing customers as well as key prospects.

In this part, we explain each of the tabs used to manage existing customers, how they connect to each other, and most importantly, how to use them so that you can quickly get up to speed to sell more, faster. We show you how you can use Salesforce to manage your sales activities, including calendared events and tasks. You discover the ins and outs of e-mail and how, by sending e-mail from Salesforce, you can connect more effectively with your contacts than you thought possible.

Chapter 4

Managing Accounts

*W*ho are your customers? What do you know about them? What are their top compelling business problems? If you have trouble answering any of these questions, pay close attention to this chapter. In this chapter, we discuss how to use Salesforce to manage your accounts.

In Salesforce, an *account* is a company that you do business with. Accounts can include all types of companies — customers, prospects, partners, and even competitors. Among the top reasons why companies implement any customer relationship management (CRM) tool is that they need a centralized place where they can store account data, and they find themselves searching all over the place for critical customer information. With Salesforce, you can keep all your important account information in one place so that you and your team can apply that knowledge to sell more and keep customers happy. For example, if you work for a pharmaceutical company, you can use the accounts area to manage your territory of hospitals, clinics, and top offices and capture everything from call reports to business plans.

In this chapter, we describe all the ways you can use accounts to manage and track companies. First, you need to get your important company lists into Salesforce and organize them according to the way that you work. Then, you can find how out to make the best use of the account record to profile your companies. Finally, you can discover how to capitalize on the account related lists to gain a 360-degree view of your customers and ensure that no one drops any balls.

Getting Familiar with the Account Record

The account record lets you collect all the critical information about the companies you interact with. That account record is supported by other records (contacts, opportunities, cases, activities, and so on) that collectively give you a complete view of your customer. From this vantage point, you can quickly take in the view from the top, and if you need to, you can easily drill into the details.

Here's a short list of valuable things you can do with accounts:

- Import and consolidate your lists of target accounts in one place.
- Enter new accounts quickly and maintain naming consistency.
- Create parent/child relationships that describe how companies' divisions or subsidiaries relate to each other.
- Realign sales territories.
- Segment your markets with ease.
- Eliminate paper-based business planning.
- Assign account teams to better serve your customers.
- Track your top customers and de-emphasize bottom-feeders.
- Define the movers and shakers within an account.
- Devise schemes to beat your competitors.
- Manage your channel partners.

Understanding standard fields

The *account record* is the collection of fields that make up the information on a company that you're tracking. The record has only two modes: an Edit mode, in which you can modify fields, and a Saved mode, in which you can view the fields and the account's related lists (which are located below the record fields).

An account record comes preconfigured with a set of fields commonly used for account management.

Most of the standard fields are self-explanatory, but in the following list, we highlight certain terms that warrant greater definition:

✔ **Account Owner:** The person in your organization who owns the account. An account record has only one owner, but many users can still collaborate on an account.

✔ **Account Name:** This required field represents the name of the company you want to track.

✔ **Account Site:** The Account Site field goes hand in hand with the Account Name field when you're distinguishing different physical locations or divisions of a company. This field, although not required, is very important if your company sells to different locations of a customer with decentralized buying patterns. For example, if you sell mattresses to Hilton Hotels, but each Hilton Hotel buys independently, this field is useful for classifying different sites.

✔ **Type:** One of the fields on an account record that classifies the relationship of an account to your company. The Type field consists of a drop-down list of values, and it's critical if you want to differentiate types of companies. For example, if you work for a software company that uses value-added resellers (VARs) to sell and service your products, you might want to select Reseller as one of your drop-down list values.

✔ **Rating:** Use this drop-down list to define your internal rating system for companies that you're tracking. Salesforce provides default values of Hot, Warm, and Cold, but you can replace these with numbers, letters, or other terms based on how you want to segment companies.

Customizing account fields

Using standard fields gives you a simple way to collect basic profiles on companies. But to get the most out of your account record, you should think about how you and your company define a target customer. For example, if you're selling corporate healthcare plans, you might want to know certain information about each of your target companies: number of employees, number of people insured, level of satisfaction, and so on.

If the fields on your account record can answer these four questions, that record has a solid foundation:

✔ What attributes describe your target customer?

✔ What are the important components of your account plan?

✔ Is a company's infrastructure important to what you sell?

✔ What information, if you had it, would help you sell to a company?

If you find your account record lacking relevance to your business, write down fields that you want and then seek out your system administrator to customize your account record. (See Chapter 20 for the how-to details on building fields, rearranging your layouts, and other design tricks.) You can have greater success with accounts if you focus on your customer.

Creating and Updating Your Accounts

Before you can begin using Salesforce to manage accounts, you must get the account records into Salesforce. In the following sections, we show you how to get started and how to update saved records.

Adding new accounts

The best way to enter a new account is to use the Create New drop-down list located on the sidebar. By using this drop-down list, you get a clear picture of the account fields that are most important to your company. To create accounts by using the Create New drop-down list, follow these simple steps:

1. **Enter the name of the account that you want to create in the Search tool on the sidebar, and then click the Go button.**

   A Search Results page appears with a list of records that match your query. If you see records that match particular account or lead records, don't throw in the towel yet. Click links listed in the Name columns to drill into the details and see whether the account is being worked. Consult with your sales manager if you have questions.

2. **If you don't get any results, select Account in the Create New drop-down list on the sidebar.**

   The Edit mode of a new account appears.

   Before adding an account (or any other record, for that matter), always search for it first. You might not be the only person to have worked with a particular company. By searching first, you avoid creating duplicate entries, potentially profit from prior history on an existing account, and don't waste time chasing accounts that don't belong to you. (Although we know this *never* happens.)

3. **Fill in the fields as much as you can or as required.**

   At a minimum, you must complete the Account Name field. Try to provide as much detail as possible to make this new account record valuable for your selling objectives. You can make this data as simple as basic phone and address information and as detailed as account segmentation data such as type, industry, annual revenue, and so on. (See Figure 4-1 for an example of a record in Edit mode.)

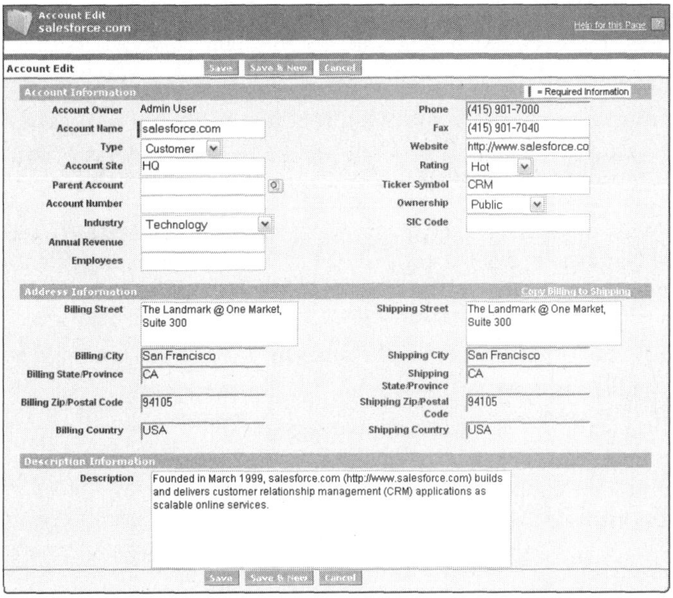

Figure 4-1:
Completing
account
fields.

When creating account records, strive for accurate and consistent spelling of the corporate name. Your customer database is only as good as the data being entered into the system. As a best practice, look up and use the name of the company from a reliable source (for example, Dun & Bradstreet, Hoover's, or the company name as displayed on its corporate Web site). For suggested naming conventions, go to salesforce. com's best practices Web site, Successforce Community (`http://success.salesforce.com`), and search for "naming convention" to see more documents and presentations from real customers on this very topic.

4. **When you're done, click one of the following buttons:**

   • **Save:** After you click the Save button, the Account detail page appears, in which you can click the Edit button at any time if you need to modify information on the record.

   • **Save & New:** Clicking this button saves the current account record and automatically opens a new, blank account record in Edit mode.

If you have an existing spreadsheet of companies that you want to import into Salesforce, you can use an import wizard tool and avoid the manual entry. See Chapter 5 for how-to details on importing accounts and contacts.

Updating account fields

In the course of working with your accounts, you inevitably collect pertinent information that you want to save directly in the account record. Every time you capture important data on your account, remember to update your record by following these steps:

1. **Enter the name of your account in the Search tool on the sidebar and click the Go button.**

   A Search Results page appears.

2. **Click the desired link in the Account Name column to go to your account.**

   The Account detail page appears.

3. **Click the Edit button on the account record.**

4. **Update the fields as necessary, and then click Save.**

   The account reappears in Saved mode, and the fields you edited have been changed.

Organizing Your Accounts

When you have all or a portion of your accounts entered in Salesforce, you can begin to organize them to suit the way that you sell.

In the following sections, we cover how to use views and other tools from the Accounts home page to provide greater focus for you and your sales teams. We also show you an important feature of the account record that lets you create parent/child relationships between accounts. Then, for even more robust organization of your account information, check out Chapter 17 for specifics on how to use standard and custom account reports.

Using account views

An *account view* is a list of accounts that match certain criteria. When you select a view, you're basically specifying criteria to limit the results that you get back. The advantage of a view, versus searching, is that you can use this view over and over again. On the Accounts home page, Salesforce comes preset with four defined views:

✔ **All Accounts:** Provides a list of all the account records entered into Salesforce. Depending on the way your company has set up your security model, you might not see this view or its results.

✔ **My Accounts:** Gives you a list of just your accounts.

✔ **New This Week:** Generates a list of accounts created this week.

✔ **Recently Viewed Accounts:** Lets you look at a list of accounts that you've recently viewed.

To try out a predefined view, follow these steps:

1. **On the Accounts home page, click the down arrow on the Views drop-down list.**

   You see the four options that we mention in the preceding bulleted list and maybe some other choices that have been created for you.

2. **Select the My Accounts view.**

   If you've already entered or imported account records, a list page appears, showing accounts that you currently own. Salesforce lays out the list with six standard columns that correspond to commonly used account fields, plus an Action column so that you can quickly modify a record.

3. **Click a column header to re-sort the list page.**

   For example, if you click the Billing State column header, the list page re-sorts by state in alphabetical order. You can click the Billing State column header a second time to re-sort in reverse alphabetical order.

4. **Click into any account by clicking a link in the Account Name column.**

   The Account detail page appears.

5. **Click the Back button on your browser and click the Edit button on the same row as the account you clicked in Step 4.**

   The account record appears in Edit mode, allowing you to make changes to the data.

Creating custom account views

If you want special lists for the way that you manage your accounts, you should build custom views. For example, if you're a new business sales rep who focuses solely on California telecom companies and always researches the prospect's Web site before calling, creating a custom view can help you be more effective because you can build your list of target accounts, define columns, and use that view over and over again.

To build a view from scratch, follow these simple steps:

1. **On the Accounts home page, to the right of the Views drop-down list, click the Create New View link.**

   The Create New View page appears.

2. **Name the view by entering text in the Name field.**

   For our fictitious California telecom example, you might call the view California Telco Prospects.

3. **Select the appropriate radio button, depending on whether you want to search All Accounts or just My Accounts.**

4. **(Optional) Filter by additional fields.**

   A basic criteria query is made up of three elements:

   • **Field:** The first drop-down list offers all the fields on the account record. One example is the Type field.

   • **Operator:** The second drop-down list offers operators for your search. That sounds complicated, but it's easier than you might think. Taking our example, you'd select Equals from the drop-down list.

   • **Value:** In the third field, you type the value that you want in the search. For our example, you'd type **Prospect** because, for this example, you go after only new business.

5. **Select the columns that you want displayed.**

   Although Salesforce's preset views take common fields, such as Phone and Billing State, you can display any of the account fields that you're permitted to see on your custom list page. In our example, you'd add another column for the Web Site field.

6. **Decide whether you want others to see your custom view.**

   Your decision is simple if you don't have an option. Otherwise, select the appropriate option, depending on whether you want to share your view with others. If you choose limited accessibility, use the two list boxes to select which users can see the view.

7. **When you're done, click Save.**

   A new view appears based on your custom view criteria. If you don't get all the results you anticipated, you might want to recheck and refine the search criteria. For example, if your company has a habit of using initials or full spelling for the State field (NY or New York, respectively), this habit impacts results.

By default, each filtering criteria for your list view is joined together with AND parameters. If you want to get fancy with your search criteria, click the Advanced Options link to use a combination of AND and OR filters.

Reassigning account ownership

You might find that after you set up your accounts in Salesforce, you need to give them to the right people. Part of organizing your accounts is getting them into the right hands. You might even want to reassign an account to yourself if that account wasn't properly given to you.

Reassigning a single account

If you're just reassigning an account on a case-by-case basis, you can transfer ownership directly from an account record. Go to the detail page of an account that you want to reassign and follow these steps:

1. **To the right of the Account Owner field, click the Change link (which appears in square brackets).**

   The Change Account Owner page appears.

2. **Select the user you're assigning the account to.**

   By selecting the Send Notification Email check box on the page, you can choose to notify the recipient with an e-mail.

3. **Select the check boxes to determine whether and how associated records change ownership.**

   See Figure 4-2 for an example.

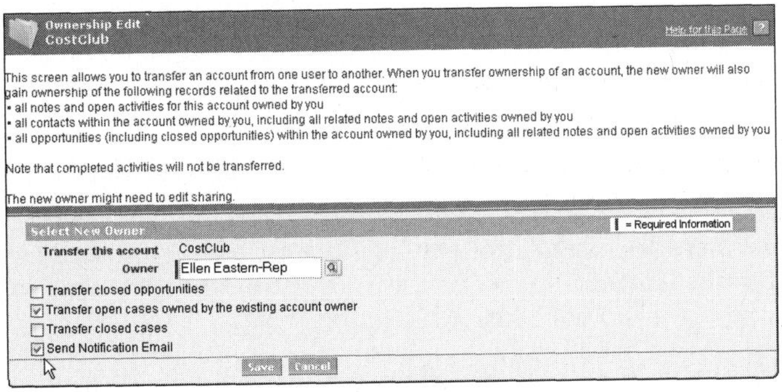

Figure 4-2:
Reassigning
an account.

4. **When you're done, click Save.**

   The account record reappears. The Account Owner field has changed to the assigned user.

Reassigning multiple accounts at the same time

Over the course of managing accounts and sales people, you'll probably need to quickly and efficiently transfer multiple accounts at the same time. For example, it's not unheard of that a sales rep leaves the company, and accounts need to be moved immediately to someone else.

If you commonly realign account territories, Salesforce's transfer tools can make this task a piece of cake. Depending on the method you or your company uses to carve up territories, plan ahead by customizing and then populating fields that define your territories. For example, if you segment by market cap and industry, those account fields should be filled in. Administrators can mass-transfer accounts to new owners. To mass-transfer accounts, follow these steps:

1. **Click the Accounts Tab to go to the Accounts home page.**

2. **Click the Transfer Accounts link in the Tools section.**

   The Mass Transfer Accounts Page Wizard appears.

3. **Fill in the Transfer From and Transfer To fields. (Use the Lookup icons, as needed.)**

   You can transfer accounts to or from any user.

4. **Select the appropriate check boxes to determine whether and how associated records change ownership.**

5. **Specify the search criteria in the drop-down lists and fields.**

   For example, if you want to transfer accounts located in California to a new rep, you can use Billing State contains California, CA as your search criteria.

6. **Click the Find button.**

   The search results appear at the bottom of the resulting page.

7. **Select check boxes in the Action column to select all or a portion of the accounts for transfer, and then click the Transfer button to complete the process.**

   The Mass Transfer Accounts page reappears, minus the records that you transferred.

Building parent/child relationships

If you sell into different locations or divisions of a company and you're currently challenged by how to keep this information organized, use account hierarchies to solve your problem. In Salesforce, you can link multiple offices of a company together by using the Parent Account field on an account record. And you can create multiple tiers to the hierarchy if your customer is organized that way.

To establish parent/child relationships, follow these steps:

1. **Create accounts for the parent and subsidiary companies (see the section "Adding new accounts," earlier in this chapter).**

   You can skip this step if the accounts are already created. You might want to type a term such as **Headquarters** or **HQ** in the Account Site field to signify which account is the parent.

2. **Click the subsidiary account (also called a child account) that you want to link and click Edit.**

   The record appears in Edit mode.

3. **To the right of the Parent Account field, click the Lookup icon.**

   A pop-up window appears, containing a Search field and a list of recently viewed accounts.

   If you see the parent account in the results, skip to Step 5.

4. **Search for the parent account by typing the name of the account in the Search field and clicking Go.**

5. **From the list of results, click the name of the company to select the parent account (as shown in Figure 4-3).**

   The pop-up window closes, and your selection appears in the Parent Account field.

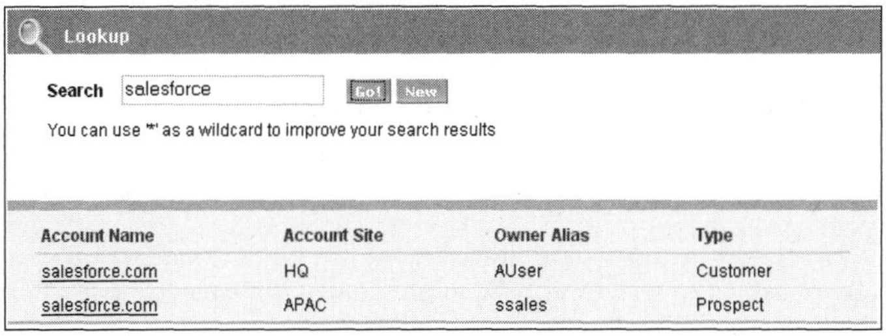

Figure 4-3: Selecting a sample parent account.

6. **If you want to further denote the child account, use the Account Site field.**

   Some companies use city, state, country, division, and so on, depending on how they organize their accounts. For example, if Staples, Inc., has locations in Dallas and Atlanta, you might want to type the city into the Account Site field for each of the child accounts so that you can tell which is which.

7. **When you're done, click Save.**

   The Account detail page appears.

8. **To view the account hierarchy, click the View Hierarchy link to the right of the Account Name field on the record.**

   An Account Hierarchy list page appears, and like other lists, you can click an item to go to a specific account.

Performing Actions with Account Related Lists

Fields on an account record are useful for storing important data specific to a company. But where do you go to capture all the critical interactions and relationships when you're working an account? To keep track of these details, use the related lists located on the Account detail page.

Many of the actions on account related lists are common to other modules. For example, major modules, such as Accounts, Contacts, Opportunities, and Cases all have related lists for Open Activities, Activity History, and Notes & Attachments. Instead of being redundant, we point you to Chapter 6 for details on using related lists to track tasks and calendar events. In the following sections, we describe certain related lists that are unique to the account record.

Defining contact roles

Many sales reps do a great job of collecting business cards for contacts within an account, but this action alone doesn't get them closer to a sale. Contacts and their titles often don't tell the whole story about decision makers and chain of command within an account. To use contact roles in Salesforce, your administrator must proactively reveal this related list on the account record — you can find details on how to do this in Chapter 20.

To better define the buying influences on an account, go to an account record and follow these steps:

1. **Review your records in the Contacts related list.**

   If important contacts are missing, add them first, which we describe how to do in Chapter 5.

2. **Click the New button on the Contact Roles related list.**

   The Account Contact Role page appears.

3. **Type the name of a contact in the Contact field and click the Lookup icon.**

   A pop-up window with your search results appears.

4. **If you find the correct contact, click the link for that contact's name.**

   If your search doesn't find the contact, refine your search or click the New button to create the contact record and then select the contact you find or create. After you select the contact, the pop-up window disappears, and the Contact field is filled in.

5. **Select Correct Role from the Role drop-down list.**

   The default roles are strategic, rather than mere job titles. People's strategic roles can change in every deal. If the right role for your contact doesn't appear, advise your system administrator to edit the roles. Many companies match these roles with their particular sales methodology identifiers.

6. **Select the Primary Contact check box if the contact is your primary contact and click the Save button or the Save & New button.**

   If you click Save, the Account detail page reappears, and your contact appears on the Contact Roles related list. If you click the Save & New button, a new Account Contact Role page appears, and you can associate another contact to a role immediately.

Displaying an account's opportunities

Over the course of managing an account, you'll hopefully uncover specific opportunities to sell that company your products or services. You can use the Opportunity related list to quickly perform the following tasks:

- ✔ Stay aware of all the open opportunities that you and your team are pursuing on an account.

- ✔ Add new opportunities and link them automatically to the account.

- ✔ Edit and delete opportunity records with a single click.

- ✔ Gauge the progress of an account by quickly seeing all open and closed opportunities at their various sales stages and amounts.

See Chapter 9 for the scoop on adding, editing, and managing opportunities.

Viewing cases

Account health is much more than measuring the growth of sales for a customer. After selling, sales reps want to stay informed of customer service issues so that they can continue to keep their customers satisfied, resolve issues early, receive warnings about potential landmines, and track potential upsell opportunities. Use the Cases related list to view all the open and closed customer service cases that relate to an account.

If your company relies on a channel sales team to manage partners, distribute leads, and bring in revenue, you may want to consider using Salesforce Partners, available in Enterprise and Unlimited Editions for an extra charge. This partner relationship management (PRM) application gets your partners on board with using Salesforce to manage all the details of their activities with your company and your joint deals. Go to Chapter 11 for a more in-depth discussion.

Maintaining Your Account Database

The more you use Salesforce for account management, the more important it is to maintain it over time.

In the following sections, we show you simple tools for keeping your account database up to date.

Merging duplicate records

Try as you might to avoid it, the best sales reps and teams still create duplicate account records. For example, say you're a new business rep, and you create and manage an account record for General Electric. Unbeknownst to you, an account manager in the cubicle right next to you has been tracking all his customer activity on an account called GE. Three months later, you both have logged multiple activities, contacts, and other records. Do you throw up your hands in despair and continue working with independent records, delete your friend's record, or fight it out? The Salesforce merge tool for accounts can help you avoid the loss of friendship and data.

To merge account records, you must be the Account Owner of the records, the Account Owner's manager (that is, the Account Owner must be subordinate to you in the Role Hierarchy), or a system administrator.

To merge accounts, follow these steps:

1. **Click the Accounts Tab to go to the Accounts home page.**

2. **In the Tools section, click the Merge Accounts link.**

   Step 1 of the Merge My Accounts tool appears.

3. **Type the name of the accounts that you need to merge and click the Find Accounts button.**

A Search Results page appears with a list of records. If you don't see one of the accounts you're looking for, you may need to rename it with a name similar to its duplicate. For example, you'd rename GE to General Electric Dupe to merge it with the other General Electric account.

4. **Select the check boxes for a maximum of three records that you want to merge, and then click Next.**

   The Step 2 page of the tool appears, containing a side-by-side comparison of the selected account records.

5. **Compare the information and click the appropriate radio buttons to select the values that you want to retain, as shown in Figure 4-4.**

   At the top of each column, you can also choose to keep all the values from one record by clicking the Select All link.

Figure 4-4:
Selecting values while merging duplicate accounts.

	salesforce.com [Select All]	salesforce.com [Select All]
Merge My Accounts		Help for this Page
Step 2. Select the values to retain		Step 2 of 2
		Previous / Merge / Cancel

Select the values that you want to retain in the merged record. Highlighted rows indicate fields that contain conflicting data. The Master Record selected will retain read-only and hidden field values. The oldest Created By date and user will be retained in the merged record.

Note: All related records including any notes, attachments, and activities will be associated with the new merged record.

	salesforce.com [Select All]	salesforce.com [Select All]
Master Record	⊙	○
Account Owner	⊙ Admin User	○ Sam Sales
Account Name	salesforce.com	salesforce.com
Type	⊙ Customer	○ Prospect
Account Site	⊙ HQ	○ APAC
Account Number		
Industry	⊙ Technology	○
Annual Revenue		
Employees		
Phone	⊙ (415) 901-7000	○
Fax	⊙ (415) 901-7040	○
Website	⊙ http://www.salesforce.com	○
Rating	⊙ Hot	○
Ticker Symbol	⊙ CRM	○
Ownership	⊙ Public	○
SIC Code		
Billing Address	⊙ The Landmark @ One Market, Suite 300 San Francisco, CA 94105 USA	○
Shipping Address	⊙ The Landmark @ One Market, Suite 300 San Francisco, CA 94105 USA	○
Description	⊙ Founded in March 1999, salesforce.com (http://www.salesforce.com) builds and delivers customer relationship management (CRM) applications as scalable online services.	○
Created By	Admin User, 7/11/2006 10:19 AM	Sam Sales, 7/16/2006 9:21 AM
Last Modified By	Sam Sales, 7/16/2006 9:20 AM	Sam Sales, 7/16/2006 9:21 AM
		Previous / Merge / Cancel

6. **When you finish reviewing, click the Merge button.**

   A pop-up window appears, prompting you to verify that you want to perform the merge. After you click OK, the account record reappears. Any records from related lists are kept.

Deleting account records

If you find that you (or a subordinate) own accounts that need to be deleted, you can delete them one at a time by using the Delete button on the account records. The one caveat here is that some companies remove your permission to delete accounts altogether. If this is the case or you want to delete many accounts at one time, consult with your system administrator. System administrators are the only users in your company who have the ability to mass-delete records. (Kind of startling to realize that geeks have all the power, isn't it?)

When deleting records, remember that you're also deleting associated records. So, if you're deleting an account, you can potentially be removing contacts, activities, opportunities, and other records linked to the account. You can rectify a mistakenly deleted record within 30 days of your deletion by retrieving it from your Recycle Bin, but be careful before deleting records.

Chapter 5

Developing Contacts

· ·

· ·

*I*f you've been selling for more than a few years, you probably have a big golden Rolodex overflowing with business contacts. And if you're just starting out, you probably wish you had one. But how much do you know about those contacts? Where do you keep track of the personal and business information that you've collected throughout the years?

Salesforce enables you to plan, manage, and capture all the important interactions that you normally have with your prospects and customers. Just imagine the value that keeping this shared information in one place can have for you and your teams.

By using the Contacts section in Salesforce, you can effectively keep all of your most important contacts together in one place, easily link them with the accounts they work for, gain insight into the relationships between contacts, and capture the critical personal drivers of each contact which are so key to your selling success.

In this chapter, we discuss how to use Salesforce for your contact management needs. You can also find out how to build your contact database by adding information directly or by importing your existing files. Later in the chapter, we describe how to organize your contacts lists so that you can quickly find the people you want to talk to. We also show you how to maintain the integrity of your contact data by editing contact records, merging duplicate records, and deleting old records. These tasks allow you to start putting your contacts to work for you.

Understanding the Contact Record

The *contact record* is the collection of fields that consists of the information on a person you do business with. Unlike a business card in your Rolodex or a lead record in Salesforce, however, a contact is linked to an account. Like other records, the contact record has only two modes: an *Edit* mode, in which you can modify fields, and a *Saved* mode, in which you can view the fields and the contact's related lists (which are located below the fields).

A contact record comes preconfigured with a standard set of fields commonly used for contact management. The exact number isn't important because your company will probably add or subtract fields based on the way you want to track your contacts. Most of the standard fields are self-explanatory, but in the following list, we highlight a few fields that are less obvious:

- ✔ **Contact Owner:** The person in your organization who owns the contact. A contact has only one owner, although many users can still collaborate on a contact.

- ✔ **Reports To:** This lookup field on the contact record allows you to organize your contacts hierarchically.

- ✔ **Lead Source:** Use this drop-down list to define where you originated the contact.

- ✔ **Email Opt Out:** This check box reminds you whether a contact should be e-mailed.

- ✔ **Do Not Call:** This check box reminds you whether a contact can be called.

Privacy is a big issue with companies and the selling tactics they employ. Nothing damages a customer relationship more than a contact who's contacted when he or she has asked not to be. To protect your contacts' privacy, be diligent about the Email Opt Out and Do Not Call fields. And users in your company should always check the contact record before calling or marketing to a contact.

Customizing Contact Information

If you complete the standard fields, you'll never have trouble knowing where to reach your contacts . . . whether they'll take your call is another question.

Precision target marketing

A leading telecommunications provider wanted to improve the coordination between sales efforts and marketing programs. Over the course of a year, the provider's marketing department planned numerous campaigns that included direct marketing, tradeshows, customer case studies, client outings, and so on. In the past, marketing managers wasted substantial time trying to extract contact information from the sales teams. By customizing the contact record to collect important personal and business information, and then training sales reps to update custom fields on contacts in Salesforce, the company has realized substantial savings in time and better productivity in targeted marketing programs.

Think about all the personal or professional information that you commonly collect on your best contacts. For example, if Michael Jordan is your client, you might like to know that he loves golf and fine cigars, is married, and has three kids. And he's always driven to be number one.

Ask yourself these questions while you customize your contact record:

- ✔ What professional information is important in your business (for example, prior employers or associations)?
- ✔ What personal information can help you build a better relationship?
- ✔ How do you evaluate the strength of your relationship with the contact?
- ✔ What probing questions do you commonly ask all contacts? (For example, what are their current initiatives and business pains?)

We always advise keeping it simple, but if any specific fields are missing, write them down and seek out your system administrator. (See Chapter 20 for the how-to details on building fields and other design tricks.) Because Salesforce can help you remember important details about your contacts, you can use that information to build better relationships.

Entering and Updating Your Contacts

Your contact database is only as good as the information it contains, so Salesforce has multiple ways for you to get your contacts into the system. You can either start from scratch and manually create new contact records, or if you already have contacts on a spreadsheet or in another tool, you can use Salesforce's simple wizard to import your contacts within minutes. In the following sections, we discuss quick and simple ways to get started and how to update records.

Entering new contacts

Because contacts belong to accounts, the best, most reliable way to create contact records is by starting from the relevant Account detail page. From the Account detail page, you can then add a contact by using either the Create New drop-down field on the sidebar or the New button on the Contacts related list. The result is the same in both situations, and Salesforce automatically pre-fills the Account lookup field. By doing this, you can always find your contact, and your contact's activities appear in a list on the overall Account detail page.

To create contacts by using the best practice, follow these steps:

1. **Search for the account and, on the Search Results page, click the appropriate Account Name link.**

   The Account detail page appears.

2. **Click the New button on the Contacts related list.**

   The Edit mode of a new contact appears. (See Figure 5-1 for an example of a new record being created.)

3. **Fill in the fields as much as you can or as required.**

   The Account field is pre-filled with the account you were working from.

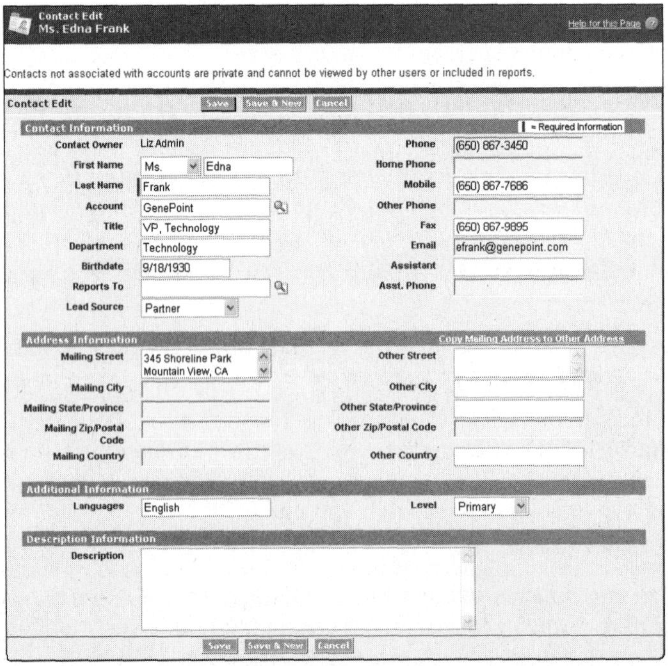

Figure 5-1: Completing fields on a contact record.

4. **When you're done, click one of the following buttons:**

   • **Save:** After you click the Save button, the Contact detail page appears. On this page, you can click the Edit button whenever you need to modify information on the record.

   • **Save & New:** Clicking this button saves the current contact info and automatically opens a new, blank contact record in Edit mode.

Importing your contacts and accounts

If you already have contact lists from another database (for example, Excel or ACT!), you can use the import wizards to create multiple contact records in Salesforce, and you'll be done in no time. The import wizards are located in the Tools sections of either the Accounts or Contacts home page.

When you're importing accounts, you can choose to import just companies and their associated information, or you have the option to import companies and their related contacts in one action. Which route you take really depends on your existing data and what you want in Salesforce.

To import your contacts and accounts automatically, follow these steps:

1. **On the Contacts home page, click Import My Accounts & Contacts under the Tools section.**

   The Import Wizard for My Contacts page appears, which includes four steps for importing records, plus helpful hints.

   If you're a system administrator for Salesforce, you can click the Import My Organizations Business Accounts & Business Contacts link, which allows you to import substantially more records at one time with different owners. If you're an administrator, that link also appears under the Tools sections of the Accounts or Contacts home pages. What's the big deal? Most users can import 500 records at a time, but if you're a system administrator, you can import 50,000 at a time and leap over tall buildings in a single bound.

2. **In your existing contact tool or file, compare your current fields with the fields in Salesforce.**

   If you can map all the information you currently have to fields in Salesforce, move on to Step 3. If you can't, add fields to the account or contact records by customizing Salesforce. (See Chapter 20 for simple instructions on adding fields.)

3. **Export your file.**

   You might have contacts and accounts in an existing database, such as ACT!, Goldmine, Microsoft Access, or Outlook. Most systems like these have simple tools for exporting data into various formats. Select the records and the fields that you want to export. Then export the file and save it in a comma-separated value format. If your accounts are already in spreadsheet format, such as Excel, just resave the file in that format.

4. **Review and prepare your data.**

Refine your accounts and contacts before bringing them into Salesforce or clean them up after the import. . . . It's up to you. Some sales reps prefer to make changes on a spreadsheet first because they're more accustomed to spreadsheets.

When preparing your import file, keep these points in mind:

- Enter your column headers in the first row. We recommend renaming column headers to be consistent with the field names in Salesforce. For example, you could rename the Company field from Outlook as Account Name.

- If you're importing data for your entire company, add a column for Record Owner to signify who should own the record in Salesforce. Otherwise, as the person importing, you own all the records from the file.

- If you sell to different locations of a company (for example, Sony in Tokyo versus Sony in New York), you might want to add a column for Account Site and update the rows on your file to reflect the different sites.

- You can link accounts in the import file by adding columns for Parent Account and Parent Site, and filling in fields as necessary to reflect the hierarchy.

- Make sure that a Type column exists and that fields are filled to correspond to the types of companies you track (customers, partners, prospects, competitors, and so on).

- If your file has more than 500 rows, divide the master file into smaller files to fit the Import Wizard's size limitation. You have to repeat the Import Wizard for each of the smaller files.

- If you're importing contacts and accounts at the same time, you might want to add a column for the billing address fields if those addresses are different from the contacts' mailing addresses.

For more hints on importing, click the Help and Training link and check out the Training and Support information in Salesforce by searching for the keyword *Importing*.

5. **After preparing the file, click the Start the Import Wizard link.**

The Select the Source step appears in a new window.

6. **Use the radio buttons to select the source and click Next.**

   You can't go wrong if you select the Other Data Source option, but the other choices are helpful because Salesforce knows how Outlook and ACT! fields map to Salesforce. When you click Next, the Upload the File step appears.

7. **Click the Browse button, shown in Figure 5-2, to locate and select your import file.**

   If you've already prepared your file, then you've done the heavy lifting on this page. Salesforce pre-fills the character coding of your file based on your Company Profile. If you have questions about character coding in general and what your company should use, ask your administrator.

8. **Select the contact matching type and click Next.**

   If you want Salesforce to avoid importing duplicate records, choose whether you want a duplicate contact to be identified by matching name or e-mail. If a contact record with the matching criteria already exists in Salesforce, Salesforce updates that record with the information in your file. When you click Next, the Map Contact Fields step appears.

Figure 5-2:
Loading the
contact file.

If you see an additional request to choose an account record type for import (right after the Contact Matching Type options), check with your system administrator to find out which one you should choose. This advanced option is available only for Enterprise and Unlimited Edition users. The default type usually is the right answer for most common uses, but better to be safe than sorry.

When you're figuring out how to import data into Salesforce, we recommend testing an import with five or so records first, just to make sure that you know what you're doing. After importing the test data, review your new records to make sure that they contain all the information you want brought in. Delete the test records, refine your import file, if necessary, and then run through the final import.

9. **Map the contact fields between your file and Salesforce, and when you're done, click Next.**

   If you're importing only accounts, skip this step. Otherwise, just go through the fields and use the drop-down lists to select the field from the file that you're importing which maps to the Salesforce field, as shown in Figure 5-3. (The fields are repeatedly listed in each of the drop-down lists.) When you click Next, the Map Contact Phone and Address Fields step appears.

   Mapping fields is simply the process by which you associate a field from one database to a field in another database so that your data appears in the right fields. For example, if you're importing your contacts from MS Outlook, you want data from the field called Company in Outlook to map to the field called Account Name in Salesforce. Take your time when making the mappings. Pay attention to which screens are for account-specific fields and which screens are for contact-specific fields.

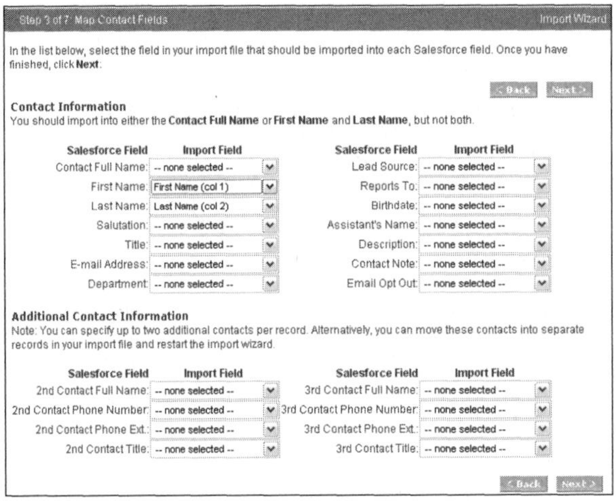

Figure 5-3:
Mapping
the contact
fields.

10. **Map the contact address and phone fields and then click Next.**

    Again, you can skip this step if you're importing just accounts. Map the relevant fields just as you did in Step 9. When you click Next, the Map the Account Fields step appears.

11. **Map the account fields and, when you're done, click Next.**

    You map these fields just like you did in Steps 9 and 10, with two exceptions: Now you're mapping account data, and you can choose to update existing data. For example, if you already have an account record for

Microsoft Corporation in Salesforce, and you entered no other information except the Account Name, you can update that existing account record with the Import Wizard and avoid creating a duplicate account record. So if you want to append existing records, select the Overwrite existing account values check box at the top of this page. When you click Next, the Map Account Phone and Address Fields step appears.

12. **Map account phone and address fields and then click Next.**

    No surprises here; by now, you should be a pro. When you click Next, the Map Extra Import Fields step appears.

13. **Map any extra import fields, and when you're satisfied, click the Import Now button.**

    This step basically warns you about problems with the data or lets you know about fields that haven't been mapped. If you discover an error, you can click the Back button and refine your mapping, or even close the wizard so you can improve your import file. You might have to start over, but at least you avoid importing bad or incomplete data. When you click Import Now, an Importing page appears to confirm that your import is in process.

14. **Click the Finish button and later check the records that you imported.**

    Salesforce sends you an e-mail after it successfully imports your file. To check your import, click the Accounts tab to go to your Accounts home page. Use the Recent Accounts section drop-down list to select the Recently Created option, and a list of the accounts that were recently created appears. Click the link for an account that you just imported to double-check that the information is accurate.

If you're importing both accounts and contacts, scroll down on an applicable account to its Contacts related list and verify that all the right contacts are linked from your import file. Click into a specific contact record and check to see that the information matches your import file.

Updating contact fields

While you work with your contacts, you might need to modify their contact information. To update a contact, follow these steps:

1. **Type the name of your contact in the Search tool and click Go.**

   A Search results page appears.

2. **Click the desired Contact Name link.**

   The Contact detail page appears.

3. **Like with any record, double-click any field that has a pencil icon to its right to edit that field.**

   If a field doesn't have an icon at the right of the field, you have to edit the whole record by clicking the Edit button at the top of the record to make changes. A padlock icon means you can't edit that field at all.

4. **Update the fields as necessary and click Save.**

   The Contact detail page reappears.

Cloning an existing contact

If you want to add a contact that's similar to an existing record, cloning can save you key strokes and time. To clone a contact, go to the existing contact and follow these steps:

1. **Click the Clone button at the top or bottom of the contact record.**

   A new contact record in Edit mode appears. All the information is identical to the previous record.

2. **Edit the information on the new contact record, where appropriate.**

   Pay attention to what's pre-filled because you want to avoid inaccurate information on the new contact record.

3. **When you're done, click Save.**

   You've created a new contact without altering your existing contact.

Organizing Your Contacts

When you have all or a portion of your contacts entered in Salesforce, you can begin to organize them to suit the way you sell.

In the following sections, we show you how you can use views and other tools from the Contacts home page to provide greater focus for you and your sales teams. We also show you an important feature of the contact record that lets you build powerful organizational charts (also called org charts) for contacts of an account. Then, for even more robust organization of your account information, flip to Chapter 17 to find out how to use standard and custom contact reports.

Using contact views

A *contact view* is a list of contacts that match certain criteria. When you select a view, you're basically specifying criteria to limit the results that you get back. The advantage of using a view versus searching is that you can use the view over and over again. For example, if you like to send out a card on a contact's birthday, you can benefit from a preset view for this month's birthdays.

The Contacts home page comes with four predefined views:

- ✔ **All Contacts:** Provides a list of all the contact records entered into Salesforce. Depending on the way your company has set up your security model, you might not see this view or its results.

- ✔ **Birthdays This Month:** Generates a list of contacts whose birthdays land in the current month (assuming you collect that information).

- ✔ **New This Week:** Generates a list of contacts that have been created since the beginning of the week.

- ✔ **Recently Viewed Contacts:** Lets you look at a list of contacts that you've recently viewed.

You use a predefined contact view in exactly the same way that you use an account view (as we mention in Chapter 4) or the predefined view for any other record.

Creating custom contact views

If you want special lists for the way that you track your contacts, we recommend building custom views, just like you do for any other record. (For an example of how to create a custom view for accounts, see Chapter 4.) For example, if you sell medical equipment, and once a month you like to call your contacts who are dentists, you can create a view to simplify your work.

Developing Organizational Charts

Having 20 contacts associated with an account is great, but you might not be any further along in understanding the pecking order. In practice, sales reps have been building organizational charts (or org charts) to strategize on accounts ever since someone thought up org charts, but often, the charts resided on whiteboards and PowerPoint presentations. (And whiteboards are tough to lug around.) By using the org chart feature in Salesforce, you can quickly define the reporting structure for your contacts and use that structure to more easily identify your relationships with your customers.

To build an org chart in Salesforce, follow these steps:

1. **Add all the contacts for an account.**

   See the section "Entering and Updating Your Contacts," earlier in this chapter, for details about adding records.

2. **Go to the contact record for a person low on the totem pole and click the Edit button.**

   The record appears in Edit mode.

3. **In the Reports To field, type the name of the contact's boss, and then click the Lookup icon to the right of the field (it looks like a little magnifying glass).**

   A pop-up window that contains search results appears.

4. **Select the correct contact or refine your search until you can select the right contact.**

   The pop-up window disappears, and the Reports To field is pre-filled with the selected contact, as shown in Figure 5-4.

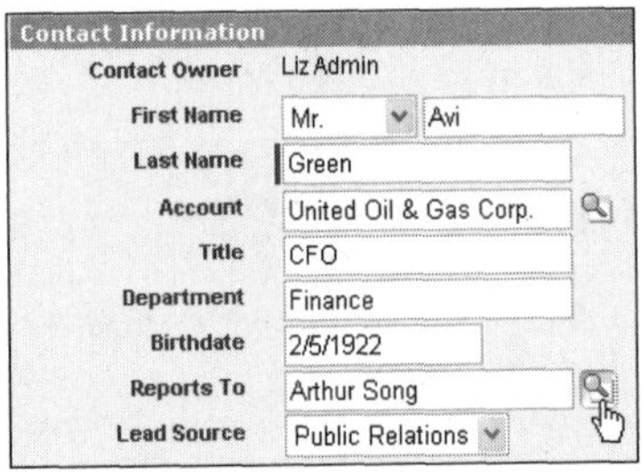

Figure 5-4:
Selecting
the boss.

Contact Information	
Contact Owner	Liz Admin
First Name	Mr. ▾ Avi
Last Name	Green
Account	United Oil & Gas Corp. 🔍
Title	CFO
Department	Finance
Birthdate	2/5/1922
Reports To	Arthur Song 🔍
Lead Source	Public Relations ▾

5. **When you're done, click Save.**

   The Contact detail page appears.

6. **To display the hierarchy, click the View Org Chart link that appears to the right of the Reports To field on the contact record.**

   An Org Chart list page appears, and like other lists, you can click a link to go to a specific contact.

Some sales reps run into certain challenges based on the way they create the org charts in Salesforce. One such challenge is gaps; you just might not know or even care about the entire reporting structure. By getting creative and building placeholder contacts, you can avoid pitfalls. For example, if you sell to both the business and the technology side of a customer, create a contact record called IT Organization and another called Business Organization, and then align your contacts accordingly. This technique also works well for *orphans,* where you know one contact in a department and don't want to leave the contact out of the org chart for the entire account.

Performing Actions with Contact Related Lists

Fields on a contact record are useful for capturing the essential contact information for a person. But where do you track and review all the interactions that you've had with a contact? To add, edit, delete, and keep track of this detail, use the related lists located on the Contact detail page.

Turn to Chapter 6 if you want to find out all the wonderful things you can do with related lists to keep track of activities with people and the companies they work for. But if you're looking for typical ways that sales people use Contact related lists, go over the following list of features that you can find in the Contact related lists:

- ✔ If you want to track, edit, or close your pending activities for a contact, use the Open Activities related list. In this list, you can click the New Task button to set up a to-do item or click the New Event button to schedule a calendared activity. See Chapter 6 for the how-to details on these activities.

- ✔ If you want to view what has happened with a contact to date, review the Activity History related list. Sales reps commonly use Log a Call to capture details for a call taking place or after the fact. Go to Chapter 7 for the ins and outs of sending e-mail.

- ✔ Ever wonder whether your contact is paying attention? If you send HTML e-mail from Salesforce, you can use the HTML Email Status related list to see how your contact is responding to your e-mail. By using this list, you can send an e-mail, find out whether your contact is viewing your e-mail, and see how quickly he or she views a message after you send it.

- ✔ If you want to store attachments that relate to a contact, use the Notes & Attachments related list. Click the Attach File button to store important documents, such as confidentiality agreements or contact resumes.

Though you can click the New Note button to jot down your comments and even keep them private, we recommend that you track your comments in tasks, instead. Using tasks to track your activities allows for better timestamping, editing, and reporting on your interactions with your contacts. See the "Tracking your tasks" section in Chapter 2 for more information on tasks.

✔ If a contact brings you a new deal, you can click the New button on the Opportunities related list and automatically associate your contact with the opportunity record. See Chapter 9 for details on creating opportunities.

✔ To keep track of or edit your contact's participation in campaigns, use the Campaign History related list. And if you want a contact to be part of an active campaign, click the Add Campaign button. For example, if marketing sends out invites to a customer event, you can use the Add Campaign feature to efficiently add a contact to the list of recipients. See Chapter 12 for more tips on campaigns.

Merging Duplicate Records

Your once-tiny Rolodex is now a gigantic contact database because you're managing more contacts and covering more territory. However, don't let those large piles of data walk all over you. You have to show that data who's boss. In this section, we show you simple tools that can help you keep your contact database in line and up to date.

Try as you might, sometimes you come across duplicate contact records in the system. Instead of deleting one or several of the duplicate records and potentially losing valuable information in those records, you can use Salesforce to merge contact records easily.

Similar to merging account records, to merge contact records, you must be the Contact Owner of the records, the Contact Owner's manager (that is, the Contact Owner must be subordinate to you in the Role Hierarchy), or a system administrator.

To merge contacts, go to the account record that has a duplicate contact and follow these steps:

1. **On the Contact related list, click the Merge Contacts button, as shown in Figure 5-5.**

   Step 1 of the Merge My Contacts tool appears.

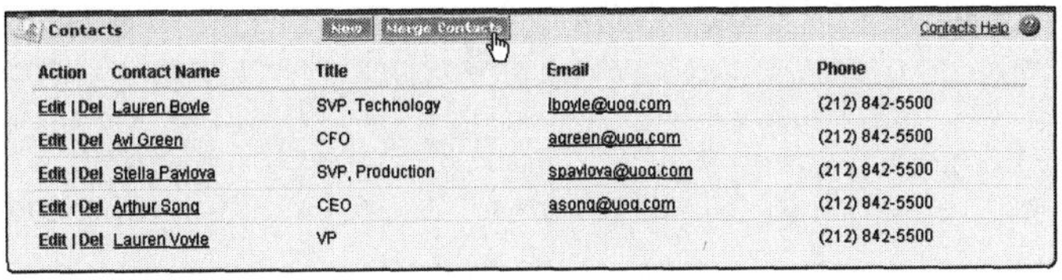

Figure 5-5:
Merging
duplicate
contacts.

2. **Type the name of the contact that you need to merge in the field to the left of the Find Contacts button and click the Find Contacts button.**

   A search results page appears, displaying a list of records.

3. **Select a maximum of three records to merge and click Next.**

   In Salesforce, you can merge only three records at a time. The Step 2 page of the tool appears with a side-by-side comparison of the selected contact records.

4. **Compare the information and select the radio buttons for the values that you want to retain.**

   At the top of each column, you can also choose to keep all the values from one record by clicking the Select All link.

5. **When you finish reviewing, click Merge.**

   A pop-up window appears, prompting you to verify that you want to perform the merge. After you click OK, the contact record reappears, and associated records from related lists are now linked on the contact record.

Chapter 6

Managing Activities

Activities in Salesforce are scheduled calendar events and tasks. In many ways, Salesforce's events and tasks are just like the activities you use in Microsoft Outlook. You can schedule events on your calendar, invite people to meetings, book a conference room, and add tasks to your to-do lists so that you don't forget to get things done.

You can synchronize Salesforce with Outlook so that you don't have to input activities twice. (See Chapter 3 to install and configure Salesforce's Outlook synchronization plug-in.)

However, Salesforce takes activities further: You can easily link events and tasks to other related records, such as accounts, contacts, and so on. So you can view activities both in the context of a relevant item (for example, all activities that relate to an account), and as a standalone from your calendar and task lists in the comfort and convenience of your home page. And, if you're a manager, Salesforce allows you to stay up to speed on your users and how they're spending their time.

By managing activities in Salesforce, you can better coordinate with your team, quickly assess what's going on in your accounts, and focus on the next steps to close deals or solve issues.

In this chapter, we first show you how to schedule events and create tasks. Then, we cover how to find and view activities, both from your home page and from specific record pages, such as accounts and opportunities.

Reviewing Activities

You can use activities in Salesforce to track all the significant tasks and events involved in acquiring, selling, and servicing customers. Think about all the actions that you and your teams currently perform to accomplish your job — meetings, calls, e-mails, letters — and imagine the value of all that information in one place at your fingertips. You can have such a place in Salesforce, and you can easily link your activities together in an organized fashion.

Salesforce features six types of activities that you can access from the Open Activities and Activity History related lists displayed on many of the major records, including accounts, contacts, leads, opportunities, and cases. In this chapter, we focus on events and tasks, but in the following list, we briefly explain all the various activity records you can track in Salesforce:

- ✔ **Task:** Essentially a to-do. Use this activity record as your online yellow sticky note. It's an activity that needs to be completed, but it doesn't have a specific time or duration associated with it. For example, if you know that you're supposed to follow up with a contact by sending a written letter, you can create a task such as Send Letter.

- ✔ **Event:** A calendared activity. An event has a scheduled time, date, and duration associated with it. Examples of common events are Meetings, Conference Calls, and Tradeshows.

- ✔ **Log a Call:** A task record of a completed call. Use Log a Call during or after a call to make sure that you capture important details. For example, use it when a contact calls you and you want to record comments or outcomes from the discussion.

- ✔ **Mail Merge:** Logs an activity for a document that you've mail merged. With Mail Merge, you can quickly merge common Microsoft Word templates with customer information and track those activities in Salesforce.

- ✔ **Send an Email:** Logs an activity for an e-mail that you send to a contact or a lead. You can send e-mails from Salesforce or Microsoft Outlook, and capture that information directly inside Salesforce.

Salesforce's online suggestion box, also known as Salesforce Ideas, let's you and a community of other Salesforce users within your company post suggestions on any topic for others (other licensed users of Salesforce within your company) to vote on and discuss. This sharing of ideas is a valuable way for your company to mine feedback from your employees that could result in product or service innovations. Ideas are ranked based on popularity over time, and you can group Ideas into multiple subject areas. You can also set up this sort of action for your customers (see what Starbucks did at `http://mystarbucksidea.force.com/home/home.jsp`). For more information on setting up and using Salesforce Ideas, visit `http://www.kao consulting.com`.

Creating Activities

Before you can begin managing your time or activities in Salesforce, you need to know the easiest and most reliable way to add events and tasks.

Creating an event

When you want to schedule activities that have a particular place, time, and duration, use event records. By using event records, you and your sales teams can keep better track of your calendars.

You can create an event from your home page, its calendar views, or the Open Activity related list of a record. The best method to choose often depends on what you're doing. If you're carving out meetings on a day, add events from your calendar's Day View. If you're working on a customer deal, you might create the event from an opportunity record. The end result is the same.

If you're just getting accustomed to filling out records in Salesforce, create events from the record that's most directly associated with the event. By using this method, many of the lookup fields are pre-filled for you. So when you save, you ensure that you can find the activity quickly because it's linked to all the right records.

To create an event from a relevant record (such as a contact or account record), follow these steps:

1. **Enter names in the sidebar Search for the record to which you want to link the event and click the Go button.**

   For example, if you want to schedule a meeting about an account, you search for the account name. When you click Go, a Search results page appears.

2. **Click a link in the Name column to go to the record you want.**

   The record's detail page appears.

3. Scroll down to the Open Activities related list on the page and click the New Event button, as shown in Figure 6-1.

A New Event page appears. If you created this event from a relevant record, the name of the person or the related record is pre-filled for you.

Open Activities								Open Activities Help
		New Task	New Event					
Action	Subject	Related To		Task	Due Date	Status	Priority	Assigned To
Edit | Cls	Send Letter	Express Logistics and Transport		✓	9/25/2008	Not Started	Normal	Liz Admin
Edit | Cls	update status report	00001005		✓		Not Started	Normal	Liz Admin

4. Fill in the relevant fields.

Pay close attention to the required fields highlighted in red. Depending on your company's customization, your event record might differ from the standard, but here are tips on some of the standard fields:

- **Assigned To:** Defaults to you. Use the Lookup icon to assign the event to another user.

- **Subject:** The event's subject, which appears on the calendar. Click the combo box icon. A pop-up window appears, displaying a list of your company's event types. When you click a selection, the window closes and your selection appears in the Subject field. To the immediate right of your selection's text, add a brief description. For example, you might click the Meeting link and then type **-Define Requirements** to explain the event's purpose.

- **Related To:** The standard event record shows two drop-down lists that you can use to link the event with relevant records, as highlighted in Figure 6-2. The first drop-down list relates to a person — a contact or lead. The second list relates to other types of records — an account, opportunity, or case. First, select the type of record, and then use the associated Lookup icon to select the desired record. For example, if you select Opportunity from the second drop-down list, you can use the Lookup icon to find a specific opportunity.

If you use the Related To fields on activities, you'll rarely have problems finding an activity later. For example, if you sell through channel partners, you might associate a meeting with a partner contact, but you might relate the meeting to an end-customer account. When you save the event, it appears on the related lists of both records.

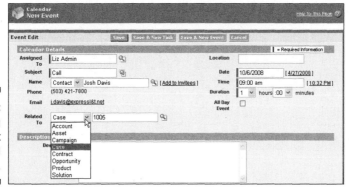

Figure 6-2:
Linking
the event
to related
records.

- **Location:** Provides you or other invitees with a hint about where the event will take place. Examples include conference rooms, cities, and office locations.

- **Time:** Lets you specify the time. You can use basic shorthand and avoid unnecessary key strokes. For example, type **9a** for 9:00 a.m. or **2p** for 2:00 p.m.

- **Duration:** Lets you specify the duration of an event in hours and fifteen-minute intervals.

5. **When you're done, click Save.**

   The page you started from reappears, and the event appears under the Open Activities related list for the associated records. The event also appears on the home page of the user assigned to the event.

   Alternatively, click the Save & New Event or Save & New Task button if you want to immediately create another activity. A new activity record appears in Edit mode.

If you're an Outlook user, Salesforce makes it easy for you to add events from Salesforce directly into your Outlook calendar. Go to an event record and click the Add to Outlook button. An Outlook dialog box appears. Review the information and click the Save & Close button. Then check your Outlook Calendar for the meeting record.

Viewing events in your calendar

From your home page or an event record, you can access your calendar to get a daily, weekly, or monthly overview of your schedule. Simply click any of the three calendar view icons displayed (see Figure 6-3).

When you're looking at a summary view of all your events in Salesforce's calendar, you can simply hover your mouse over an event to get a pop-up glimpse of that event's details. This feature can really save you time because you can stay on the same browser page, so you don't have to wait for any additional pages to load.

Using pop-up reminders

Similar to Microsoft Outlook, Salesforce triggers pop-up reminders about events at a set time before the event is scheduled to start. If you live your life daily in Salesforce and have the application constantly logged in on your machine, this feature makes sure you don't forget an important meeting with a customer.

Make sure that your browser's pop-up blocker protection is set to allow pop-ups that come from the Salesforce domain. Otherwise, if your browser has the pop-up blocker feature turned on, when you create an event, a little warning box appears every time your browser attempts to display a reminder box.

If, on the other hand, you're the type that lets pop-up reminders pile up on your computer screen, or you log in to Salesforce infrequently (what sacrilege!), you can disable this feature. Simply go to Setup⇨Personal Setup⇨My Personal Information⇨Reminders and uncheck the Trigger Alert When Reminder Comes Due check box. Remember to hit Save after you finish.

Creating a task

Some sales reps refer to tasks as *ticklers;* others call them reminders or to-dos. Whatever your favorite term, use task records when you want to remind yourself or someone else of an activity that needs to get done.

You can create a task from the My Tasks section of your home page or from the Create New drop-down list on any page within Salesforce. We use both methods, depending on whether we're planning out our weeks or strategizing about a particular account, contact, or other record.

To create a task from the relevant record, follow these steps:

1. **Enter a name in the sidebar Search tool for the record to which you want to link the task and click the Go button.**

   For example, if you want to set a task to review a proposal that relates to an opportunity, search for the opportunity name. After you click Go, a Search results page appears.

2. **Click a link in the Name column to go to the record you want.**

   The record's detail page appears.

3. **Select Create Task from the sidebar or click the New Task button on the Open Activities related list of a record, as shown in Figure 6-4.**

   Either way, the result is the same. A New Task page appears.

   When creating tasks, go to the record that the task is most directly related to before adding the task. By taking this path, you ensure that your task is easy to find because it's automatically associated with the correct record and its account. For example, if you're creating a task to follow up on a letter to a contact, you most likely add the task from the contact record.

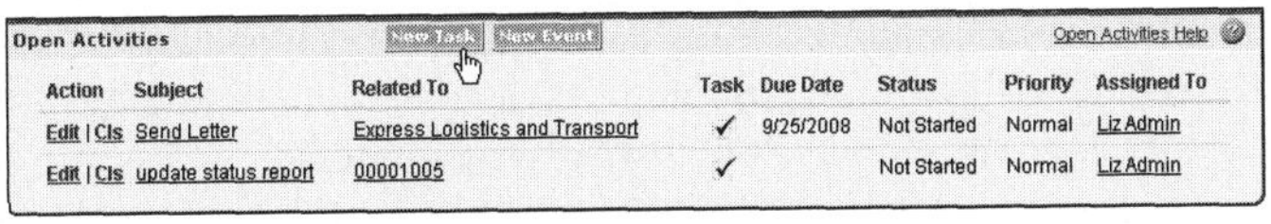

Figure 6-4:
Creating a
new task.

Open Activities		New Task New Event					Open Activities Help
Action	Subject	Related To	Task	Due Date	Status	Priority	Assigned To
Edit | Cls	Send Letter	Express Logistics and Transport	✓	9/25/2008	Not Started	Normal	Liz Admin
Edit | Cls	update status report	00001005	✓		Not Started	Normal	Liz Admin

4. **Fill in the relevant fields.**

   Like the event record, your fields may vary, but here are some tips on adding a task:

   • **Assigned To:** Defaults to you. Use the Lookup icon to assign the task to another user.

   You can choose to add multiple assignees to the task, too. Each assignee gets his or her own copy of this task. Use multiple assignees if you need to send the same task out to several people (for example, to turn in your monthly expense report). This approach doesn't act like a queuing system. If one of the assignees completes and closes his or her task, that action doesn't close or remove the open tasks belonging to the other assignees.

- **Subject:** The task's subject, which appears on the My Tasks section of the Assigned To's home page. Click the combo box icon. A pop-up window appears, displaying a list of your company's activity types. When you click a selection, the window closes and your selection appears in the Subject field. To the immediate right of your selection, add a brief description. For example, you might click the Send Letter link and then type **-Introduction** to explain the task's purpose.

- **Related To:** The standard activity record shows two drop-down lists that you can use to link the task with relevant records similar to the event fields. First select the type of record, and then use the associated Lookup icon to select the desired record.

- **Priority:** Denotes the task's importance. High priority tasks display an exclamation mark (!) to the left of the activity on the assigned user's home page.

- **Status:** Defines the status of the task.

- **Due Date:** The date by which you expect the task to be completed. This is typically an optional field — but an important one if you want to make sure a task gets done when it's supposed to. Hovering your cursor over this field makes a calendar window pop up, and you can select a date from this calendar.

5. **Select the Send Email Notification check box if you want to notify the user to whom you're assigning this new task.**

   You can't guarantee that every user will log in to Salesforce daily, so e-mail notifications are an effective way to make sure that tasks are delivered to the right people in a timely fashion.

6. **When you're done, click Save.**

   The page that you started from reappears, and the task displays under the Open Activities related list for the associated records. The task also appears in the My Tasks section of the home page of the user who's assigned to the task.

Make sure that you set your My Tasks view on the home page so that your tasks are included in the filter. The view defaults to Overdue, which can confuse some people when they don't see a recently created task in that area.

Always link your tasks with the relevant records in Salesforce. Otherwise, you run the risk of losing valuable customer information that might have been captured in that task.

Logging a call

Sometimes, you perform a task and just want to log the activity after the fact. For example, a contact calls you on the phone, or you get stopped in the coffee room by your boss to talk about a customer issue. In these situations, instead of creating a task and then completing it, use the Log a Call feature.

When you click the Log a Call button, you're simply creating a task record that has a Completed Activity Status. To log a call, go to the record that the call relates to (an account or lead record, for example) and follow these steps:

1. **Scroll down to the Activity History related list and click the Log a Call button.**

   The Log a Call page appears, displaying fields for a completed task at the top of the page and fields for a follow-up activity at the bottom of the page.

2. **Fill out or modify any of the fields to log the call.**

   The Status field is preset to Completed, as shown in Figure 6-5.

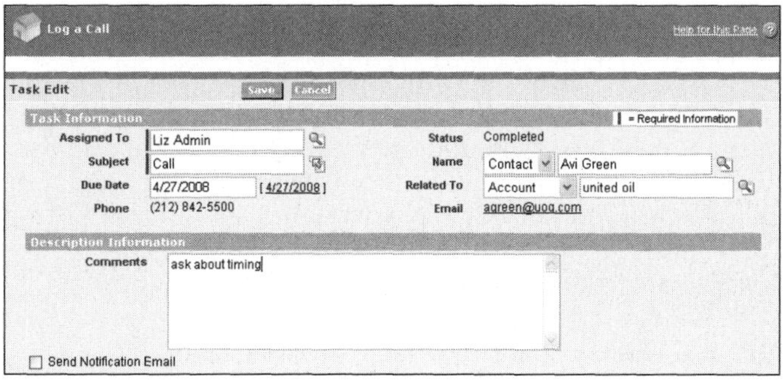

Figure 6-5:
Logging
a call.

3. **If applicable, add another related task by filling out the fields below the Schedule Follow Up Task header.**

   Although certain fields are labeled as required, the follow-up task is optional.

4. **Select the Send Notification Email check box for the logged call (and for the follow-up task if you choose to schedule that) and click Save when you're finished.**

    The detail page that you started from reappears. The call record appears under the Activity History related list. If you set up a new follow-up task, that record appears under the Open Activities related list.

Rather than using the Notes feature in Salesforce to track details of your interactions with customers and prospects, we recommend using Log a Call to record this type of information. Tasks allow for easier reporting, timestamping, editing, and viewing capabilities.

Organizing and Viewing Activities

You can view your activities from the home page and from a specific record's Open Activities or Activity History related lists. If you're planning out your calendar, use the home page. If you're working from a particular account, contact, or other item, you can get better context on pertinent activities from the related lists on the record.

After you create (or are assigned to) activities, you probably want to view them so that you can prioritize and complete them.

If you're planning around a specific record, such as a contact or opportunity, you can view linked activities from the Open Activities and Activity History related lists located on a detail page.

The two related lists work hand in hand. An event record automatically moves from the Open Activities related list to the Activity History related list when the scheduled date and time passes. A task record remains on the Open Activities related list until its Status is changed to Completed; then, the record appears on the Activity History related list.

To view activities from a detail page, follow these steps:

1. **Open a saved record.**

    The detail page of the record appears. The saved record appears at the top, and related lists are at the bottom of the page.

2. **Scroll down until you see the Open Activities and Activity History related lists.**

    If you've already created related activities, activity links appear in the lists.

3. **Click an item listed under the Subject column.**

   The activity record appears.

Updating Activities

Things happen: Meetings get cancelled, and small tasks suddenly become big priorities. With Salesforce, you can perform many of the actions that a normal time-management tool would allow you to do, including delegating activities to other users, rescheduling, editing information, deleting records, and so on.

You can do the following basic functions by clicking buttons at the top of an activity record:

- ✔ **Edit:** Update any of the fields in the record whose fields now appear, and make sure you save.
- ✔ **Delete:** Delete the record. A pop-up window appears in which you can confirm the deletion.
- ✔ **Create a Follow Up Task:** Generate a related task. A New Task page opens, pre-filled with information from the prior record.
- ✔ **Create a Follow Up Event:** Schedule a related meeting. A New Event page appears, pre-filled with information from the prior record.

Assigning activities

Sometimes, you may create activities and decide to delegate them later. Salesforce lets you easily reassign tasks and events, and notify users of assignments.

To assign an activity, open the activity record and follow these steps:

1. **Click the Edit button.**
2. **Click the Lookup icon to the right of the Assigned To field.**

   A pop-up window appears, displaying a list of your Salesforce users.

3. **Use the Search field to search for the user or select the user from the list.**

   After you make a selection, the pop-up window disappears, and your selection appears in the Assigned To field.

4. **Select the Send Email Notification check box if you want to alert the user by e-mail and then click Save.**

   The activity record reappears, and the Assigned To field has been modified.

Completing a task

When you're done with a task, you want to gladly get it off the list of things to do. You can mark a task as complete from your home page or from the Open Activities related list in which the task link is displayed.

To complete a task, follow these steps:

1. **If you're viewing the task from an Open Activities related list, click the Cls link to the left of the task. If you're looking at the task on the home page, click the X link in the Completed column.**

   Both links create the same result: The task appears in Edit mode, and the Status field has been changed to Completed. (Your company might have its own terminology for the Completed status.)

2. **Type any last changes and click Save.**

   Some reps update the Comments field if they have relevant new information. The detail page reappears, and the completed task now appears under the Activity History related list.

You can synchronize your activities with Microsoft Outlook. Refer to Chapter 3 for more information.

Chapter 7

Sending E-Mail

· ·

· ·

E-mail is a fundamental method for communicating with customers, prospects, and friends. By using e-mail correctly, you can manage more sales territory and be responsive to customers. However, by sending e-mail inappropriately, you can leave a bad impression or lose a client.

If e-mail is an indispensable part of your business, you and other users can send e-mail from Salesforce and track the communication history from relevant records, such as accounts, contacts, opportunities, and cases. This capability is helpful if you inherit a major customer account; you can potentially view all the e-mail interactions from a single account record.

Sending an e-mail is a cinch, and if that were all this chapter covered, we'd have summarized it in just one section. But Salesforce provides additional e-mail tools to help you better sell to, service, and wow your customers. In this chapter, we show you all the tricks and best practices for sending a basic e-mail, mass e-mailing, using templates, and tracking responses.

Understanding E-Mail Fields in Salesforce

An e-mail in Salesforce is an activity record comprising fields for the message and for the people you want to keep in the loop on the message.

The e-mail record comes with standard fields that people commonly use when sending e-mail. Most fields are self-explanatory if you've ever sent an e-mail before. This list summarizes some additional fields:

✔ **Related To:** Use this field to relate the e-mail to an account, opportunity, product, campaign, solution, or case record in Salesforce, depending on your edition. By completing this field, the e-mail is stored under the Activity History related list of that record.

✔ **Additional To:** Use this field to type in additional primary recipients. They don't have to be contacts or leads in Salesforce.

✔ **Attachment:** You can attach files up to 10MB per e-mail.

Setting Up Your E-Mail

Before you begin e-mailing people from Salesforce, check out a couple of setup options that can save you time and headaches. In the following sections, we show you how to personalize your outbound e-mail and how to build personal e-mail templates for common messages that you send to people.

Personalizing your e-mail settings

When you send an e-mail by using Salesforce, the recipient can receive the message just as if you sent the e-mail from your current e-mail program. The e-mail message appears as if it came from your business e-mail address, and you can use a standard signature to go with your message. And if the recipient replies to your e-mail, that reply e-mail comes right to your existing inbox. To pull this off, you need to personalize your e-mail settings in Salesforce.

To set up your e-mail, follow these steps:

1. **Go to Setup⇨Personal Email⇨Email⇨My Email Settings.**

   The My Email Settings page appears in Edit mode.

2. **Modify the two required fields, as necessary, to specify the outgoing name and the return e-mail address.**

3. **Select the Yes radio button if you want to send a blind copy to your existing e-mail inbox.**

   If, for example, you like to keep e-mails in customer folders in your e-mail application, you don't have to give up this practice.

4. **Modify the Email Signature field.**

   If you're personalizing your e-mail settings for the first time, you might notice a default signature from Salesforce. This message appears at the bottom of your e-mail in lieu of your signature. Unless you're using Personal Edition, go ahead and change it.

5. **When you're done, click Save.**

   The Email page under Personal Setup appears, and your settings are modified.

Building personal e-mail templates

If you ask your top sales reps about sending e-mail, they probably tell you that they don't re-create the wheel every time they send certain messages to customers. It's a waste of their time, and time is money.

In your standard sales process, you probably send out a variety of e-mails to customers, including

✔ Letters of introduction

✔ Thank-you notes

✔ Responses to common objections

✔ Answers on competition

Although you do need to personalize a message to fit the specific details of a customer, you probably use certain effective phrases and sentences over and over again. Instead of searching for a prior message and cutting and pasting, you can create personal e-mail templates and improve your productivity.

To create a personal template, follow these steps:

1. **Go to Setup⇨Personal Setup⇨Email⇨My Templates.**

   An Email Templates page appears. Select the My Personal Email Templates folder in the drop-down list, if it's not already set to that.

2. **Click the New Template button.**

   Step 1 of the template wizard appears.

3. **Select the radio button for Text, HTML, or Custom to set the type of e-mail that you want to create and click Next.**

   The HTML and Custom options are both in HTML; the HTML option uses letterhead, and the Custom option doesn't.

The next page of the wizard appears, and the content of the page depends on the choice you made. HTML has certain advantages, from an appearance and tracking standpoint, but not all e-mail programs can receive HTML e-mail.

4. **If you select Text in Step 3, complete the template fields provided (see Figure 7-1) and click Save.**

   You can use the template only after you select the Available for Use check box. After clicking Save, a Text Email Template page for your new template appears in Saved mode with an Attachments related list, which you can use if you want to attach a standard document. If you're only interested in creating text e-mail templates, your work is done.

Figure 7-1:
Creating
a text
template.

5. **If you select either HTML option (HTML or Custom) in Step 3, enter the properties for the e-mail template and click the Save & Next button.**

   If you choose to build your e-mail template with a letterhead, you have to select the letterhead and layout by using the drop-down lists provided. After you click the Save & Next button, the Step 3 page of the wizard appears.

   You can create HTML or Custom e-mail templates only if you have the Edit HTML Templates permission.

6. **Create the HTML version by typing and formatting the content and copying and pasting merge fields.**

7. **Click Preview to review your work and, when you're done, click the Save & Next button.**

   The Step 4 page of the wizard appears.

8. **Enter the text version of the e-mail template.**

   Some of your customers can't or don't want to receive HTML e-mails, in which case they receive the text version. If the message is similar or identical to the HTML version, click the Copy Text from HTML Version button and modify the content, as needed.

9. **When you're done, click the Save & Done button.**

   An HTML or Custom Email Template page for your new template appears in Saved mode with an Attachments related list, which you can use for attaching standard documents.

Saving Third-Party Emails to Salesforce

Salesforce allows users to send e-mails to Leads and Contacts; however the management of the conversations (that is, the back and forth of e-mail dialogue that occurs) happens in your company's e-mail management system of choice.

Many companies today are moving their e-mail systems online to reduce the costs of using and maintaining a traditional e-mail software system like Microsoft Outlook. Don't get us wrong, Outlook (and Lotus Notes) are the big gorillas of the e-mail (officially called "productivity tools") space. At the same time, acceptance of using e-mail systems like Google Gmail or Yahoo! Mail for business purposes is gaining momentum.

Chapter 3 explains how to download the Connect for Microsoft Outlook plug-in to synchronize e-mails in Outlook with Salesforce Leads and Contacts.

If you're using a third-party online e-mail system, you can save your outbound emails to Salesforce, too.

Activating Email to Salesforce

To first activate Email to Salesforce, have your administrator go to Setup⇨ Administration Setup⇨Email Administration⇨Email to Salesforce. The brief Email to Salesforce page provides two checkboxes for you to check. Click the Edit button in the middle of the page, to check the box to the left of the Active field, to enable Email to Salesforce.

If you've got some sophisticated e-mail security policies, and know if your e-mail domains support any of following protocols: SPF, SenderID, or Domain-Keys, also check the box to the left of the Advanced Email Security Settings. Salesforce uses these protocols to verify the legitimacy of the sender's e-mail server. If the e-mail server passes at least one of these protocols, then Salesforce processes that e-mail and proceeds to log it as an activity under a Lead or Contact.

Once you've made your checkbox selections and click the Save button in the middle of the page, a pop-up box appears that optionally allows you to notify all your Salesforce users about the Email to Salesforce feature.

Identifying your Email to Salesforce address

Once your administrator has activated Email to Salesforce, a new link appears within the Setup⇨Personal Setup⇨Email section. Within this section, click the My Email to Salesforce link to get to the My Email to Salesforce page. In the middle of the page, a highlighted field notes your Email to Salesforce address. Whenever you're writing an e-mail in your online e-mail system (let's use Gmail as the example), paste that address into the BCC: field of your e-mail. When you send your e-mail, it will also be logged as an activity in Salesforce, under whichever Lead or Contact record whose e-mail address matches that in the TO: field.

If you send and receive e-mail from multiple addresses (and possibly from the same inbox), you can list out all your e-mail addresses so Salesforce can associate correspondence from those e-mail addresses to the automatically-generated Email to Salesforce address. To edit your e-mail addresses, follow these steps:

1. **Click the Edit button in the middle of the My Email to Salesforce page.**

2. **In the My Email Addresses field, add all the e-mail addresses that apply, separated by commas.**

Saving an e-mail to Salesforce

Now that you have your Email to Salesforce special e-mail address, it's time to use it.

Keeping your web browser open to Salesforce and the My Email to Salesforce page, open a new browser window to access your online e-mail system and compose an e-mail (again, we'll use Google Gmail as the example) to a person whose e-mail you know is in Salesforce, associated with a Lead or Contact. (Make sure your relationship with this person allows you to send test e-mails to them or you might have some explaining to do!) Simply copy the special e-mail address and paste it into the BCC: field. When you're done writing the body of the e-mail, send it, and voila! Almost instantaneously, it will appear as an activity associated with that Lead or Contact.

Sending E-Mail from Salesforce

You can send an e-mail to any lead or contact stored in Salesforce that has a valid e-mail address. By sending from Salesforce, you can ensure that you and your team members can keep track of critical outbound communications to customers and prospects.

Creating and sending e-mail

You can initiate your outbound e-mail from many different records in Salesforce, including opportunity, account, case, campaign, lead, and contact records. To create and send an e-mail, go to the relevant record and follow these steps:

1. **Click the Send an Email button on the Activity History related list.**

   A Send an Email page appears. The Email format is in Text, with a Switch to *Format* link appearing to the right of it. Alternatively, click the Send an Email button in the HTML Email Status related list to default to HTML format. Either way, if you change your mind, you can always switch formats on the Send an Email edit page.

2. **Click the Switch to Text Only link if you don't want to send the message in HTML. (In that event only, a dialog box appears to warn you that any HTML formatting will be removed. When you click OK, the box disappears, and the format is switched.) Similarly, click the Switch to HTML link to send your message in HTML format.**

3. **Type the recipient's name in the To field and click the Lookup icon on the right of the field to search for the contact or lead.**

   A pop-up window appears, containing a search tool and a list of search results.

   If you send an e-mail from the relevant lead or contact record, you can eliminate this step because the To field is pre-filled. But remember to use the Related To field to associate to other records, such as an opportunity.

4. **Select the correct person by clicking the name or refine your search by modifying the name or using wildcards, and then click the Go button.**

   When you select the recipient, the pop-up window disappears, and the To field is populated with your selection.

5. **Use the Related To drop-down list to associate the e-mail with the correct type of record, and then click the Lookup icon to the right of the adjacent field to find the exact record — similar to the process in Steps 3 and 4.**

   Depending on which record you started from, the Related To drop-down list might already be filled.

6. **In the Additional To field, type in additional primary recipient e-mails.**

   These folks get their e-mail on the To list when they receive and open up your message. They don't have to be contacts or leads.

7. **Click the CC link or the BCC link to copy other contacts or users to the e-mail.**

   A pop-up window appears, containing a drop-down list for co-workers at your company and contacts of the account.

8. **Select names in the Contacts list box, use the double arrows to include them as recipients, and when you're done click Save.**

   The pop-up window disappears, and the CC and BCC fields reflect your selections.

9. **Click in the CC or BCC fields and add additional e-mail addresses, as needed.**

   Salesforce allows you to send e-mails to people who aren't contacts, leads, or users. Just type the e-mail address directly into this field.

10. **Complete the Subject and Body fields of the message and, when you're done, click Send.**

    If your contact or lead in the To field doesn't yet have an e-mail address, this absence will be flagged before you send the e-mail. A Click Here to Edit the Email Address link appears that allows you to associate an e-mail with the record without having to leave your Send an Email page.

    The record that you started from reappears, and a link to a copy of your e-mail appears in the Activity History related lists of the records that you linked. (See the Bonus Chapter on the book's Web site for details on using the standard formatting tools.)

Using e-mail templates

In the section "Building personal e-mail templates," earlier in this chapter, we show you how to create a personalized template. In this section, you can find out how to send an e-mail that uses a template you've created. First, create an e-mail (as described in the preceding section), and then follow these additional steps before you send it:

1. **Before you modify the Subject and Body fields, click the Select Template button at the top of the page, as shown in Figure 7-2.**

   A pop-up window appears, displaying a list of available templates.

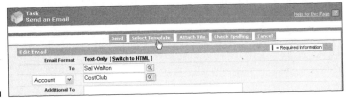

Figure 7-2:
Using
an e-mail
template.

2. **Click the Folder drop-down list and select the desired folder.**

   The pop-up window refreshes, displaying a list of available templates based on your folder selection.

3. **Select the desired template by clicking the relevant link in the Name column.**

   The pop-up window disappears, and the page reappears with content based on the template that you selected.

4. **Modify the message to further personalize the e-mail and, when you're done, click Send.**

   The record you started from reappears, and a link to a copy of your e-mail appears under the Activity History related lists of the linked records.

Sending Mass E-Mail

If you struggle to stay in touch with prospects or customers on a regular basis, you can use Salesforce to send mass e-mails and shorten your workload. Mass e-mail is particularly helpful for sales reps who send common messages that don't require high levels of personalization. For example, if you're an institutional sales rep selling shares of a hedge fund, you might want to send a monthly e-mail newsletter to sophisticated investors specifically interested in your fund.

When sending mass e-mail, Professional Edition users can send a maximum of 250 e-mails at a time. Enterprise Edition users can send up to 500 e-mails, and Unlimited Edition users can send up to 1,000 e-mails. A company is limited to 1,000 e-mails a day.

You can send a mass e-mail to contacts or leads — the method is similar.

To send out a mass e-mail, go to the Contacts home page or Leads home page, and follow these simple steps:

1. **Click the Mass Email Contacts link or the Mass Email Leads link (depending on which home page you're on) under the Tools section.**

   The Recipient Selection page appears.

2. **Use the View drop-down list to specify the recipients that you want to include in the e-mail and, if you find what you want, skip to Step 5.**

3. **If you can't find the view that you want in the View drop-down list, click the Create New View link.**

   The Create New View page appears. In most circumstances, you need to create a custom view.

4. **To create the new view, fill in the information that you want to use to filter the recipients for your mass e-mail and click Save.**

   For example, if you want to send an e-mail to all customer contacts that are located in New York, you can build a view. (See Chapter 5 for details on creating custom views for contacts.) When you click Save, the Recipient Selection page reappears, displaying a list of contacts that meet your criteria. Any of your leads or contacts that have the Email Opt Out box checked are automatically omitted from these lists.

5. **Review the list and select the check boxes to designate the contacts to whom you want to send the mass e-mail.**

   Contacts or leads that don't have e-mail addresses lack an available check box in the Action column.

6. **When you're satisfied with your selections, click Next.**

   A Template Selection page appears, in which you can select an e-mail template from the e-mail template folders and associate lists.

7. **Use the Folder drop-down list to locate the right folder and template.**

   You can skip this step if you already see the desired e-mail template on the list results.

8. **Select the desired e-mail template by clicking the appropriate radio button in the Name column, and then click Next.**

   A Preview Template appears.

9. **Review the content for the mass e-mail and click Next.**

   A Confirmation page appears, summarizing the number of contacts that will receive the mass e-mail.

10. **Select the appropriate check boxes if you want to receive a blind copy, store an activity, and/or use your signature. Give this mass e-mail a name in the Mass Email Name field. Use the radio buttons to select whether you want to send the e-mail now or schedule it for delivery at a later time and date that you specify in the Schedule for delivery on and Time Zone fields. When you're done, click Send.**

A Complete page appears, confirming the delivery of your mass e-mail.

Tracking E-Mail

By sending and storing important business-related e-mails in Salesforce, you and your teams can get a more complete picture of what's happening with your accounts, contacts, and so on. In the following sections, we show you the basic ways to view your e-mail records and a special feature in Salesforce that allows you to track HTML e-mails.

Viewing e-mails in Activity History

When you send an e-mail from Salesforce, a copy of your message is logged as a task record on the Activity History related list of related records. For example, if you send an e-mail from an opportunity record in Salesforce, you can view that e-mail from the related Opportunity, Contact, and Account detail pages. See Figure 7-3 for an example.

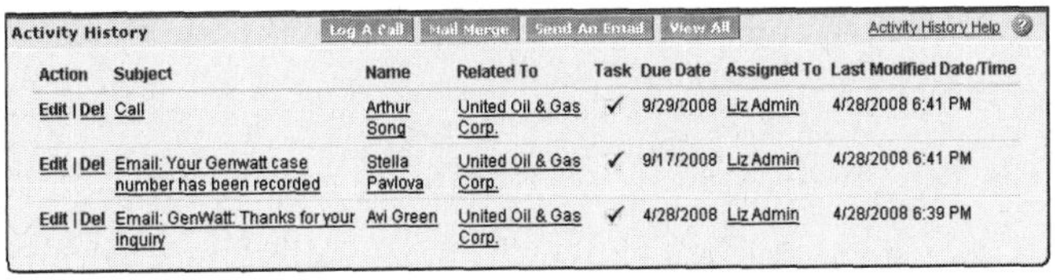

Figure 7-3:
Viewing e-mail records on an Activity History related list.

On an Activity History related list, you can also click the View All button if you want to see the completed activities (including e-mail) on a single page.

Tracking HTML e-mails

If you often wonder whether customers pay attention to e-mails that you send them, you can use the HTML Email Status related list for confirmation that the e-mail was opened. Sales reps can use this feature to see whether contacts and leads are opening and viewing important e-mails on quotes, proposals, and so on.

Simply put, when you send an HTML e-mail from Salesforce, the e-mail is embedded with an invisible pixel that can be used for tracking.

You can view that e-mail not only on the Activity History related list, but also on the HTML Email Status related list of a lead or contact record.

The HTML Email Status related list shows data on a number of key elements, including the date the e-mail was sent, first opened, and last opened, and the total number of times it was opened. Although this information isn't a sure-fire way to determine whether your customer wants to buy, some reps use this feature to measure interest on a single e-mail or even mass e-mails.

Integrating with Outlook E-Mail

If your company uses Microsoft Outlook for e-mail, you can work from within that application and still track your e-mails in Salesforce. You may be accustomed to receiving and sending your e-mails from Outlook, so this Salesforce feature can help you capture both inbound and outbound e-mail on relevant records in Salesforce. For more information on installing and using the free Connect for Microsoft Outlook plug-in, see Chapter 3.

Part III
Driving Sales

The 5th Wave   By Rich Tennant

"Oh wait – this says, 'Lunch Ed from Marketing', not 'Lynch', 'Lunch.'"

In this part . . .

Sales is pretty straightforward, right? Your company makes widgets, you help sell them to new prospects or existing customers, and in return, you get a nice commission check for your efforts. The cycle starts all over, and hopefully you get to knock on the door of existing customers, since you've built up a rapport with them. Or so you'd hope. For many companies, life may not be that cut and dried.

First, in this day and age, never take your existing customers for granted. With easier access to information, your customer has more negotiating power and is more likely hop to a competitor (or to you) if the value's there. That means you should always be courting new leads and moving them along the various stages of your sales process. Your pipeline should have no dry spells.

Second, you better know what the next steps are to move them closer to winning that deal. Spreadsheets show outdated information, and aren't enough help when you need to be more nimble than your competitors. And what if your company sells a whole laundry list of products and services to a wide range of customers in varying industries. . . and even the prices of your offerings differ depending on the customer? How do you organize that in a spreadsheet? Or what if your company depends heavily on an indirect sales force to help bring in deals from across the globe? How will you track all those moving parts to get an accurate view of what's really in your pipeline? Don't worry. Salesforce helps sales organizations manage their deals.

In this part, we cover how to track sales scenarios, such as the ones just described, in Salesforce. We show you how to use Salesforce to track the various products and pricebooks that you deal with and better involve your partners to close more deals. Whatever the size of your sales organization, read ahead if you'd like to take your use of Salesforce to the next level.

Chapter 8

Prospecting Leads

. . . .

. . . .

*O*ften, we hear frustrated sales people say, "We could hit our numbers if we just had enough leads to fill our pipeline." Leads are the building blocks by which many companies drive their sales.

Loosely defined, a *lead* is a person or a company that might be interested in your services. Some organizations refer to them as *suspects* because that person might not even be aware of you. Others call them *prospects* because a lead has to be someone who has expressed interest in your service. Whatever your favorite terminology is, you can use leads to efficiently follow up on sales inquiries, aggressively attack new markets, and vastly improve your sales pipeline.

In this chapter, you can discover all the basic tricks you need to convert leads into revenue. You need to get your existing leads into Salesforce, organize them in a logical fashion, and update them when you follow up with them. Also, we discuss how to convert a lead into an actual opportunity that you can link to an account and a contact. And, finally, if you're a lead manager or administrator, we devote an entire section to how you can manage and maintain your lead database.

Introducing the Lead Record

A *lead record* consists of a number of fields that you use to capture information about a potential lead. A lead record has only two modes: an Edit mode, in which you can modify the fields, and a Saved mode, in which you can view the fields and related lists.

Building an effective lead process

The key to a successful lead program that contributes to sales is a well-constructed lead process built into your Lead Status drop-down list. Salesforce provides a default list of four statuses: Open, Contacted, Qualified, and Unqualified. These statuses may appear straightforward, but they require definition. And those four choices might not mirror your process or your terminology. The good news is that after you define the statuses, your administrator can quickly modify the values. The process starts with the Lead Status field, but it doesn't end there. Here are some additional suggestions for how you might construct your lean, mean, lead-generating machine:

✔ Build fields to capture qualification criteria.

✔ Make it clear at what point in the process a lead should be converted to an opportunity.

✔ Decide who'll manage the lead program and what that entails. Make sure that he or she has sufficient permissions to administer the lead database.

✔ Figure out at what point in the process a lead should be deleted or archived.

✔ Set up queues, if it makes sense, to manage the workload and drive the competitive spirit.

✔ When you figure out your process, train your users so that everyone knows what's expected of them.

The standard record comes predefined with several fields. Most of the terms are immediately clear, but if you want specific definitions, click the Help and Training link in the top-right corner of Salesforce. In the following list, we describe the most important standard fields:

✔ **Lead Owner:** The person or queue who owns the lead. A person can own a lead, or Salesforce can automatically place it in a queue. You can then assign a group of users, who can take leads from the queue.

✔ **Lead Status:** One of three required fields on a lead record. Lead Status is a drop-down list of values, and this field is critical if you want to follow a standard lead process.

✔ **Lead Source:** A standard, but not required, field on a lead record. If you use it, you can define and track the sources of your leads by using this field.

 When you first get a lead, you'll likely want to qualify that lead to make sure there really is a sales opportunity for you. For example, perhaps you want to be certain that they have the budget and a real interest, and aren't just kicking tires. A qualified lead is a lead that meets your qualification requirements.

You'll have your own definition of what qualifies a lead, so jot it down, and then seek out someone to customize your lead record. (See Chapter 20 for the how-to details on building fields, rearranging your layouts, and other design tricks.) You have greater success with leads if you collect the right information.

Setting Up Your Leads

Before you can begin working your leads, you need to add the lead records into Salesforce. In the following sections, we show you three quick approaches for lead creation, and if needed, how to share your leads with the right people. Then, if you want to capture leads from your Web site, see Chapter 12 for details on generating Web-to-Lead forms.

Adding new leads

The best way to create a lead is to use the Create New drop-down list on the sidebar. To create a lead using this method, follow these simple steps:

1. **Select the Create Lead item in the picklist.**

   A New Lead page appears in Edit mode. The only pre-filled field is the Lead Status field.

2. **Fill in the fields as much as you can.**

   At a minimum, you must complete the Last Name and Company fields. (See Figure 8-1 for an example of a record in Edit mode.)

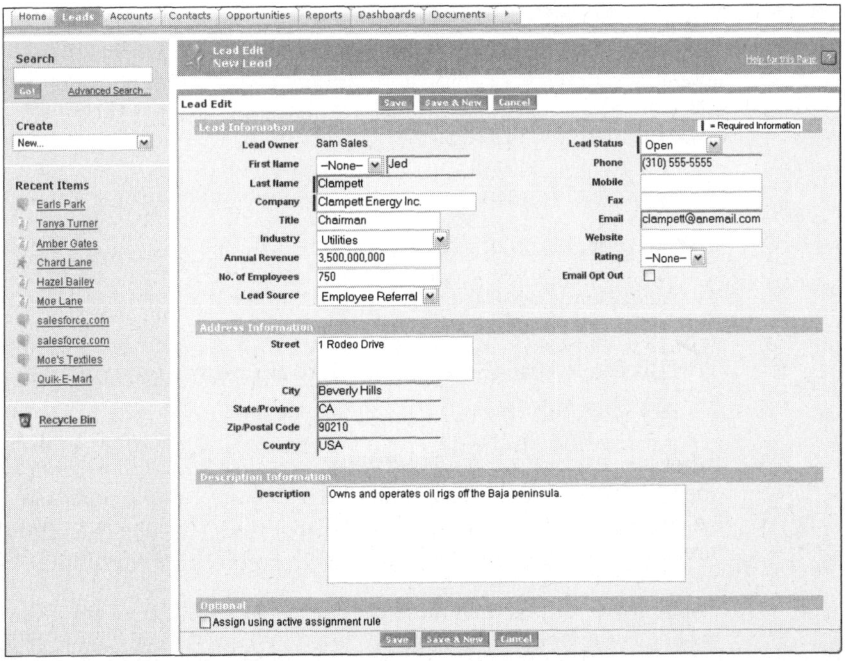

Figure 8-1: Filling out a lead record.

You can add a list of target companies as leads, even if you don't yet know the names of the right people. In certain cases, you might have only the name of a company because you know you want to target it but you don't yet know who to call. You can work with incomplete information; in these cases, we recommend that you type **?** or **unknown** in the Last Name field so that you know this information is missing.

3. **When you're done, click the Save button or the Save & New button.**

   If you click Save, the lead record appears in Saved mode, and your changes are displayed in the fields.

   Salesforce knows that sales people commonly add multiple leads before working them. If you click Save & New, the lead is saved, and a New Lead page appears in Edit mode.

When entering or editing records, click the Save button or the Save & New button when you're done. Otherwise, you don't save the information that you just typed in for that record. If you make this mistake and haven't yet logged out of Salesforce, try clicking the Back button on your browser (as opposed to hitting your head in frustration), which hopefully gets you back to the record in Edit mode. Then, click Save and breathe a sigh of relief.

Cloning an existing lead

If you're working a particular company and want to enter multiple leads for that company, you can save time by cloning leads. For example, say you already created a lead record for Sergey Brin at Google. When you talk to his assistant, she courteously refers you to Larry Page. In this case, cloning can save you many extra steps.

To clone a lead record from an existing lead, follow these instructions:

1. **Click the Clone button at the top of the lead record.**

   A new lead record appears in Edit mode. All the information is identical to the previous lead record.

2. **Edit the information on the new lead, where appropriate.**

   Pay attention to what's pre-filled because you want to avoid inaccurate information on the new lead record.

3. **Click Save when you're done.**

   The newly created lead reappears in Saved mode. To verify this, simply click the link to the older lead, which you can find in the Recent Items section on the sidebar.

Importing your leads

If you already have a file of leads, you probably want a faster way to get them into Salesforce than entering them manually. You must be an administrator to import leads, so if you're not, find your administrator, tell her what you're trying to do, and have her read this section.

Though you can import up to 50,000 leads at the same time, you should test an import with five or so leads first, just to make sure that you know what you're doing. After the test data is imported, review your new lead records to make sure they contain all the information that you want brought in. Delete the test records, refine your import file, and then run through the final import.

To import lead files, use these steps:

1. **On the Leads home page, click the Import Leads link at the bottom of the page, below the Tools heading.**

   The Import Wizard for Leads page appears, providing you with a four-step process to import your records, plus helpful hints.

2. **In your existing lead file or system, compare your fields against the lead fields in Salesforce.**

   If you can map all the necessary fields, move to the next step. If not, add fields to the lead record by customizing Salesforce. (See Chapter 20 for simple instructions on adding fields.)

   Mapping is a technical term for matching one field to another field, typically in different databases, in order to properly move data. For example, in Microsoft Outlook, you type a corporation's name into the Company field. In Salesforce, you typically use the field Account Name. These two different labels have the same meaning. Mapping is the process by which you decide that data from the Company field in Outlook should correspond to the Account Name field in Salesforce.

3. **Export your file.**

   You might have leads in an existing database, such as ACT, Goldmine, or Microsoft Access. Most systems like these have simple tools for exporting data into various formats. Select the records and the fields that you want. Then, export the file and save it in a `.csv` format. If your leads are already in spreadsheet format (such as Excel), just resave the file in `.csv` format.

4. **Review your lead data.**

   You've probably heard the old adage "garbage in, garbage out." Clean up your information before you bring it into Salesforce so that you can save yourself the effort after.

5. When you're done with the preparation, click the Start the Import Wizard link.

A pop-up window labeled Step 1 of 3 Upload the File appears.

6. Complete the fields in Step 1 of the wizard, as shown in Figure 8-2.

Assuming that you've already prepared your file, you probably just need to follow these steps:

a. Load the file by clicking the Browse button and selecting the correct file on your computer.

b. Select a default lead source, if relevant.

c. Apply an assignment rule if you want leads to route directly to assigned reps.

If you don't use an assignment rule, all the leads that you import are assigned to you unless you otherwise specify a Lead Owner in the file. (See the section "Creating assignment rules for automatic routing," later in this chapter.)

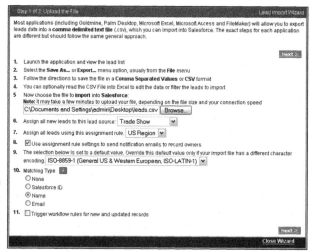

Figure 8-2:
Uploading
the lead file.

d. Select the check box if you want to use assignment rule settings to send e-mail notifications to the record owners.

e. Verify the character coding.

Salesforce pre-fills this picklist based on your Company Profile, and you rarely have to change it.

f. Select the matching type.

If you want Salesforce to avoid importing duplicate records, choose whether you want to identify a duplicate lead by matching

Salesforce ID, name, or e-mail. If a lead record with the matching criteria already exists in Salesforce, that record will be updated with the information in your file.

g. **Select the check box if you want to trigger workflow rules to new and updated records.**

See Chapter 21 for tips on improving workflow.

7. **When you're done with Step 1 of the wizard, click Next.**

The Field Mapping page appears.

8. **Map the fields between your file and Salesforce and then click Next.**

The Field Mapping Page displays all the Salesforce lead fields as labels with drop-down lists that correspond to the fields in your file. Simply go down through the list of fields and select the field from the corresponding file that you're importing which maps to the Salesforce field, as shown in Figure 8-3.

After you click Next, the review and confirm page appears, displaying a list of warnings, if any, on your impending import.

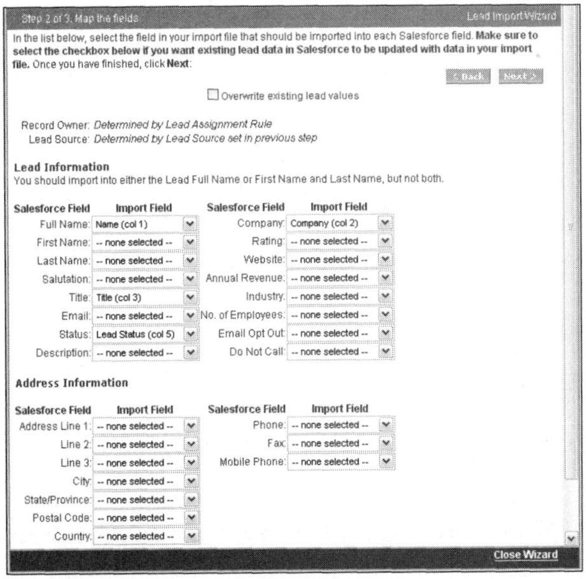

Figure 8-3:
Mapping the
lead fields.

9. **Review the messages for possible errors.**

This step basically warns you about problems with the data or lets you know about fields that you haven't mapped. If you discover an error, you can click the Back button and refine your mapping, or even close the wizard so that you can improve your import file. You might have to start over, but at least you avoid importing bad or incomplete data.

10. **When you're completely satisfied with your mapping, click the Import Now button.**

    An Importing page appears to let you know that the import is in progress, including an estimate of how long it will take.

11. **Click the Finish button.**

    The pop-up window closes.

12. **Check the lead records that you've imported.**

    Salesforce sends you an e-mail after your file has been successfully imported. To check your handiwork, click the Leads tab to go to your Leads home page. In the Views drop-down list, select Today's Leads to see a list of the leads that were created today. Click the link for a lead that you just imported and review the information for accuracy.

Importing leads is one of the fastest ways for you to set up your leads in Salesforce so that you can begin working them.

Sharing your leads

Depending on how your company has set up its Salesforce sharing model, you may see a Share button on the top section of your Lead record.

The Sharing button allows you to share varying levels of access to your lead record to any user or group that you designate. For example, a new inside sales rep may want to share a lead with a more senior teammate so that they can tackle a new prospect together.

To share a specific lead record, follow these steps:

1. **Click the Sharing button on the top of the lead record.**

    The Sharing Detail page for the lead appears. By default, you're the only user with full access to your lead. This page also includes an explanation of access levels.

2. **Click the Add button.**

    The New Sharing page appears.

3. **Select members from the list of users, roles, roles and subordinates, or groups.**

4. **Choose the level of lead access that you want to provide.**

5. **When you're done, click Save.**

    The Sharing Detail page reappears for the lead.

Breaking into unchartered waters

A leading Internet performance monitoring company wanted to sell its services to a variety of new, untested markets. This salesforce.com customer had a stronghold in financial services but wanted to extend its client base to other Fortune 500 companies. Due to the specific nature of its business, the actual names of the decision makers that it wanted to target was publicly unavailable.

Marketing simply imported the Fortune 500 list and set the Last Name field as Unknown. Then, the company used Salesforce and a pool of cost-efficient telemarketers to generate leads and set up appointments between actual buyers and the company's outside field reps. In just six months, this use of Salesforce helped dramatically improve qualified lead generation and increased the pipeline and new bookings while breaking ground in new markets.

Organizing Your Leads

When you have some leads in Salesforce, you want to organize them to make them productive. When we work with companies, we often hear this request from sales people: "I just want to see my data, and it needs to be the way that I want to look at it." Just like Goldilocks, you want your leads to look just right.

In the following sections, we show you how you can use views on the Leads home page to provide greater focus for you and your sales teams. Then, for even more robust organization of your lead information, see Chapter 17 for specifics on how to build custom lead reports.

Using lead views

When you select a view, you're basically specifying criteria to limit the results that you get back. For example, if you're one of many sales reps, you might not want to waste your time sifting through all your company's leads, you want to see just the ones that you own. With Salesforce, you can do that in one click. On the Leads home page, Salesforce comes with four predefined views:

- ✔ **All Open Leads:** Provides a list of all the lead records in which the Lead Status is still Open

- ✔ **My Unread Leads:** Gives you a list of your leads that you haven't yet viewed

✔ **Today's Leads:** Shows you only leads that were created today

✔ **Recently Viewed Leads:** Lets you look at a list of leads that you've recently viewed

To try out a preset view, go the Leads home page and do the following:

1. **Click the down arrow on the Views drop-down list.**

   The four options in the preceding bulleted list appear, maybe along with some other choices that have been created for you.

2. **Select one of the views.**

   For example, if you select the My Unread Leads view, a list page appears, displaying any of your unread leads. From this list page, you can perform a variety of standard operations, including editing, deleting, and viewing a record. See Chapter 2 for details on using list pages.

Creating custom lead views

For many users, the preset views are a good start. But if you want special lists for the way that you follow up on your leads, you should build custom views. For example, if you call only on companies in the manufacturing industry located in the State of Florida with revenue over a billion dollars, take a minute and build a custom view.

To create a view from scratch, follow these simple steps:

1. **On the Leads home page, to the right of the Views drop-down list, click the Create New View link.**

   A New View page appears, which includes a wizard to help create your view.

2. **Enter a name for the view.**

   For example, you might call the view Big Florida Manufacturers.

3. **Decide whether you want this view to search the entire leads database, your leads, or a queue.**

   If your company's marketing department creates marketing campaigns in Salesforce to help generate leads, you can further limit your view to leads associated with a specific campaign.

   This feature is part of Salesforce's integrated campaign builder feature. (Marketing managers: See Chapter 12 for details on how to set up this feature.)

4. **Under the Search Criteria step, select the criteria for your search, as displayed in Figure 8-4.**

A basic criteria query is made up of three elements:

- **Field:** The first box is a drop-down list that contains all the fields on the lead record. For example, you could choose the Industry field.

- **Operator:** The second box is a drop-down list that contains operators for your search. That sounds complicated, but it's easier than you think. Taking the example from the preceding bullet, you'd select Equals from the drop-down list.

- **Value:** In the third box, you type the value that you want in the search. For this example, you'd type **manufacturing**.

5. **Select the columns that you want displayed on your list page.**

   Although Salesforce's preset views display common fields, such as Email and State, you can select any of up to 11 lead fields to display on your list page.

6. **Under the Visibility step, decide whether you want others to see your custom view and select the appropriate radio button.**

   Your decision is made simple if the Visibility step doesn't appear. Otherwise, think about whether other users can benefit from this view when you complete this step.

7. **When you're done, click Save.**

   You're taken to a new list page, which is completely customized based on the search criteria that you chose in Step 4.

Accepting leads from a queue

If you're a rep assigned to a queue, you can access the queue in the View drop-down list on the Leads home page. The queue list page looks just like a regular list page, but you can use it to grab and claim leads. (See the section "Making use of lead queues," later in this chapter, for details on setting up queues.)

To pull leads from a queue and make them your own, go to the Leads home page and follow these steps:

1. **Select the queue name from the View drop-down list.**

   The queue list page appears.

2. **Select check boxes in the Action column to the left of leads that you want to claim.**

Your manager might have specific guidelines. This is your chance to click into some records and try to pick the hottest leads.

3. **Click the Accept button.**

   The queue list page reappears, minus the lead or leads that you selected.

Following Up on Leads

After you receive a new lead, you want a quick way to follow up and determine what you caught: a big one, a warm one, or just another student looking for a freebie. Your company might already have a standard lead qualification process, but the following sections talk about some of the ways that you can use Salesforce to pursue leads.

Finding and merging duplicate lead records

Before following up on a new lead, use the Find Duplicates button to see whether a record already exists. You probably know that duplicates frequently occur with leads. For example, if you capture leads from your Web site, the same visitor might fill in your Web form multiple times, even with the best of intentions. Instead of wasting your time or upsetting the existing lead, check first for duplicates.

By checking for duplicates, you might up your chances of a qualified lead. When you merge duplicate records, the remaining record inherits not only the information you select, but also linked records on related lists.

To merge lead records, you must be the Lead Owner of the records, the Lead Owner's manager (that is, the Lead Owner must be subordinate to you in the Role Hierarchy), or a system administrator.

To find and merge duplicate leads, follow these steps:

1. **Go to a lead record that you suspect or know has duplicates.**

2. **Click the Find Duplicates button at the top of the lead record.**

   A Search for Duplicates page appears, in five sections. The first section determines how you want to search Salesforce for duplicates. By default, Salesforce looks for a duplicate with a matching name, company, e-mail address, or phone number. The remaining four sections show any matching lead, contact, account, or opportunity records, based on the default matching criteria.

3. **Check or uncheck search criteria boxes to narrow or expand your search. Click the Search button to return updated results.**

   Records matching any of the selected search criteria appear in their appropriate sections.

4. **Review the duplicate lead records and select a maximum of three records to merge.**

   In Salesforce, you can merge only three records at a time.

5. **Click the Merge Leads button on the Matching Leads related list.**

   A Merge Leads page appears, displaying side by side the selected records and any fields that have been completed.

6. **Compare the information and click the radio buttons to select the values that you want to retain, as shown in Figure 8-5.**

   At the top of each column, you can also choose to keep all the values from one record by clicking the Select All link.

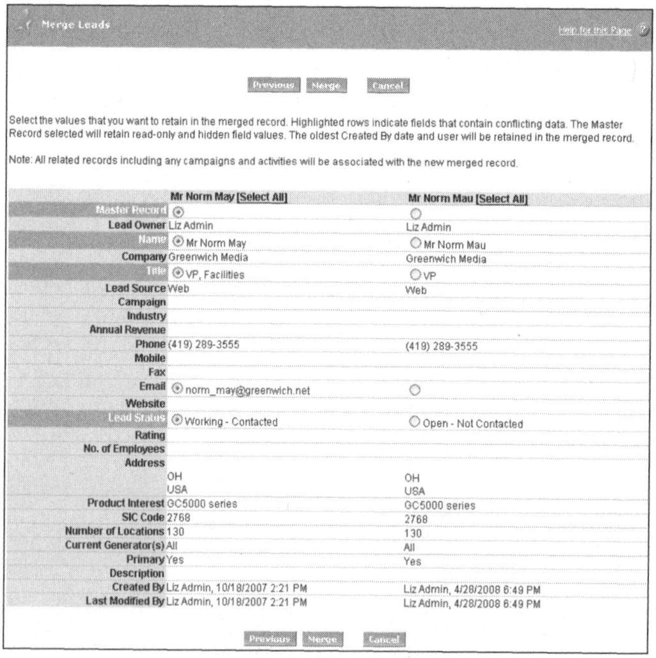

Figure 8-5: Merging duplicate lead records.

7. **When you finish reviewing, click the Merge button.**

   A pop-up window appears, prompting you to validate that you want to perform the merge. After you click OK, the merged lead reappears. Any records from related lists are kept.

Tracking leads with related lists

How can you remember all the interactions that took place with a lead? Some of us have a hard enough time remembering what we did yesterday, let alone three months ago with 200 leads. Related lists on a lead record can help you capture all that information so that it's at your fingertips the next time you talk to a lead.

If you're looking for typical ways that sales people use lead related lists, read the following list and look at Figure 8-6 for an example:

- ✔ **Log a Call:** The next time you respond to a lead and want to record what you said to the lead's assistant, click the Log a Call button and type in the details.

- ✔ **New Task:** You plan to call the lead back next Friday when you know the assistant is on vacation. Click New Task and set a tickler for yourself for Friday.

- ✔ **Send an Email:** You get through to the lead, and he asks you to send him an introductory e-mail about your company. Click the Send an Email button to send and track the e-mail directly from Salesforce.

- ✔ **New Event:** The lead agrees to a demo. Click New Event and schedule a meeting so that you don't forget.

- ✔ **Mail Merge:** Before you demo your new product, you need the lead to sign your standard non-disclosure agreement (NDA). Click the Mail Merge button and quickly create the NDA that has the lead's information pre-filled.

- ✔ **Add Campaign:** You decide to invite the lead to the annual customer golf outing, a campaign tracked in Salesforce. Add the lead to the campaign so that your marketing team remembers to send the lead an invitation.

Updating lead fields

In the course of your lead qualification, you inevitably collect pertinent information that you want to save directly on the lead record. Every time you capture important data on your lead, update your lead record by doing the following:

1. **Double-click a field on the lead record to modify that field.**

   If you see a padlock icon in that field, you can't modify it.

2. **Complete the fields, as necessary, to determine whether the lead is qualified.**

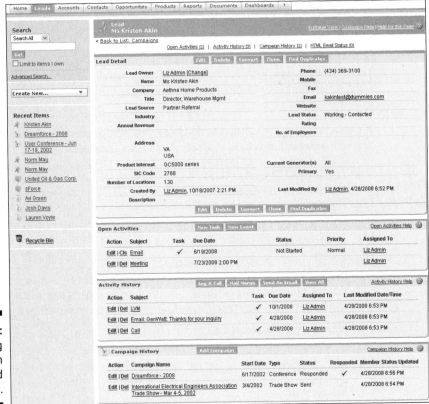

Figure 8-6:
Tracking
activity with
lead related
lists.

3. **Update the Lead Status field when you make progress.**

   Even if you discover that the lead is a waste of your time, that's progress.

   Click Save when you're done making changes.

At some point, you might decide that a lead can't become a qualified opportunity at this time. In that case, you can archive the lead by changing its status. Archiving inactive leads allows you to get a sense of how many leads are still being worked.

Converting qualified leads

When you decide that a lead is actually a qualified opportunity, you can start using Salesforce's full opportunity tracking system. To do so, you must convert the lead to an opportunity. This conversion gives you two benefits:

✔ Converting a lead to an opportunity allows you to track multiple contacts within an account, which you can do more easily than tracking a single individual lead. In other words, if you have ten leads from Microsoft, none of them are linked with each other in Salesforce. But, if by converting a lead, you create an account called Microsoft, you can link all the Microsoft co-workers as contacts for the same account.

✔ Your goal is to ABC (always be closing), so the sooner you can start managing opportunities and not just leads, the healthier your pipeline and wallet. For a qualified lead, your sales process begins where your lead process ends.

When deciding whether to add names of companies or business people as leads or as accounts with contacts, remember that the leads module of Salesforce is non-relational from lead to lead. If you're serious about going after a particular company, and the inter-relationships of business contacts will be important, we recommend that you add the target as an account, rather than as a lead.

To convert a lead to an opportunity, follow these steps:

1. **Click the Convert button on a lead record that you want to convert.**

   The Convert button is located at the top and bottom of the lead record. A Convert Lead page appears.

2. **Complete the required fields.**

   Required fields are highlighted in red. Here's a summary (see the example in Figure 8-7):

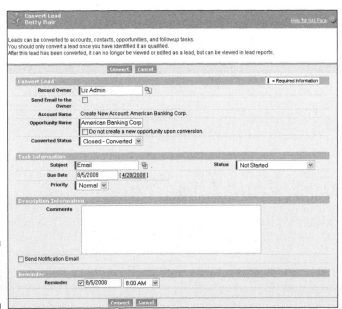

Figure 8-7:
Converting a lead.

- **Record Owner:** If the Lead Owner remains the Record Owner, don't change the selection. If the owner changes, click the Lookup icon and choose from the list of users. Select the Send Email to the Owner check box, if needed.

- **Account Name:** If Salesforce doesn't find an account that closely matches the Company field from your lead, it creates a new account record. In the event that it does find a match, select an option from the drop-down list, depending on whether you want to create a new account or associate the lead to the existing account.

- **Opportunity Name:** If you want to create an opportunity, complete this field by giving the opportunity a name. (We typically recommend that the name of an opportunity be the Account Name followed by a hyphen and then a summary of the product interest. For example: Amazon – New Hardware.) You don't have to create an opportunity record when you convert a lead. Sometimes, the lead that you're converting is associated with an existing opportunity. In these situations, select the Do not create a new opportunity upon conversion check box to avoid creating a new opportunity. Then see Chapter 9 for details on how to link contacts to existing opportunities.

- **Converted Status:** Salesforce pre-fills this field with the default value that your company has chosen for a qualified lead. Don't change this field unless your company has multiple selections for a qualified lead.

- **Task Information:** You can create a follow-up task right in these fields, but you don't have to. Complete these fields only if it saves you a step.

3. **When you're done, click the Convert button.**

   If Salesforce finds a contact record that matches your lead, you can then decide to associate with the existing contact record. Otherwise, a contact record appears for your former lead. That contact is linked to an account corresponding to the lead's Company field, and all associated records from related lists are carried over. If you chose to create an opportunity in Step 2, you can see the opportunity on both the account and contact record's Opportunity related lists.

Maintaining Your Lead Database

If you're a system administrator or a lead manager who has the right permissions (we specify those permissions in the following sections), one of your greatest challenges is administering what hopefully will become a large pool of leads.

Lead databases can become unwieldy over time, so you need to keep them clean. For example, if you work for a company that regularly collects leads from industry conferences, after a year your leads database might have many duplicates and plenty of garbage. Salesforce provides a number of simple tools to make short work of cleaning your leads and other tasks.

The biggest problems we see with leads surround assigning, de-duping, transferring, archiving, and deleting. We know: You hate to get rid of anything. However, sometimes it's necessary and relatively painless.

Making use of lead queues

If you have a sales team made up of multiple reps responsible for attacking leads collectively, you might want to set up lead queues. For example, some companies hire telemarketers to handle leads on a first-come, first-serve basis. You might just find that your reps work harder if they all have an equal chance to go after a fresh pool of leads.

If you're an administrator or user who has permission to customize Salesforce, you can set up lead queues. Follow these steps:

1. **Go to Setup⇨Customize⇨Leads⇨Queues.**

   A New Lead Queue page appears.

2. **Click New to create a new queue.**

   The New Lead Queue page appears in Edit mode.

3. **Name the queue and specify the users, groups, or roles in your company who'll be part of the queue.**

   For example, you might label the queue Telemarketers and then choose users who make up the telemarketing team. (See Figure 8-8 for an example of creating a queue.)

4. **When you're done, click Save.**

   You can now use this queue when you organize and reassign lead records.

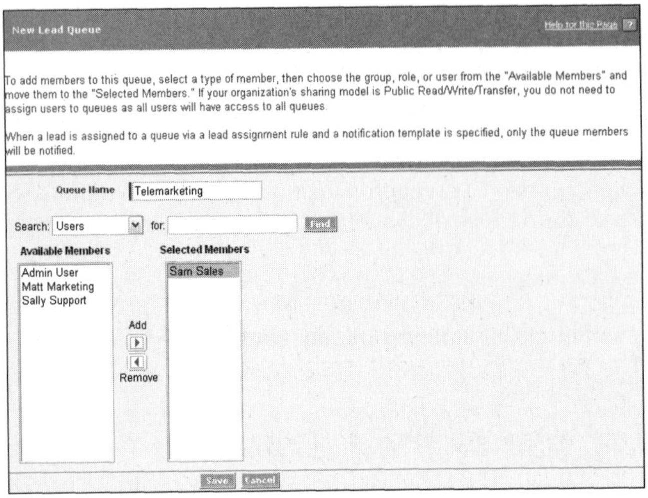

Figure 8-8:
Creating a
lead queue.

Creating assignment rules for automatic routing

If your company generates a lot of leads, assignment rules can help distribute the workload and get leads to the right users. Assignment rules give you a better chance to keep leads from becoming stagnant. A lead *assignment rule* is a feature that lets the administrator define who should receive a lead and under what conditions. For example, if your reps have sales territories defined by ZIP Codes, you can use those ZIP Codes to dictate who should get what leads.

To create a lead assignment rule, follow these steps:

1. **Click Setup➪Customize➪Leads➪Assignment Rules.**

   If you haven't yet set the default lead owner, the Lead Settings page appears, asking you to select the default lead owner. The buck stops with this person or queue, as far as lead routing goes. After you make this selection, Salesforce returns you to the Lead Assignment Rules page.

2. **Click New to create a new assignment rule.**

   The New Lead Assignment Rule page appears in Edit mode.

3. **Enter a title in the Rule Name field, select the check box if you want to make it the active assignment rule, and click the Save button.**

The Lead Assignment Rule page reappears. You can have only one active rule at any time, but the rule can have multiple entries. Click the rule name to the detail page for that rule.

4. Click New on the Rule Entries related list.

A Rule Entry Edit page appears.

5. Complete the steps as follow:

> **a. Enter a number in the Order field to set the order.**
>
> **b. Select criteria to define the rule.**
>
> See the section "Creating custom lead views," earlier in this chapter, for details on selecting criteria. In this case, you might put ZIP Code Equals 02474.
>
> **c. Use the drop-down list and Lookup icon to select the user or queue.**
>
> **d. Use the Lookup icon to choose a Notification Template.**
>
> You can set the assignment rules to send e-mail alerts to recipients of new leads.

6. When done, click the Save button or the Save & New button.

If you click the Save button, the New Lead Assignment Rule reappears.

If you click the Save & New button, a new Rule Entry Edit page appears, and you can repeat Steps 5 and 6 until you finish.

Transferring leads

You might need to transfer leads for a variety of reasons. For instance, after you set up your lead records in Salesforce, you need to give them to the right people. Or maybe some reps just weren't following up, so you took their leads away after swatting their noses with a rolled-up newspaper.

To transfer leads, you must be an administrator or a user with Manage Leads and Transfer Leads permissions. If you want to reassign many leads at the same time, take these steps:

1. From the Leads home page, select a view from which you can see some leads that you want to reassign.

The list page appears.

2. In the Action column of the lead list, select the check boxes to the left of the lead records that you want to assign to someone else.

  3. **Click the Change Owner button at the top of the page.**

     The Change Lead Owner page appears.

  4. **Select the user or queue that you intend to reassign leads to, and then click Save.**

     The lead list reappears, and the lead owners have been changed.

 If you're an administrator, you can use the Mass Transfer Leads tool in Setup to accomplish the same goals of reassigning en masse. See Chapter 23 for details on mass-transferring leads.

If you're reassigning one lead at a time, you can transfer ownership directly from a lead record. Follow these steps:

  1. **On the lead record, to the right of the Lead Owner field, click the Change link.**

     The link is in square brackets. The Change Lead Owner page appears.

  2. **Select the user or queue that you're assigning the lead to.**

     This is the same page that you use when you're assigning multiple leads, but here, you can choose to notify the recipient with an e-mail.

  3. **When you're done, click Save.**

     The lead record reappears, displaying your ownership change. The new owner instantly receives an e-mail if you selected the Send Notification check box.

Changing the status of multiple records

An administrator or a user who has Manage Leads and Transfer Leads permissions can change the status of multiple records at the same time. This feature comes in handy if, during a process, a lead manager reviews leads prior to assigning them to reps.

To change the status of multiple leads at the same time, follow these steps:

  1. **From the Leads home page, select a view.**

     The list page appears.

  2. **In the Action column of the lead list, select the check boxes to the left of the lead records that require a status change. If you're sure that you want to select all the leads in this view, select the check box to the left of the Action column header, which selects all the leads on this page.**

     For example, if you're eyeballing a list of leads from a tradeshow, you might select obviously bogus leads.

3. **Click the Change Status button at the top of the page.**

   The Change Status page appears.

4. **Select a status from the New Status drop-down list and click Save.**

   The lead list reappears.

 If you require industrial strength de-duplication tools, a number of proven technology partners handle de-duplication with Salesforce, plus a variety of other data management tasks. You can check out these offerings on the AppExchange directory in the Sales⇨Data Cleansing category.

Mass-deleting lead records

 Periodically, be sure to delete records that are unqualified or of no value to your company. You must be an administrator to mass-delete records.

Some companies add a To Be Deleted value to their Lead Status field to denote garbage. Then, periodically, the administrator deletes those records.

If you want to delete multiple records at a time, check out these steps:

1. **On the Leads home page, click the Mass Delete Leads link below the Tools heading.**

   A Mass Delete Leads page appears, including a three-step deletion wizard.

2. **Review the steps, and then type the search criteria for the leads that you want to delete.**

   For example, if you want to delete unqualified leads, enter a filter in which Lead Status Equals Unqualified.

3. **Click the Search button.**

   The page reappears, displaying your results at the bottom of the page.

4. **Select all records or just the records that you want to delete by clicking the appropriate check boxes.**

   To select all the search results for deletion, click the Select All link at the top of the list.

 When deleting records, always be cautious but don't overly stress out. When you delete records, that information is placed in your Recycle Bin, and you can access it for 30 days. To undelete a record, click the Recycle Bin link on your sidebar, find the record, and undelete it. Then, count your blessings and breathe into a paper bag until the panic attack subsides.

Chapter 9

Tracking Opportunities

*Y*our sales pipeline is the lifeblood of your business. It's the list of deals that can help you achieve your sales targets. But try as you might, you can probably never close every deal in your pipeline. Things happen: Budgets get slashed, projects get tabled, roles change. So you need enough deals to give yourself the chance to hit and exceed your goals in a given time frame.

An *opportunity* in Salesforce is a sales deal that you want to track. The opportunity record has tools to help you efficiently track and close a sale. By using Salesforce, you can manage more opportunities at the same time and pursue each opportunity with greater precision. For example, if you're a Salesforce sales rep, you can use opportunities to follow a standard process, link distribution partners, associate products, strategize against competition, record your actions and other notes, and more. And you don't have to waste precious time updating a pipeline spreadsheet. Instead, you or your manager can generate the current pipeline with the click of a button.

In this chapter, we show you the techniques and best practices for using opportunities to track sales. First, you can find out the most reliable way to create opportunities. Then, we discuss how to view them in the manner that makes sense to you. You can also discover how to update your records so that your information is current.

Getting Familiar with the Opportunity Record

The *opportunity record* is the collection of fields that make up the information on a deal you're tracking. The record has only two modes: The Edit mode allows you to modify fields, and the Saved mode lets you view the fields and the opportunity's related lists.

An opportunity record comes preconfigured with several standard fields. Most of these fields are self-explanatory, but be sure to pay attention to these critical ones:

- ✔ **Amount:** The estimated amount of the sale. Depending on the way your company calculates the pipeline report, you might use numbers that include total contract value, the bookings amount, and so on.

- ✔ **Close Date:** Use this required field for your best guess as to when you'll close this deal. Depending on your company's sales process, the close date has different definitions, but this field is commonly used to track the date that you signed all the paperwork required to book the sale.

- ✔ **Expected Revenue:** This read-only field is automatically generated by multiplying the Amount field by the Probability field.

- ✔ **Forecast Category:** This field is typically hidden, but it's required. Each sales stage within the Stage drop-down list corresponds to a default forecast category so that higher probability opportunities contribute to your overall forecast after they reach certain stages. See the special Bonus Chapter online for details on forecasts.

- ✔ **Opportunity Owner:** The person in your organization who owns the opportunity. Although an opportunity record has only one owner, many users can still collaborate on an opportunity.

- ✔ **Opportunity Name:** This required text field represents the name of the specific deal as you want it to appear on your list of opportunities or a pipeline report.

When naming opportunities, you and your company should define a standard naming convention for the Opportunity Name field so that you can easily search for and distinguish opportunities. We recommend that the Opportunity Name start with the Account Name, then a hyphen, and then the name of the customer's project or the product of primary interest. This naming convention makes for readable reports later.

- ✔ **Private:** If you want to keep an opportunity private, select this check box to render the record accessible to only you, your bosses, and the system administrator. This field isn't available in Team or Personal Editions.

- ✔ **Probability:** The *probability* is the confidence factor associated with the likelihood that you'll win the opportunity. Each sales stage that your company defines is associated with a default probability to close. Typically, you don't need to edit this field; it gets assigned automatically by the Stage option that you pick. In fact, your administrator might remove write access from this field altogether.

- ✔ **Stage:** This required field allows you to track your opportunities, following your company's established sales process. Salesforce provides a set of standard drop-down list values common to solution selling, but your system administrator can modify these values.

- ✔ **Type:** Use this drop-down list to differentiate the types of opportunities that you want to track. Most customers use the Type drop-down list to measure new versus existing business, but your system administrator can modify it to measure other important or more specific deal types, such as add-ons, up-sells, work orders, and so on.

When customizing your opportunity fields, always remember the patience and attention span of your end users. Keep the record as simple as possible to ensure that all your important fields actually get filled out. If you add many fields, you might make the opportunity record harder to use, which then puts user adoption of Salesforce at risk. At the same time, you'll have greater success with opportunities if you can easily capture what you want to track.

Entering Opportunities

Before you can begin using Salesforce to close opportunities, first you must get the records into Salesforce. In the following sections, we discuss the best ways to create opportunities so that they link to the correct accounts, contacts, and other records.

Adding new opportunities

The best method for creating a new opportunity is to start from the relevant account or contact record, which guarantees that the opportunity associates to the correct record, making the opportunity easily trackable. And, if you add the opportunity from a contact, you link both the account and contact at the same time.

To create an opportunity, go to the relevant Account or Contact detail page and follow these steps:

1. **Select the Create Opportunity option in the Create New drop-down list on the sidebar.**

   Alternatively, scroll down the detail page to the Opportunities related list and click the New button. The result is the same. The Edit mode of a new opportunity appears. The Account Name field is conveniently filled in for you.

2. **Fill in the fields as much as you can or as required.**

   At a minimum, you must complete the required fields. Depending on how you set up your opportunity record, you might have to fill in other required fields, which are highlighted in red. (See Figure 9-1 for an example of a record in Edit mode.) See the section "Getting Familiar with the Opportunity Record," earlier in this chapter, for more detail on common required fields.

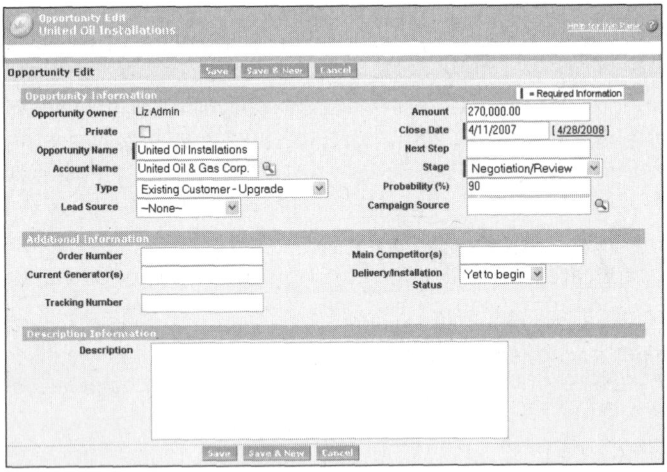

Figure 9-1: Completing opportunity fields.

3. **Click Save when you're done.**

   The Opportunity detail page appears. You can click the Edit button on this page at any time if you need to modify the record.

If you have the good fortune to need to enter multiple opportunities, one after another, instead of clicking the Save button, click the Save & New button. A new opportunity record appears in Edit mode. You have to fill in the Account Name field, but this technique can save you time.

Cloning an opportunity

If you commonly create opportunities that are similar to each other, use the cloning feature to reduce unnecessary retyping. For example, if you're an account manager who creates work order opportunities for additional purchases from the same customer, you might want to clone an existing record and change the details.

To clone an opportunity, go to the opportunity record that you want to clone and follow these steps:

1. **Click the Clone button at the top of the record.**

   A new Opportunity Edit page appears, pre-filled with all the data from the previous record.

2. **Modify the fields, as necessary.**

   Pay close attention to content in required fields such as Close Date, Stage, and Opportunity Name — the information pre-filled in those fields might be incorrect for the new opportunity. Review data in other fields to ensure that the information is applicable to this new opportunity.

3. **If your opportunity has products, select the Clone Products and Associated Schedules check box at the bottom of the page, as needed.**

   If your company uses products in Salesforce, you can use this check box to duplicate the products underlying an existing opportunity. See Chapter 10 for more information on using products.

4. **When you're done, click Save.**

   An Opportunity detail page for your cloned opportunity appears.

If your company has legacy databases that contain opportunities, and you want this data in Salesforce, you currently can't use an import wizard to migrate your records like you can with leads, accounts, and contacts. If this is a current challenge, seek out your technical staff, system administrator, or Salesforce rep. With business guidance, a person with the technical know-how can use the Apex Data Loader to import opportunities and other records through the backend of Salesforce, which can help you avoid wasting time manually re-inputting opportunities. See Chapter 23 for additional tips and tricks on migrating data.

Modifying Opportunity Records

After you add opportunities into Salesforce, you can make changes to your records when deals progress, stall, or fade away. In the following sections, we cover three common practices: editing, sharing, and reassigning.

Updating opportunity fields

In the course of working with your opportunities, you inevitably collect information that you want to save directly in the opportunity record. Every time you capture important data on your opportunity, remember to update your record by doing the following:

1. **Click the Edit button on the opportunity.**

   You can also hover your mouse over the field. If a pencil icon appears to the right of the field, double-click the field to edit it.

   Alternatively, if you're already in an account or contact record that's linked to the opportunity, scroll down to the Opportunities related list and click the Edit link to the left of the desired opportunity. The result is the same. The Opportunity Edit page appears.

2. **Update the fields, as necessary, paying particular attention to keeping fields such as Amount, Close Date, and Stage up to date.**

   Nine out of ten times, those fields play a key role in your company's sales pipeline reports. By keeping your information up to date, you and other users can get a true measure on the opportunity's progress.

3. **When you're done, click Save.**

   The opportunity reappears in Saved mode. The fields that you edited have been changed.

You can keep track of certain critical updates to your opportunity record by using the Stage History related list. Any time you or one of your team members who has read-write access to your record modifies the Stage, Probability, Close Date, or Amount fields, you can see who modified the record and when. Sales managers can use this data in reports to measure progress and trends on opportunities. See Chapter 17 for further details on using and customizing opportunity reports.

Rolling up opportunity data onto the account record

The opportunity record carries a great deal of information about an account. By collecting key opportunity field information onto an account record, a sales rep can quickly see how valuable a particular customer is by viewing the total number of licenses a customer currently has, how much business a customer has closed with your company, and the highest deal closed with that customer, to name a few examples.

You can aggregate this summary information in two ways:

✔ Run a report that summarizes this information for you (see Chapter 17 for more details on creating reports).

✔ Your Salesforce administrator can choose which opportunity fields you want summarized automatically on the account record.

To create a custom roll-up of your opportunity data onto the account record, go to Setup⇨App Setup⇨Customize⇨Accounts⇨Fields and follow these steps:

1. **In the Account Custom Fields and Relationships section, click the New button.**

   The New Custom Field Wizard opens.

2. **Select the Roll-Up Summary radio button and click Next.**

   The read-only field appears, displaying the sum, minimum, or maximum value of a field that you pick on the opportunity record.

3. **Enter the name of what you're summarizing in the Field Label field and click Next.**

   The Field Name field automatically populates itself based on what you enter in the Field Label. In this example, you type **Total Deals Closed**.

4. **In the Summarized Object picklist, select Opportunities.**

   Identifying the Summarized Object tells Salesforce which records you want combined and summarized on the account record.

5. **Select the roll-up type from the selection of radio buttons in the Select Roll-Up Type section in the middle of the page.**

   This selection tells Salesforce how you want the field of your choice to be summarized. You can choose a count of records, the sum, the minimum, or the maximum value. If you choose any of the latter three options, you also have to identify which field in the opportunity you want summarized, by using the Field to Aggregate picklist to make their choice.

You can filter out certain criteria in your result set.

If you want to summarize only records that meet certain criteria, select the Only Records Meeting Certain Criteria Should Be Included in This Calculation radio button to reveal a set of filter criteria. For example, you may want a sum of all the Amount fields for opportunities in which the Stage equals Closed Won. (Figure 9-2 shows an example of defining the field calculation.)

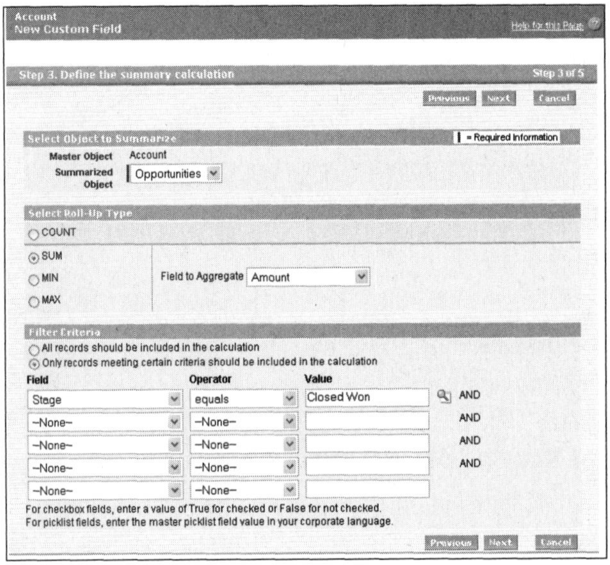

Figure 9-2: Defining an opportunity roll-up field calculation.

Reassigning opportunity ownership

You might find that after you set up your opportunities in Salesforce, you need to give them to the right people. Or your sales teams might be set up in a hunter/farmer configuration, in which you reassign closed opportunities from new business reps to account managers at a certain time.

If you want to reassign an opportunity, open the Opportunity detail page and follow these steps:

1. **To the right of the Opportunity Owner field, click the Change link, which appears in square brackets.**

   The Ownership Edit page appears.

2. **Select the user that you're assigning the opportunity to.**

   By selecting the Send Notification Email check box on the page, you can choose to notify the recipient with an e-mail.

3. **Select the Keep Sales Team check box to retain the Sales Team.**

   If your company doesn't use Sales Teams, you don't see that particular check box. See Figure 9-3 for an example.

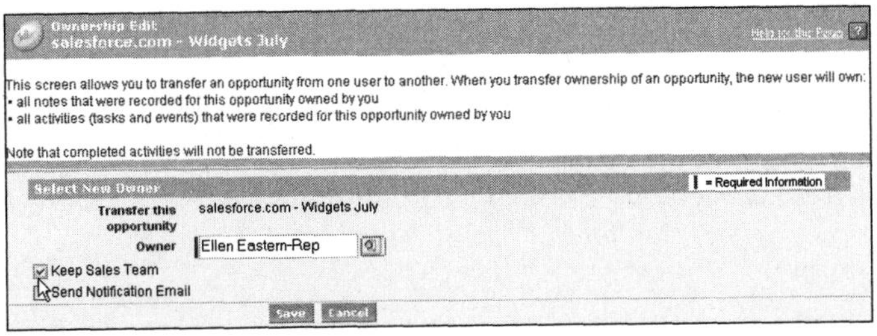

Figure 9-3:
Reassigning
an
opportunity.

4. **When you're done, click Save.**

   The opportunity record reappears. The Opportunity Owner field has changed to the assigned user.

Organizing Your Opportunities

When you have all or a portion of your opportunities entered in Salesforce, you can begin to organize them to suit the way that you sell.

In the following sections, you can find out how you can use views and other tools from the Opportunities home page to provide greater focus for you and your sales teams. Then, for even more robust organization of your opportunity information, check out Chapter 17 for specifics on how to use standard and custom opportunity reports.

Using opportunity views

An *opportunity view* is a list of opportunities that match certain criteria. When you select a view, you're basically specifying criteria to limit the results that you get back. The advantage of a view, versus searching, is that you can use this view over and over again. For example, if you're one of many sales reps, you probably want to see only your opportunities. On the Opportunities home page, Salesforce comes preset with several defined views:

- ✔ **All Opportunities:** A list of all the opportunity records entered into Salesforce. Depending on the way your company has set up your security model, you might not see this view or its results.

- ✔ **Closing Next Month:** Displays opportunities in which the close date falls in the following month.

- ✔ **Closing This Month:** Displays opportunities in which the close date falls in the current month.

- ✔ **My Opportunities:** Gives you a list of just the opportunities that you own in Salesforce.

- ✔ **New This Week:** Generates a list of opportunities that have been created since the beginning of the week.

- ✔ **Recently Viewed Opportunities:** Lets you look at a list of opportunities that you've recently viewed.

- ✔ **Won:** Shows opportunities to which you have access that have been closed and won.

To try out a predefined view, do the following:

1. **On the Opportunities home page, click the down arrow on the Views drop-down list.**

   Depending on how your company has customized the views, you might see all or none of the options in the preceding bulleted list and maybe some other choices that have been created for you.

2. **Select the My Opportunities view.**

   A list page appears, showing opportunities that you currently own. Salesforce lays out the list with six standard columns that correspond to commonly used opportunity fields, plus an Action column so that you can quickly modify a record.

3. **Click a column header to re-sort the list page.**

   For example, if you click the Close Date header, the list page re-sorts by the close dates entered on your opportunity records.

4. **Click into any opportunity by pointing and clicking an underlined link in the Opportunity Name column.**

   An Opportunity detail page appears.

5. **Click the Back button on your browser, and then click the Edit link on the same row as the opportunity you just clicked.**

   The opportunity record appears in Edit mode, and you can make changes to the data.

Creating custom opportunity views

If you want special lists for the way that you manage your opportunities, you should build custom views. For example, if you want to see only open opportunities closing this month at or above 50 percent, you can create a view that helps you focus on just that part of the pipeline.

To build a view from scratch, follow these simple steps:

1. **On the Opportunities home page, to the right of the Views drop-down list, click the Create New View link.**

   The Create New View page appears.

2. **Name the view by entering text in the Name field.**

   In the example used in the preceding section, you might call the view Closing This Month >= 50%.

3. **Select the appropriate radio button, depending on whether you want to search All Opportunities or just My Opportunities.**

4. **In the Search Criteria step, select your search criteria.**

   A basic criteria query is made up of three elements:

   - **Field:** In the first drop-down list, you can find all the fields on the opportunity record. An example is the Probability field.

   - **Operator:** The second drop-down list offers operators for your search. That might sound complicated, but it's easier than you think. Taking the example a step further, you'd select the Greater or Equal option from the drop-down list.

   - **Value:** In the third box, you type the value that you want in the search. For our example, you'd type **50** because you want to see only those opportunities that are greater than or equal to 50 percent probability.

5. **Select the columns that you want displayed.**

   Although Salesforce's preset views display common fields, such as Stage and Amount, you can select any of up to 11 opportunity fields to display on your custom list page.

6. Decide whether you want others to see your custom view.

Your decision is simple if you don't see the Visibility step. Otherwise, select the appropriate option, depending on whether you want to share your view with others. Your options are basically all, none, or limited. If you choose limited accessibility, use the Available for Sharing and Shared To list boxes to select which users can see the view.

7. When you're done, click Save.

A new view appears, based on your custom view criteria. If you don't get all the results you anticipate, you might want to recheck and refine the search criteria.

Defining contact roles

Depending on your sales process, at some early point, you need to identify the decision makers who'll influence the buying decision. Contacts and their titles often don't tell the whole story about decision makers and the chain of command within an opportunity.

To better define the buying influences on an opportunity, go to an opportunity record and follow these steps:

1. Click the New button on the Contact Roles related list.

The Contact Roles page appears for that specific opportunity, displaying a list of the available contacts linked to the related account.

2. For each relevant contact, use the Role drop-down list to select the appropriate role, as shown in Figure 9-4.

Salesforce comes preconfigured with a standard list of contact roles, but your company can customize this drop-down list if you need to modify the list of values. You don't have to classify a role for every contact on the list; you can just leave the Role default value of None.

If the right role for your contact doesn't appear, advise your system administrator to edit the roles.

3. Select a radio button to designate the Primary Contact.

The Primary Contact typically refers to the person who's currently your point of contact. One of the benefits of selecting a Primary Contact is that you can list out who the primary contact is on a basic opportunity report.

Figure 9-4:
Selecting
the contact
role.

4. **If necessary, click the Lookup icon to the right of empty fields in the Contact column to add other contacts who are critical to your opportunity.**

If you work with multitier selling models, or if you collaborate with business partners on your deals, use contact roles to add contacts who aren't employees of an account. For example, if your customer's legal gatekeeper works for an outside law firm, you can use the Contact Roles related list to highlight the attorney's role.

5. **When you're done, click Save.**

The Opportunity detail page reappears, and your Contact Roles related list is updated to reflect contacts involved in the opportunity. If you need to add more contact roles, click the New button on the Contact Roles related list again.

Chapter 10

Tracking Products and Price Books

A product, as its name implies, is a product or service that you sell to customers. Products are the individual line items that make up an opportunity. Depending on your goals for Salesforce, you might not need to immediately incorporate Salesforce's product-type features into your opportunities. But if you do sell multiple products and services, and you struggle with product-level visibility, Salesforce provides powerful and easy tools to implement solutions for Enterprise and Unlimited Edition users. Professional Edition customers may also use products for an additional charge.

Using products in Salesforce benefits sales reps and people in product marketing, management, and development throughout your organization. Sales reps can quickly locate the price of a product and select products to calculate an opportunity's amount. Marketing, management, or development professionals can get vital sales information to support strategic business planning, new product development, and product lifecycle management.

In this chapter, we show sales teams how to use products and price books with opportunities (if your administrator has already set it up). Administrators, before setting up products and price books, first need to do some advance planning. We discuss how to create a product catalog, set up schedules, and build price books. We then show you how to maintain products and price books on an ongoing basis to facilitate your sales goals.

Discovering Products and Price Books

You need to know two key and interrelated terms before you can begin planning your product strategy in Salesforce.

✔ **Products:** Individual items that you sell on your opportunities. All products belong to one universal product catalog. After you create a product, you can associate it to one or multiple price books with identical or different prices. For example, you may use multiple price books if you use one set of prices when selling to qualified non-profit agencies and a different price list for companies in the private sector.

A product can have an associated *schedule* based on quantity, revenue, or both. If you currently sell products and break out schedules to forecast revenue recognition or for planning, you can use Salesforce to reflect important schedules for products linked to opportunities.

✔ **Price book:** A collection of products and their associated prices. A product with its associated price is called a *price book entry.* You can also create custom price books based on your unique sales model.

You can associate a price book, add products, and build schedules on an opportunity through the *Products related list* on an Opportunity detail page.

Defining standard product fields

A product record consists of a number of fields that you use to capture information about a product you sell. If you're involved in shaping products for your company, most of the standard fields are obvious. If you want specific definitions, click the Help and Training link in the top-right corner of Salesforce.

The following are a couple of important pointers on understanding the standard product record fields:

✔ **Product Name:** This is the name of your product. Make sure to use titles that are clear and familiar to your sales reps and customers.

✔ **Product Code:** An internal code or product ID used to identify your product. If your existing products and product codes reside in a financial database, and you want to plan for integration, make sure the product codes are consistent.

✔ **Product Description:** Text to distinguish products from each other. If you're in product management or marketing, describe your products so that they're obvious and useful for your sales teams.

✔ **Product Family:** The category of the product. Use this drop-down list if you plan to build reports that reflect sales data by product category. For example, if you work for a technology value-added reseller (VAR), you might want to reflect your pipeline by families that include hardware, software, services, training, and maintenance. You can set up products in Salesforce so that each product automatically maps to a product family.

✔ **Active:** This check box must be selected to make the product available to your users.

✔ **Quantity Scheduling Enabled:** Select this check box to enable quantity scheduling for a product. If you don't see this check box, then your administrator hasn't enabled it.

✔ **Revenue Scheduling Enabled:** Select this check box to enable revenue scheduling for a product. If you don't see this check box, then your administrator hasn't enabled it.

Understanding the different types of pricing

Salesforce lets you customize your pricing based on the way you sell. If you use products in Salesforce, your company has three different options for pricing:

✔ **Standard Prices** are the default prices that you establish for your products when you set up your standard price book.

✔ **List Prices** are the prices that you set up for custom price books.

✔ **Sales Price** is the price of a product determined by the sales rep when he or she adds a product to an opportunity. See the following section for details on adding products to opportunities.

Using Products and Price Books

Sales reps can add products with specific prices to their opportunities, and Salesforce automatically calculates the Amount field on an opportunity record. If you're a sales rep selling multiple products and managing multiple opportunities at the same time, you can take the frustration out of remembering what you offered to a customer. If you're a sales manager, you can segment your pipelines and forecasts by product lines. And if you're in product management or marketing, products in Salesforce can give you real insight into product demand from your markets.

Adding products to opportunities

To take advantage of products, your company must first set up a product catalog, and one or more price books. See the section "Building the Product Catalog," later in this chapter, for the how-to details on setting up your products and price books. After this is done, sales reps can add products to an opportunity by going to a specific opportunity and following these steps:

1. **Scroll down on the Opportunity detail page to the Products related list and click the Choose Price Book button.**

   A Choose Price Book page appears. If your company has made only one price book available to you, you can bypass this step.

2. **Select the appropriate price book from the Price Book drop-down list and click Save.**

   The Opportunity detail page appears again. The Products related list now shows the name of the price book in parentheses.

   On an opportunity, you can use only one price book at a time.

3. **Click the Add Product button on the Products related list.**

   A Product Selection page appears, as shown in Figure 10-1.

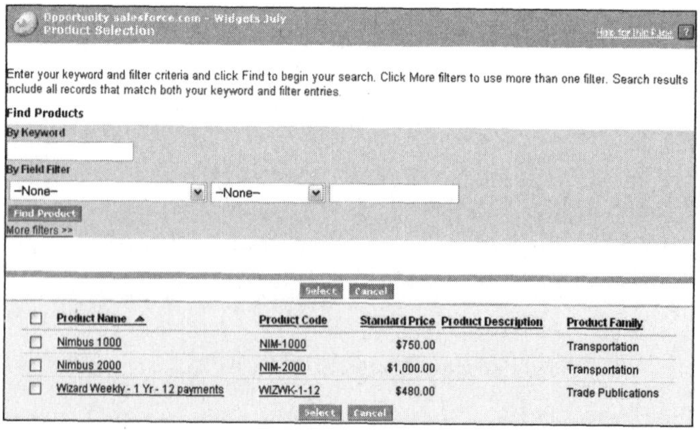

Figure 10-1: Finding your products.

	Product Name ▲	Product Code	Standard Price	Product Description	Product Family
☐	Nimbus 1000	NIM-1000	$750.00		Transportation
☐	Nimbus 2000	NIM-2000	$1,000.00		Transportation
☐	Wizard Weekly - 1 Yr - 12 payments	WIZWK-1-12	$480.00		Trade Publications

4. **If you need to, enter a keyword and filter criteria, and then click the Find Product button to begin your search.**

The page reappears with your search results in a table at the bottom of the page.

5. **Select the check boxes next to the products that you want, and then click the Select button.**

   An Add Products page appears with your selections and fields for you to provide line item details. The Sales Price field is pre-filled with the default sales price from the price book that you selected.

6. **Fill in the line item details.**

   You must, at a minimum, fill in the Quantity and Sales Price fields for each selected product. The Date field is typically used to reflect an expected shipping or delivery date for the product.

7. **When you're done, click the Save button or the Save & More button.**

   Clicking the Save & More button takes you back to the Product Selection page. If you click the Save button, the Opportunity detail page reappears. Notice the Amount and Quantity fields on the opportunity record have changed based on the total from the products you added.

Updating product details for an opportunity

If you need to change the details on your product selections in the course of the sales cycle, you can do this easily on the Products related list of the opportunity record. For example, if your customer wants to add another product, increase product quantities, or demand a better product discount, you need to know how to modify products.

To modify products on your opportunity, we suggest the following:

✔ To delete a product from the opportunity, click the Del link next to the product on the Products related list.

✔ To edit all the products on the opportunity, click the Edit All button.

✔ To edit one product at a time, click the Edit link next to the product on the related list.

✔ To reorder the products on your Products related list, click the Sort button.

If you find yourself unable to modify the sales price on your products, you may want to politely confirm the intent with your sales manager. Some companies lock in the sales price for sales reps so they can follow a pre-defined discount approval policy.

Adding and updating schedules on opportunities

If you manage opportunities in which your products or services are delivered over time, you can create schedules for your products by quantity, revenue, or both. By using schedules, you and your users can benefit in multiple ways:

- ✔ If you're on a sales team, you get a gauge on revenue recognition, which could be significant if that affects compensation.

- ✔ If you're in product management, you can better forecast and plan for the amount of units that you'll have to deliver in future quarters.

- ✔ If you're part of a services organization, schedules updated by reps provide a real-time gauge in planning your resources and projects.

- ✔ Your system administrator must first set up your products with scheduling. (See the section "Setting Up Schedules," later in this chapter, for more specifics on schedules, and see Chapter 21 for the details on customizing Salesforce.)

After scheduling is enabled for a product, set up a schedule by going to the Opportunity detail page and following these steps:

1. **Click the desired product in the Product Name column of the Products related list.**

   An Opportunity Product page appears with a Schedule related list.

2. **Click the Establish button on the Schedule related list.**

   An Establish Schedule page appears.

3. **Complete the fields and click Save.**

   Your fields might vary, depending on whether the product is set up for quantity, revenue, or combined scheduling. When you click Save, a schedule appears based on your choices.

4. **Review and modify the schedule.**

   If the revenues or quantities aren't equal over the periods that you first established, you can type over the values in the schedule.

5. **When you're done, click Save.**

   The Opportunity Product page reappears with the schedule you established.

Over the course of an opportunity, you can adjust the schedule on a product if terms change by clicking the buttons on the Opportunity Product page. To access an Opportunity Product page, go to the relevant opportunity record, scroll down to the Products related list, and click the desired product link from the Product column. The Opportunity Product page for the selected product appears with a Schedule related list. You can do the following with the schedule:

- ✔ Click the Edit button if you want to modify the schedule.
- ✔ Click the Delete button if you want to delete the schedule.
- ✔ Click the Re-establish button if you want establish the schedule all over again.

Searching for products

You can search for specific products easily by using the Find Products search tool on the Products home page.

Instead of searching from the Products home page, you can search for products from your main home page. Your administrator must set this up for your company. For details on adding this home page tool, see Chapter 21 for customizing Salesforce and consult with your administrator.

To search for a product, go to the Products home page and follow these steps:

1. **Enter keywords in the Find Products search tool and click the Find Product button.**

   A Product Search page appears with a list of possible selections, as shown in Figure 10-2.

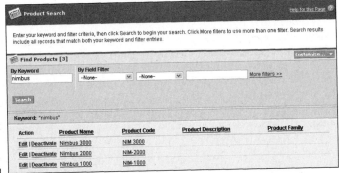

Figure 10-2: Looking at product search results.

2. **If necessary, use the Find Products search tool to enter more key-words or filters to refine your search and again click the Find Product button.**

   The list results change based on your criteria.

3. **Click a link in the Product Name column to go directly to the product.**

   The Product detail page appears.

Creating custom views for products and price lists

If the existing lists don't provide the views that you want, you can create custom views for products and price lists. You can define your views to see additional standard or custom fields in list form. See Chapter 4 for details on creating custom views.

Building the Product Catalog

If you have a vested interest in your product strategy, be aware and take advantage of all the options that Salesforce provides for customizing products and price books. The more you plan ahead, the better you can implement products and price books for the way your sales teams sell. As you make products and price books active, your sales reps can start associating products to their opportunities.

Planning products for success

For products, consider the characteristics of your products outside the standard realm that you want to analyze. In most companies, the product management or marketing teams own and maintain these records. You should pull together a cross-functional team made up of sales, marketing, finance, and product management users to decide what you want to achieve from products in Salesforce. Then work with your system administrator to customize the product record to meet your specific needs. For more details on customization, see Chapter 21.

For pricing, consider whether you have set pricing on your products or whether you'd prefer to keep the pricing simple at the beginning. Many customers of Salesforce, for example, set the prices on their products at $0 or $1, and depend on their sales reps to fill in the sales prices when they prepare an opportunity. Other companies invest time and effort in creating actual standard or list prices on products to provide guidance to their sales reps.

Adding products to the product catalog

Before your sales reps can begin linking products to their opportunities, you need to add the products into Salesforce.

To add a product, log in to Salesforce and follow these steps:

1. **Select the Create Product option in the Create New drop-down list on the sidebar.**

   A New Product page appears.

2. **Complete the fields, as shown in Figure 10-3.**

   Your exact fields might vary, but see the section "Defining standard product fields," earlier in this chapter, for info on the standard fields.

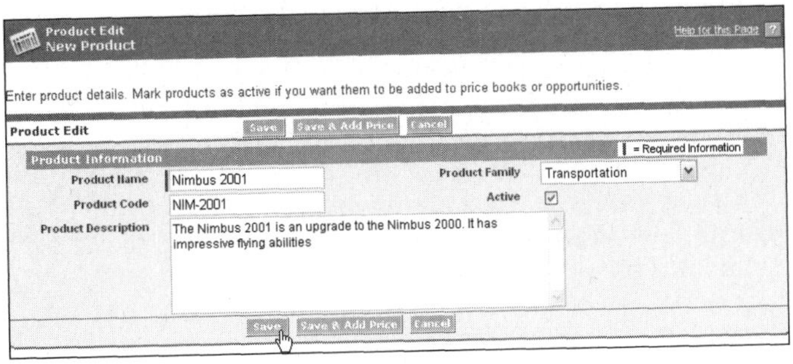

Figure 10-3:
Adding a product to the product catalog.

3. **When you're done, click Save.**

   The Product detail page for your new product appears with related lists for standard prices and price lists.

Changing product details in the product catalog

Over time, marketing or product managers may need to update details about a product. You can make most of your changes to a product from its detail page. Go to a specific product and take a look at this list of actions that you can perform. (You must have "edit" permissions on products to perform the steps below. See Chapter 20 for details on granting the right permissions to the right people.)

- ✔ **To edit the product record,** click the Edit button. For example, if the name of your product changes, you can change the product name, and then save and automatically update all opportunities that include that product with the modified name.

- ✔ **To delete the product,** click Delete and then click OK on the dialog box that appears. In circumstances in which you're no longer offering a product but it's linked to opportunities, it's better that you deactivate or archive the product, rather than delete it.

- ✔ **To deactivate the product,** click the Edit button, deselect the Active check box, and then click Save. Take this path if you might offer the product in the future.

- ✔ **To delete and archive,** click Delete and then click OK on the dialog box that appears. In the event that your product is linked to opportunities, a Deletion Problems page appears with suggested options. Click the Archive link if you're still intent on deleting the product but not altering the existing opportunities.

Setting Up Schedules

If your company wants to track annuity streams, stay aware of key shipping dates, or estimate when revenue will be recognized on products, you can also set up schedules on all or some products.

Enabling schedules for your company

Your administrator first needs to enable schedules before you can add them on specific products.

If your company wants to track shipping dates with Salesforce, you need to enable quantity scheduling. If your company wants to measure revenue recognition or anticipate upcoming payments, be sure to enable revenue scheduling. If your company wants to do both, you'd enable both types of scheduling.

To set up schedules, follow these steps:

1. **Go to Setup⇨Customize⇨Products⇨Schedule Setup.**

   The Schedule Setup page appears.

2. **Select the appropriate check boxes, as shown in the example in Figure 10-4.**

   You can choose to enable schedules based on quantities, revenue, or both. You can also choose to enable schedules for all products.

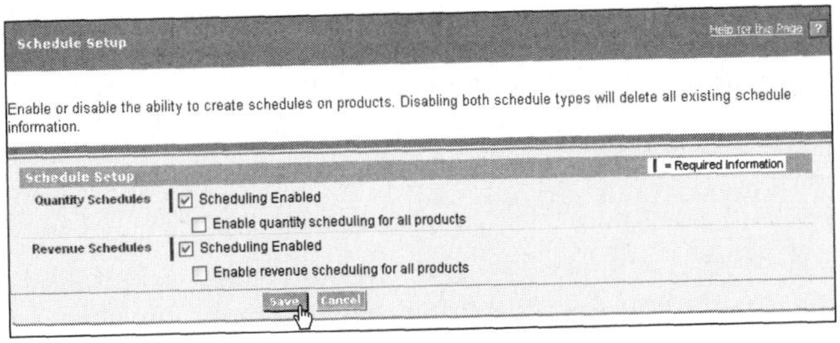

Figure 10-4: Enabling schedules for your company.

Schedule Setup

Enable or disable the ability to create schedules on products. Disabling both schedule types will delete all existing schedule information.

Schedule Setup		= Required Information
Quantity Schedules	☑ Scheduling Enabled	
	☐ Enable quantity scheduling for all products	
Revenue Schedules	☑ Scheduling Enabled	
	☐ Enable revenue scheduling for all products	

Save   Cancel

3. **When you're done, click Save.**

   The Products page reappears.

Adding and updating a default schedule

After schedules have been enabled, you can create default schedules on existing products or as you're adding new products.

By creating default schedules, you can simplify repetitive tasks for sales reps. With this setting, a default schedule is created when a sales rep adds a product to an opportunity. A sales rep can still re-establish a product schedule on an opportunity. The product date determines the start date for the installments.

If you sell a basic service with different payment plans, you might consider creating a unique product for each payment plan, and then using default revenue schedules. By doing this, you can simplify the data entry for the rep and reduce the chance of error.

To create a default schedule, follow these steps:

1. **Select the Create Product option on the sidebar or click the Edit button on a product record.**

   A Product page appears in Edit mode. If scheduling is enabled, you see additional fields for quantity and/or revenue scheduling.

2. **Complete the fields, as appropriate.**

   Here are some tips on completing the default schedule:

   • For the **Schedule Type,** select Divide if you want to divide the opportunity amount into installments. Select Repeat if you want to repeat the quantity or revenue on each installment.

   • Use **Installment Period** to define the frequency.

   • Use **Number of Installments** to define the duration.

3. **When you're done, click Save.**

   The Product detail page appears.

If your product has both quantity and revenue default scheduling, quantity scheduling is calculated first and drives the total amount. Then, revenue scheduling divides the amount.

To update a default product schedule, follow these steps:

1. **From the Products home page, search for the product whose schedule you'd like to update, using your preferred method.**

   See the "Searching for products" section, earlier in this chapter, for specifics. A Product Search page appears.

2. **Click the product name of the specific product to edit.**

   The Product page appears.

3. **Click the Edit button to update schedule information.**

4. **When you're done, click Save.**

   The Product page for your product appears with the updated information.

Managing Price Books

Some companies require just one universal price book. Many other companies, however, want custom price books based on their unique selling needs. Examples include price books that are

✔ **Based on geography:** For a global company, the Japanese sales team might sell a subset of the products sold by their North American counterparts (and at different prices and in different currencies).

✔ **Based on partner tiers:** In some companies that sell through partners, strategic partners might get preferential pricing.

✔ **Based on sales teams:** If your company is divided into sales teams that sell different products, you can use custom price books to simplify the product selection for groups.

✔ **Based on volume discounts:** Some companies build price books based on volume purchases.

✔ **Based on seasonality:** Some companies change their pricing based on seasonal buying patterns. You can use custom price books to communicate pricing changes to your sales reps during these periods.

If the standard price book meets your objectives, keep it simple. Otherwise, in the following sections, we show you how to set up your price books.

Adding to the standard price book

Every time you add a standard price to a product, you automatically associate it to the standard price book. You can do this while you're creating products or you can add the standard prices after you've built the product records.

Adding standard prices while creating products

The easiest way to add a standard price is while you're creating products. To use this method, start creating a product record as you normally would (see the section "Building the Product Catalog," earlier in this chapter), but instead of clicking Save, follow these steps:

1. **Click the Save & Add Price button, as shown in Figure 10-5.**

   An Add Standard Price page appears.

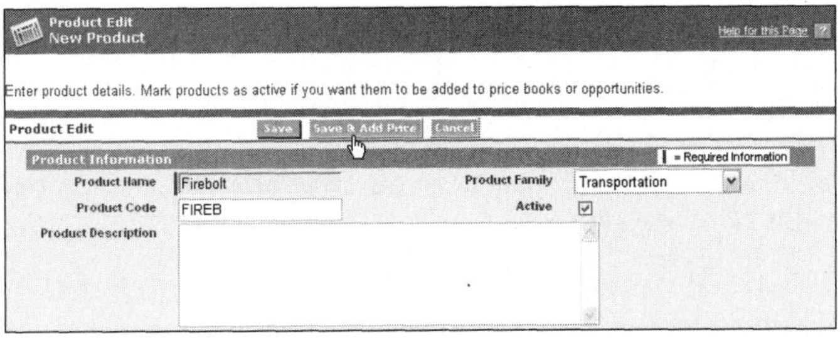

Figure 10-5:
Adding a
product and
price at the
same time.

2. **Complete the field and click Save.**

   The Product detail page appears, and a standard price displays on the Standard Price related list.

Adding or editing standard prices for existing products

If you want to create the products first and add prices later, you can do so. To add or edit a standard price, go to the desired Product detail page and follow these steps:

1. **Click the Add button on the Standard Price related list.**

   In the event that standard prices exist already, you can click Edit or Edit All. The result is the same: An Add or Edit Standard Price page appears.

2. **Complete or modify the Standard Price field, as necessary, and click Save.**

   The Product detail page reappears with any changes reflected on the Standard Price related list.

Creating a custom price book

If you want to create a price book, you need to be an administrator or have permission to manage price books.

To create a price book from scratch, go to the Products home page and follow these steps:

1. **Click the Manage Price Books link under the Maintenance section.**

   A Price Book page appears with related lists for active and inactive price books.

2. **Click the New button on the Active Price Books related list.**

   A New Price Book page appears in Edit mode.

3. **Complete the fields.**

   Remember to select the Active check box if you want to make the price book available.

4. **When you're done, click Save.**

   The Price Book detail page for your new price book appears with a Products related list.

Adding products to a custom price book

After the price book has been established, you can add products to it. A product listed on a price book is also referred to as a *price book entry*. To add products to an existing price book, go to a price book and follow these steps:

1. **Click the Add button on the Products related list.**

   A Product Selection page appears with a search tool and a list of products.

2. **Enter keywords and filter criteria, and then click the Search button to narrow your search.**

   The Product Selection page reappears with a list of products based on your search criteria.

3. **Use the check boxes on the search results to choose products and click the Select button, as shown in Figure 10-6.**

   An Add List Price page appears.

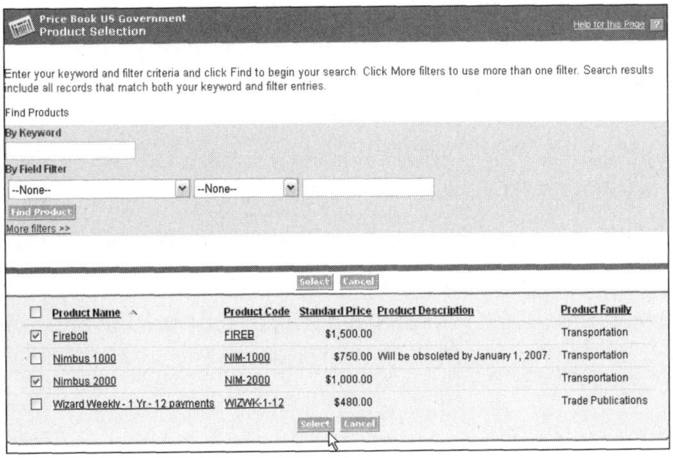

Figure 10-6:
Selecting
products
for the price
book.

4. **Complete the fields.**

   Select the check boxes in the Use Standard Price column if you want to use the standard price for the list price of a product or just enter a list price. You can use the Active check boxes to make products immediately available in the price book.

5. **When you're done, click Save (or Save & More if you want to find more products).**

   After you save the product, the Price Book detail page reappears, and your selected products have been added to the Products related list.

Making global changes to price books

Maintaining accurate and up-to-date product and price lists is challenging, especially if you have an extensive product catalog and/or complex pricing. If you're responsible for such a daunting task, you can use tools that are located on the Products home page to save time.

Changing activation on price books

If you want to make a price book unavailable to sales reps, you can deactivate one or more price books almost instantly.

To deactivate a price book, go the Products home page and follow these steps:

1. **Click the Manage Price Books link under the Maintenance section.**

   The Price Book detail page appears with related lists for active and inactive price books.

2. **On the Active Price Books related list, click the Deactivate link next to a price book that you want to make unavailable.**

   The Price Book detail page reappears, and the selected price book now appears on the Inactive Price Books related list.

To activate price books, you follow a similar process, the difference being that you would click the Activate link adjacent to a price book listed on the Inactive Price Books related list.

Cloning price books

On occasion, you might want to create a price book that closely resembles an existing price book. Instead of starting from scratch, you can clone from an existing price book and then make changes, as necessary.

To clone a price book, follow these steps:

1. **Click the Manage Price Books link under the Maintenance section.**

   The Price Book page appears with related lists for active and inactive price books.

2. **Click the New button on the Active Price Books related list.**

   A New Price Book page appears.

3. **Complete the fields and use the Existing Price Book drop-down list to select a price book to clone.**

4. **When you're done, click Save.**

   The new Price Book page appears with a Products related list cloned from the existing price book.

5. **If needed, click Edit or Edit All on the Products related list to change the list prices.**

6. **If needed, click Add or Delete on the Products related list to add or delete price book entries.**

Deleting price books

You can delete price books, but if the price book is associated to existing opportunities, beware. In those circumstances, we recommend the following actions:

- Deactivate (rather than delete) the price book so that the linkage between opportunities and products stays intact.

- Delete the associated opportunity records first, and then delete the price book.

- Archive the price book entries prior to deleting. Then, even if you delete the price book record, the products associated with opportunities are retained.

If you still want to delete a price book, follow these steps:

1. **On the Products home page, click the Manage Price Books link under the Maintenance section.**

   The Price Book detail page appears with related lists for active and inactive price books.

2. **Click the link for the desired price book.**

   The specific Price Book page appears.

3. **Click Delete and then OK on the dialog box that appears.**

   If you select a price book that isn't associated with opportunities, you're returned to the Price Book detail page with the lists of price books. If a Deletion Problems page appears, follow the suggestions provided in the preceding bulleted list and on the Deletion Problems page.

Chapter 11

Managing Your Partners

. . . .

. . . .

*N*ow that Salesforce can get sales reps and managers on board to track all their opportunities and sales-related activities, the big pipeline picture should be getting clearer for everyone. Partners, which may also be known in your business as third-party companies, value-added resellers (VARs), original equipment manufacturers (OEMs), wholesalers, or distributors, can also be accurately managed in Salesforce almost as if they were full-time dedicated company sales reps. It used to be difficult to create and maintain unique messages and branding for specific groups of partners. Not any longer.

Salesforce Partners extends the existing Salesforce product to partners, and the leads and deals they bring in. Additionally, channel managers and channel reps within a company can more easily manage their partner relationships in Salesforce.

A detailed discussion of Salesforce Partners could take up a whole book on its own, so in this chapter, we provide a high-level overview of what life is like for partners and channel reps. We then discuss how a channel team manages its partners with Salesforce Partners. For partners asked by their vendors to use this application, we discuss how to access and navigate Salesforce from the Partner Portal. Finally, we give channel managers and administrators some pointers on how to set up Salesforce Partners and begin giving partners access. For more detailed insights, check out the PRM Success Blog:

```
http://blogs.salesforce.com/prm
```

Understanding the Partner Lifecycle

Using an indirect sales force of partners to help sell your products allows you to quickly and cost-effectively expand your company's reach into markets that you might otherwise not have the resources to tackle. Some industries that are more partner-intensive include high-tech, insurance, and manufacturing. In this section, we set the stage for two types of business users and how Salesforce Partners can help.

Here are some helpful Partner Relationship Management (PRM) terms:

- ✔ **Vendor:** The company that's using Salesforce and for whom the channel managers work.

- ✔ **Channel managers:** The employees within your company that manage a set of partners.

- ✔ **Channel conflict:** What happens when your direct sales force and your indirect sales force find the same prospect to woo and start bickering about who's entitled to that lead. A clear sign that your current PRM system is ineffective.

- ✔ **Deal registration:** Minimizes channel conflict. These programs get your indirect sales channel registering deals with you (the vendor) to reduce the chances of other partners or the direct sales force competing for a deal.

- ✔ **Partner Portals:** Customizable Web portals hosted by salesforce.com that allow partner users to access Salesforce. Your company can set up multiple portals for multiple partners, if you need to use different branding.

- ✔ **Partner accounts:** Account records that are used by channel managers to manage partner organizations, partner users, and partner activities.

- ✔ **Partner users:** Salesforce users with limited capabilities and visibility into your instance of Salesforce. They're associated with a specific partner account and access Salesforce via a Partner Portal.

Understanding a day in the life of a channel manager

Channel managers and their direct reports, channel reps, manage relationships with various types of partners and partners-in-waiting. The channel team does whatever it can to empower its indirect sales force with the right selling tools, sticks and carrots, to make sure that the relationship is a win-win one.

Measuring partner performance

A major communication services company drove its channel sales strategy by partnering with leading wireless equipment manufacturers. Sometimes, the company was introduced to the end customer; other times, the company was involved in opportunities completely managed by the manufacturer. But in all circumstances, the company's channel managers leveraged Salesforce Partners to track the partner sales performance, to improve mindshare with strategic partners, and to deepen its relationships with end customers.

With Salesforce Partners, channel managers now have access to Salesforce's dashboards, leads, opportunities, accounts, and document records. Dashboards provide a graphical snapshot of the channel's performance so you can see how much revenue the channel is bringing in. Leads are potential business that either come from a partner or that come to your company and are automatically or manually reassigned to the best partner for the job. Opportunities are the deals sourced or nurtured by your partners. Accounts can be resellers, distributors, agents — any type of partners that your business tracks. Channel managers can also use documents to publish copies of sales tools, price lists, or product information for partners.

In addition to these standard tabs, you can also track partner budgets and fund claims if you run joint marketing programs, create and promote rebate programs with your partners, and more. Your administrator will need to set this up, so make sure he or she reads the "Setting Up Salesforce Partners for Your Channel Team" section, later in this chapter.

Understanding a day in the life of a partner

A partner's perspective is the flip side of the relationship managed by the channel manager. For example, one type of partner could be reselling your company's products. That partner works in a territory that's managed by a channel manager. With Salesforce Partners, partner users can now access a limited view of your Salesforce information via a Partner Portal. The Partner Portal provides a centralized view of leads to pursue, opportunities in your pipeline, vendor documents to help with the sales cycle, and optional tabs to help with additional responsibilities, such as making fund requests. Partners get to see leads specifically assigned to them or grabbed from a general "shark tank" in which first come is first served. Additionally, partners can receive other key targeted messages on the Web site, update their company's information for the vendor to see, and e-mail their channel rep, as needed. Figure 11-1 shows a sample Partner Portal that salesforce.com might set up for their partners.

Figure 11-1: Accessing the Partner Portal.

Managing Your Channel with Salesforce Partners

Once your administrator has set up your organization with Salesforce Partners, the channel team will be able to easily access it from the AppExchange app menu in the upper-right of your Salesforce window. This section provides a high-level overview of how the channel team can now use Salesforce Partners to gain better visibility into their partner relationships. We also recommend you skim Chapters 4 and 8, which talk in more detail about navigating accounts and leads.

Creating partner accounts and contacts

First, you should make sure that all your partners are represented as accounts in Salesforce, with the respective channel managers owning the partner account records. This then allows channel managers to monitor and record all activities related to partners in their territory.

To create a new partner account, follow these steps:

1. **Use the Create New drop-down list on the sidebar and select the account option.**

   See Chapter 4 for more information on managing accounts.

2. **After creating the account record, click the Enable as Partner button on the account record.**

   If you don't see this button, you don't have the permissions to manage partners, or you don't have Salesforce Partners enabled for your organization — check with your Salesforce administrator.

3. **Associate partner users to this partner account record by adding contacts.**

   See Chapter 5 for details on creating new contacts.

4. **After you create a new contact, click the Enable Partner Portal Login button on the contact record for your partner user to receive his or her login and password notification via e-mail.**

Assigning leads to partners

By assigning leads to partners, channel managers ensure an organized way of seeing what potential business their partners are working on.

Leads may be assigned to partners by manually switching the record ownership, by assigning partner leads to a queue (also known lovingly as the "shark tank"), or by adopting a "round robin" method, in which leads are routed evenly to a number of queues. Partners then have access to the queue to grab leads. (You can keep them from getting too greedy by setting a ceiling on how many leads they can accept to work at one time.) Additionally, lead assignment rules may be set up by your administrator to automatically assign leads to partner users or partner queues based on certain rules.

To reassign a lead to a partner user, follow these steps:

1. **On the lead record, next to the Lead Owner field, click the Change link.**

   The link is in square brackets. The Change Lead Owner page appears.

2. **Select the partner user or partner queue that you're assigning the lead to.**

   Note that this is the same page that you use when you're assigning multiple leads, but here you can choose to notify the recipient with an e-mail.

3. **When you're done, click Save.**

   The lead record reappears with your ownership change. The new partner owner instantly receives a customizable e-mail if you selected the Send Notification check box, and the lead appears in their Lead Inbox the next time they access the Partner Portal

You may also reassign leads in bulk. See Chapter 8 for more information.

TIP

Salesforce to Salesforce

Salesforce to Salesforce is an amazing complementary feature to Salesforce Partners that allows partners with their own instance of Salesforce to seamlessly share lead and opportunity records with vendors, in real-time. Traditionally, this sharing occurred through a hairy, expensive, and drawn out integration process. If a lot of your partners also use Salesforce, think about what partner processes you want to track.

✔ If you have very specific custom processes that are more focused on a high volume of lead and opportunity management, you may lean toward using Salesforce to Salesforce.

✔ At the same time, if you send out a lot of customized partner communications, including collateral and content distribution, and you deal with both a Salesforce-owning and non-Salesforce-owning indirect sales force, you may want to lean more towards the Partner Portal.

We don't have one correct answer to give you, so make sure you run things by your Customer Success Manager. Salesforce.com charges extra for an organization that invites others to share information, but the invited organization can accept that invitation for free.

Reducing channel conflict with deal registration

Without a well-thought-out PRM process, companies often run into channel conflict when their direct sales and indirect sales forces butt heads over who found which lead first. As the channel manager, you often have to waste time arguing with a direct sales rep and her manager over who has dibs, while the prospect waits for the internal bickering to stop. This isn't an efficient way to close a deal, and it's frustrating for the customer to often hear multiple messages (or even price quotes!) from what's supposed to be a united front. In addition, if the partner loses out on that opportunity, you've just lost some of their trust in how supportive you really are in their efforts . . . so why should they reveal their pipeline data early or adopt your processes?

By taking the time to design a deal registration process, concisely and consistently communicate the status of deal registrations to partners, efficiently carry out the approval for all submissions, and then be able to measure related conversion and close ratios, you can eliminate channel conflict. The deal registration capabilities of Salesforce Partners help provide clarity on what your deal registration processes are, from start to finish, which can increase adoption of your partner program and help increase partner sales because the channel conflict inefficiencies disappear. However, this setup can be successful only if you invest the time to think out your deal registration process. If you have a hard time explaining it or whiteboarding it, how do you think your partners feel?

Here are some key questions to ask before establishing any deal registration program:

- ✔ How would you describe your deal registration process, from start to finish?

- ✔ What do partners get for registered deals? (Exclusivity? A rebate? A different tier or status?)

- ✔ What do you think would increase deal registrations?

- ✔ What information do you need when a deal is registered? (Balance your quest for knowledge with the partner's patience in filling out fields.)

- ✔ What's your process for approving deal registrations?

- ✔ What criteria do you evaluate to determine who officially owns a deal?

- ✔ Does this approval process work the same for all partners? For which categories would it be different?

- ✔ What metrics matter to you?

Accessing Salesforce Partners as a Partner

Partners are now able to strengthen their vendor relationship by accessing their vendor's instance of Salesforce from a Web portal and getting first-hand access to leads, accounts, opportunities, and other tabs to manage their deals. Now you can get leads assigned to you in real-time — no waiting forever after a trade show ends to see which leads to pursue. You can also provide your channel managers with real-time updates on the status of deals that you're trying to bring in. That way, if you need some assistance, your channel manager can view all deal-related activity that occurred up to a certain point and provide you with the appropriate resources to close the deal. In the following sections, we give you a quick overview on accessing and navigating your Partner Portal.

Understanding your Partner Portal home page

As a partner sales rep, you'll receive two e-mails from your vendor's Salesforce administrator once they're ready for you to start accessing the Partner Portal. The first e-mail welcomes you to the Salesforce service. The second e-mail contains your Salesforce login, temporary password, and Partner Portal URL.

In this e-mail, click the appropriate link to log in directly to your Partner Portal and change your temporary password. Make sure you remember to bookmark the portal's URL for easy access later. After logging in and changing your password, you're brought to the home page for your Partner Portal. Every time you log in to the Partner Portal, you begin at your home page. You'll see that the Partner Portal is organized into a series of tabs, similar to the navigation of Amazon.com.

The look of your portal may resemble your vendor's branding, or your own. In Figure 11-1, the fictitious portal resembles the vendor's branding.

Verifying your account information

On the left side of the home page is the sidebar. Near the top of the sidebar, you see your name as registered within Salesforce. Make sure your company's information is up to date by following these steps:

1. **Click the My Account Profile link below your name, as shown in Figure 11-2.**

   Information about your company appears. This reflects the information your vendor has about you, so you should make sure it's accurate.

Figure 11-2:
Viewing your account profile.

Welcome

Tom Reseller
My Company Profile
My Profile

Channel Manager:
undefined

2. **Click the Edit button to make updates, as needed. When finished, click Save.**

   Your account profile page reappears.

Contacting your channel manager

Below your user name is the name of your main contact for your vendor —
usually this is labeled "channel manager," but your vendor can set it to the
most appropriate title. If at any time you can't remember your channel manager's name, head to the home page. If you need to contact your channel manager at any time, just click on the manager's name and his or her e-mail will
appear in a new message in your e-mail application.

Creating new records

Below your channel manager's name, you'll see a set of links to easily create
new records under the aptly named Create New section. The types of new
records you can create depend on what your vendor wants you to track.
Below are a few examples of links you may see:

- ✔ **Deal Registration** allows you to submit information on a potential lead
  that looks like it'll bear fruit. After creating this type of new record, your
  deal registration will be submitted for review and approval by your
  channel manager.

- ✔ **Sales Lead** tracks the submission of prospects that you have for your
  vendor. Actively referring leads shows your channel manager that
  you're pounding the pavement.

- ✔ **Fund Request** associates a request for funding to a justifiable marketing
  activity. Your channel manager reviews this and provides the appropriate funding for a booth at a tradeshow that may help bring in revenue
  for both of you, for example.

- ✔ After the marketing activity, create a new **Claim** to get reimbursed.

Browsing the Lead Inbox

In the main body of the page, below the company message, you'll see the
Lead Inbox, which contains unviewed leads that have either been assigned
to you specifically or to a general partner lead pool. The lead pool allows
channel managers to fairly make leads available to their partners, while
also avoiding multiple partners working on the same lead since once you've
claimed a lead from the lead pool, no other partner may claim it.

Take note to play nicely. Your vendor can set a maximum number of leads
that each partner user may claim so that a partner with an itchy trigger finger
doesn't make away with all the goodies. Don't worry, if you can close the lead
or re-assign it to someone else, you can claim leads again until you hit your
maximum.

The leads in your inbox are listed according to columns set by your vendor. Click any column heading to re-sort your inbox list according to that column's criteria. Click the same column header a second time to re-sort your inbox list in reverse order.

If you see a record in your inbox that's in bold, then that means a new lead is already assigned to you and hasn't yet been viewed. You can

1. **Click the Edit link for that record to be taken to the Lead Edit page.**

   From there, you may review more information about your lead and update the lead status to begin pursuing this suspect.

2. **Click Save when you've updated the record.**

   The Lead page reappears.

If you see a record in plain text, then that's a lead in a pool that you should claim if you think you're the right partner to pursue it. You'll see that the Action column displays Accept for these types of leads.

To claim a lead from a lead pool, follow these steps:

1. **Click the Accept link for that record.**

   The Lead record appears with your name as the lead owner. Note that you can't first look at the details of a lead record and then accept it. That'd be similar to biting a piece of chocolate from the candy box and putting it back if you didn't like the coconut filling — not very nice, is it?

2. **Click Edit to update the lead.**

   After all, you want to be able to work on all the leads that you've claimed so your channel manager sees some results.

3. **Click Save when you've updated the record.**

   The Lead page reappears.

The Lead Inbox displays only new leads that haven't been opened. After you've viewed a lead, even if you didn't make any changes, the record won't show up in your inbox. You can access it instead from the Leads tab.

Viewing and updating your leads

Once you've looked at leads in your lead inbox, they become regular leads that you need to close. You manage these leads from the Leads tab. To view a list of active leads that you're working, follow these guidelines:

1. **Click the Leads tab.**

   The Leads home page appears. You may see a company message, and below that, a drop-down list of views for your leads, as in Figure 11-3. Views are created by your vendor to help you see a subset of your leads, according to certain pre-defined criteria.

2. **Select a view from the drop-down list.**

   In our example, we select My Open Leads. A list of leads in that view appears.

Depending on the column names your vendor has set up, you should see a Company heading. Column headings here, as in all lists, can be clicked to re-sort your list according to that column's content.

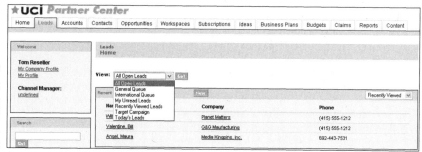

Figure 11-3: Selecting your lead view.

After you've qualified the prospect and believe a viable opportunity exists, update the lead status to your vendor's pre-defined status that notifies your channel manager to approve pursuit of this deal.

Managing your opportunities

Once your channel manager approves your deal, you'll be notified via e-mail and may begin filling in the details about the opportunity — what you'll be selling, how much revenue you think will be brought in, and where you are in the sales cycle.

You track this information under your Opportunities tab, which may have a similar look to your Leads tab. Click the Opportunities tab. Note the company message in the top part of the page, with an opportunities drop-down list below it. See the preceding section to find out how to navigate the Opportunities home page and get to an opportunity record.

Once you're viewing an opportunity record, make sure that you keep information on there updated. (For more information about standard opportunity fields, review Chapter 9.) Ultimately, what you should be driving for is, of course, a won deal, and there should be an appropriate stage that matches this concept.

Setting Up Salesforce Partners for Your Channel Team

Before setting up Salesforce Partners, your Salesforce administrator should meet with a member of the channel sales team to confirm your PRM needs. Discuss the following questions:

- ✔ What percentage of your sales force is indirect versus direct?

- ✔ What types of partners do you work with?

- ✔ Do you message differently to each type of partner?

- ✔ What are the objectives, challenges, and participation benefits for each type of partner in your program?

- ✔ How are your channel territories broken out?

- ✔ How are channel managers tracking partners' sales and marketing activities today?

- ✔ How do channel managers put together their channel forecasts? How long does it take, and how accurate is the information?

Armed with this information, make sure you set an appointment with your salesforce.com Customer Success Manager for some free advice or a blessing to go forward with using Salesforce Partners. Chances are that if answers to the above questions show that your business relies heavily on an indirect sales force, yet your visibility into the channel pipeline is as clear as mud, then you probably need Salesforce Partners. Again, the information we give you is meant to prepare you to successfully implement Salesforce Partners. The details of the all the cool features you can activate are more thoroughly discussed on salesforce.com's PRM Success Blog:

```
http://blogs.salesforce.com/prm
```

Granting partners access to Salesforce Partners

Granting partners access to the Partner Portal is a four-step process once your company is using Salesforce Partners. First, you have to create a profile for partner users (which is needed to enforce licensing), then you need to enable Salesforce Partners, then you create a partner user, and finally, you associate that partner user with a contact under a partner account.

For more detailed instructions on implementing the Partner Portal, look for the latest Implementing PRM Portal whitepaper on the PRM Success Blog:

```
http://blogs.salesforce.com/prm
```

Customizing the Partner Portal

Enabling Salesforce Partners will create a default portal for your administrator to further customize. You may create additional portals to target different partner audiences. For example, you may want to inform resellers of some promotional pricing this month, while telling your OEMs about new products coming out this week. Each partner can be associated with a Partner Portal that you've customized for it.

Part IV
Optimizing Marketing

The 5th Wave   By Rich Tennant

In this part . . .

You can expect to ask the most out of your sales teams only if you're capable of providing all the raw materials necessary to make them successful. They need effective marketing to help generate leads so they don't have to do it all on their own. Sales reps also need to know the products and services that are available, the way to position those offerings, and they must have the documentation that customers require to make buying decisions.

As you can imagine, these raw materials rely not only on sales managers, but on other people in your company: marketing, product management, finance, and so on. With Salesforce, those people can manage their sales-related activities, coordinate with sales teams, and instantly provide the raw materials in one convenient interface. And because users can access Salesforce anywhere at anytime, you don't have to worry about getting calls from reps sitting in airports in the middle of the night.

This part is devoted to the unsung heroes of marketing (although salespeople will find these chapters useful, too). First, we cover the exciting world of marketing campaigns and how you can use Salesforce to manage and measure campaigns and demonstrate your contribution to the bottom line. Next we provide an overview of Internet Marketing, and how the responsibilities of your Search Engine Marketing manager can now be tracked with Salesforce for Google AdWords. We then review the default Document Library where you can store your sales collateral, as well as Salesforce Content, for organizations that need to take document management to the next level.

Chapter 12

Driving Demand with Campaigns

Companies want to increase revenue by spending marketing dollars intelligently. However, because of the disconnect between sales and marketing teams, managers have a harder time executing campaigns, let alone tracking and measuring the results of their marketing programs. If this sounds familiar to you, campaigns in Salesforce can help you manage and track your marketing programs more effectively, resulting in lower acquisition costs, better leads, and potentially greater sales.

A *campaign* is any marketing project that you want to plan, manage, and track in Salesforce. Depending on your current or planned strategies, types of campaigns include tradeshows, search-engine marketing, direct marketing (including e-mail), seminars, Web events, and print advertising, although this is by no means a complete list.

In this chapter, you find out how to create and manage campaigns, segment target lists, execute campaigns, track responses, and analyze campaign effectiveness.

To administer campaigns, you must be a system administrator or a user with permission to manage campaigns (that is, a marketing manager type). See Chapter 20 for details on configuring your user information and profile to manage campaigns.

Understanding Campaigns

Available for Professional, Enterprise, and Unlimited Edition users, the Campaign module in Salesforce is a set of tools that enable you to manage, track, and measure your outbound marketing programs. Its foundation is the campaign record, which can be manually or automatically linked to lead, contact, and/or opportunity records to provide real metrics on campaign effectiveness.

A Campaign record comes standard with a set of fields that help you manage and track your campaigns. The following list describes the fields you use most often to measure campaign effectiveness:

- **Campaign Name:** This is the name of your marketing project. Choose a name that's readily obvious to sales reps and other users whose leads or contacts might be included in the campaign. For example, if you send out monthly e-mail newsletters, you might distinguish each campaign by month, as in "Newsletter — May 07" and "Newsletter — June 07."

- **Type:** This drop-down list includes the types of campaigns you run within your marketing mix (Direct Mail, Email, and so on).

- **Status:** This drop-down list defines the statuses of a campaign. Salesforce provides a simple default drop-down list of statuses to measure a campaign's progress. By using this field, you and others can make sure that the campaign is on track.

- **Start Date:** A date field you use to track when a campaign begins.

- **End Date:** A date field you use to track when a campaign ends.

- **Expected Revenue:** Use this currency field to estimate how much revenue the campaign will generate.

- **Budgeted Cost:** This is the amount that you have budgeted for the marketing project.

- **Actual Cost:** This is the amount that the project actually cost.

- **Expected Response:** This percentage field is your best guess of the response rate on a campaign. For example, if your direct mail campaigns typically receive a 2 percent response rate, you might use this value to benchmark the effectiveness of the campaign.

- **Num Sent:** This is the amount of people targeted in the campaign. For example, if you executed an e-mail campaign to 10,000 e-mail addresses, that would be your Num Sent.

- **Active:** Use this check box to mark whether a campaign is active or not. If you don't select it, the particular campaign doesn't appear in reports, or on related lists and other campaign drop-down lists on lead, contact, and opportunity records.

- **Description:** This field allows you to describe the campaign so that other users who want more detailed information on the campaign can get a solid snapshot.

Depending on your marketing processes, terminology, and goals, you or your system administrator should modify the drop-down list values and change the fields on the record. (See Chapter 21 for details on customizing Salesforce.)

If you're a marketing manager, you can plan and manage the majority of your campaign preparation inside Salesforce. You can

✔ Lay out your entire marketing plan of projects.

✔ Build the basic framework and business case for a project.

✔ Define statuses and success metrics for campaign responses. By *success metrics,* we mean how you determine whether the campaign was worth your company's time, money, and effort.

✔ Develop a detailed project plan so that important tasks get accomplished.

In the following sections, we show you where and how to accomplish these tasks.

Creating a new campaign

To create a campaign, log in to Salesforce and follow these steps:

1. **Select the Campaign option on the Create New drop-down list on the taskbar.**

   A New Campaign page appears, as shown in Figure 12-1.

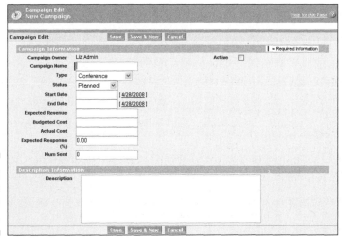

Figure 12-1: Filling in the campaign record.

2. **Fill in the fields as much as possible or as required.**

   If you currently manage marketing programs for your company, you should see few surprises in the campaign fields. Refer to the preceding section for a summary of the standard entry fields.

3. **When you're done, click Save.**

   The campaign page reappears with the information you've entered, as well as additional system-generated fields that automatically update as your company makes progress on a campaign.

You can associate campaigns to a parent campaign and see the aggregate performance statistics in one place. So your iPhone Launch Event could be a parent campaign to other campaigns such as Email Drop, Banner Ad, and Webinar, for example. To group campaigns into a campaign hierarchy, have your Salesforce administrator add the Parent Campaign field to your Campaign page layout. Refer to Chapter 21 for more information on page layouts.

Modifying the member status

A campaign *member* is a lead or a contact who's part of a specific campaign. Depending on the type of campaign you're running, you can modify the campaign to have a unique set of member statuses. For example, the member statuses that you track for an e-mail campaign (Sent, Responded) are typically different from those of a tradeshow that you're sponsoring.

To customize member statuses for a specific campaign, follow these steps:

1. **Go to the campaign record and click the Advanced Setup button.**

   The Campaign Member Status page for your campaign appears. When you first begin to create campaigns, Salesforce sets up a default set of member status values of Sent and Responded.

2. **On the Member Status Values related list, click the Edit button.**

   The Campaign Member Status page appears in Edit mode.

3. **Modify statuses by clicking into a field in the Member Status column and entering a new value.**

   For example, if you're sponsoring a booth at a conference, the preregistrants list is part of the package, and you want to invite attendees to visit your booth. In such a case, you might type member statuses of Registered, Invited, Attended, Visited Booth, and Met at Show.

4. **Select the check box in the Responded column to classify a status as responded.**

   This field tracks the Expected Response Rate field against the actual response rate.

5. **Use the Default column to select a default value and then click Save.**

   The Campaign Member Status page reappears with your changes.

Building Target Lists

One of the biggest challenges that marketing managers face is developing the right target lists for a campaign. *Target lists* are the lists of people you're targeting in your campaign. Depending on the type of campaign that you're planning, your lists might come from different sources, such as rented or purchased lists from third-party providers or existing lists of leads and contacts already entered in Salesforce. If your target list is composed of the latter, you can create your target list directly from the Salesforce Reports tab and associate specific campaigns to those leads and contacts, or you may add leads and contacts directly to specific campaigns.

Using rented lists

With a rented list, your options are limited. Depending on the circumstances, sometimes you don't know who's on the list because the list is controlled by the vendor. Other times, you enter into limited use terms, such as one-time usage. In these circumstances, simply use the external list as the target list, instead of importing the list into Salesforce.

You can use Salesforce to improve the quality of rented lists. Many third-party vendors de-duplicate their database against your customer database when they're generating the record count for a rented list. As long as you can trust the vendor, you can quickly use Salesforce to generate a file of your existing contacts to compare. By getting rid of duplicates first, you can stretch your marketing dollars by making sure that you're not paying for contacts you already have. And if you're doing a mixed campaign of rented and owned lists, you stand a better chance of not upsetting a customer with duplicate mail.

Importing new campaign members

If you own or purchase a list, and you intend for your teams to follow up on all the records, you can import the list into Salesforce as lead records and automatically link the records to a campaign.

To import a list and attribute it to a campaign, follow these steps:

1. **On the campaign record, click the Advanced Setup button, verify that the member statuses are accurate, and then return to the campaign record by clicking the Back button on your browser.**

2. **Click the Manage Members button.**

   The Manage Members: *Campaign Name* page appears.

3. **Click the Add Members — Import File link.**

   A pop-up window appears for the Campaign Member Import Wizard.

4. **Click the Import Leads button.**

   Step 1 of the Lead Import Wizard appears.

5. **Prepare your file, following the instructions that the wizard gives you.**

   Here are the main steps to perform:

   • Add and fill in a column for Member Status unless all records will use the default member status.

   • Add and fill in a column for Lead Owner unless you'll be the owner or you're applying lead assignment rules.

   • Save the file in a .csv format on your computer.

6. **In the wizard, click the Browse button to select the file from your computer.**

   A Choose File dialog box appears.

7. **Locate your file and click Open.**

   The dialog box closes, and the file name appears in the field.

8. **Use the drop-down list to select a lead source.**

9. **Use the next drop-down list if you want to select an assignment rule.**

10. **Select the check box if you want the assignment rules to send e-mail notifications to record owners.**

11. **Verify the campaign to which your leads will be assigned.**

12. **Verify the default member status.**

13. **Leave the character encoding unchanged unless necessary.**

14. **Select the check box if you want workflow rules to work on new or updated records.**

15. **When you're done, click Next.**

    Step 2 of the wizard appears.

16. **Map the fields by comparing the Salesforce Field columns against the corresponding drop-down lists in the Import Field columns.**

17. **When you're done, click Next.**

    Step 3 of the wizard appears.

18. **Review and confirm the import, and when you're done, click the Import Now button.**

Targeting existing members with the Integrated Campaign Builder

Assuming that your company has already imported users' leads and contacts, you can build your target lists directly in Salesforce three ways: by associating existing leads and contacts en masse to a campaign, by adding members from custom reports, and by adding members from a list view. After you've linked your desired leads or contacts with a specific campaign, you can begin to target them.

Adding members from a campaign record

To associate existing leads or contacts to a campaign you're planning, make sure you're able to first see the leads or contacts via a list view. See the organization sections in Chapter 5 (contacts) or Chapter 8 (leads) for information on using list views. You'll be able to add up to 250 leads or contacts per list view page. Next, follow these steps:

1. **From the specific campaign record, click the Manage Members button.**

   The Manage Members: *Campaign Name* page appears.

2. **Click the Add Members — Existing Leads (or Contacts) link, as appropriate.**

   In this example, we'll choose to add existing leads. The Add Members from a List of Leads Wizard appears.

3. **Confirm the campaign to which members will be added.**

   Use the Lookup icon if you need to find the correct campaign.

4. **Specify the member status that will be applied to these leads.**

5. **Click Next to continue.**

   Step 2 of the wizard appears.

6. **Select a lead view to display a list of members to be added to the campaign, as shown in the example in Figure 12-2.**

7. **Check the box next to the appropriate leads.**

   If a lead is already associated to this campaign, their name will be displayed with a read-only check mark next to it.

8. **Click the Add to Campaign button when ready to associate your choices to the campaign.**

   Salesforce notifies you when the members have been added. Repeat Steps 6 through 8, selecting new views, as needed.

9. **Click the Done button to finish.**

   The campaign record reappears.

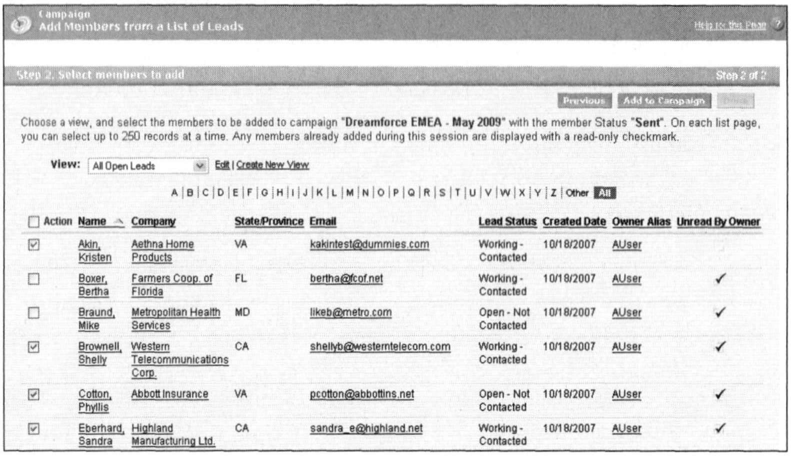

Figure 12-2:
Viewing
leads to
associate
with a
campaign.

Adding members from a custom report

Up to 50,000 leads or contacts in a single lead, contact, or campaign report may be associated to a campaign. To add existing members by running a report, follow these steps:

1. **From the Reports home page, click a custom report of the leads or contacts that you'll be targeting.**

   A Reports page appears.

2. **Click the Add to Campaign button, as shown in our example contact report in Figure 12-3.**

   The Add Members Wizard appears.

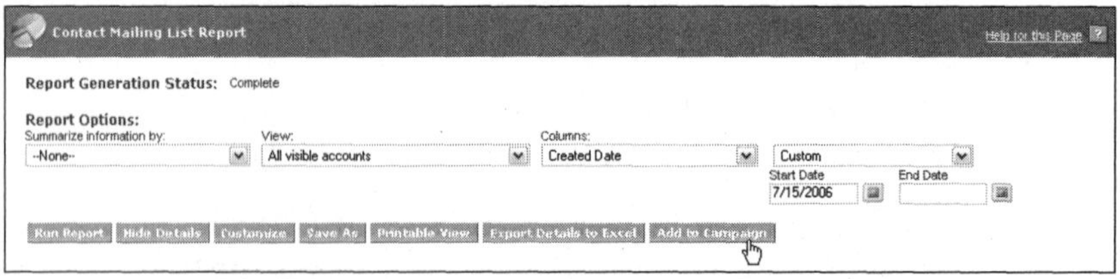

Figure 12-3:
Adding
report mem-
bers to a
campaign.

3. **Select an existing campaign for the Campaign field. Use the Lookup icon to search for your match.**

4. **After a campaign is selected, choose the appropriate status from the Member Status drop-down list.**

5. **Use the radio buttons to toggle whether you want the existing member statuses to be overridden by this member status.**

   The default is to not override existing member statuses.

6. **Click Add to Campaign to continue.**

   Step 2 of the wizard appears with a status message of your attempt.

7. **Click Done when information has been verified.**

   You're returned to your custom report page.

Adding members from a view

Now, from any lead or contact view page, members may be added to campaigns, as well. Note that this only allows marketing managers to select and add members one page at a time — so it's best for adding a small amount of members. If your view is more than one page, then you have to advance to that page and then add members. To add a member from a list view, make sure the view has already been created and follow these steps:

1. **At the view's results page, check the box next to the appropriate member names that you wish to add to your campaign.**

   In our example in Figure 12-4, we add some contacts to a campaign.

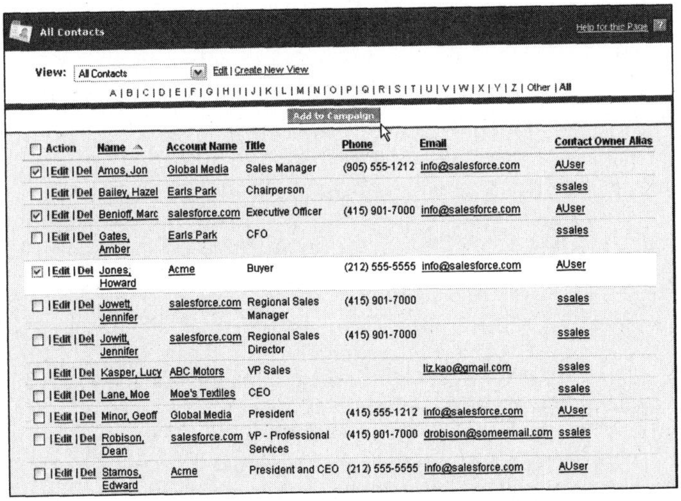

Figure 12-4:
Adding list members to a campaign.

2. **Click the Add to Campaign button once your members have been selected.**

   The Add Members Wizard appears.

3. **Select an existing campaign for the Campaign field. Use the Lookup icon to search for your match.**

4. **After a campaign is selected, choose the appropriate status from the Member Status drop-down list.**

5. **Click Add to Campaign to continue.**

   Step 2 of the wizard appears with a status message of your attempt.

6. **Click Done when information has been verified.**

   You're returned to your view page.

Executing Campaigns

Depending on the type of campaigns you're running, you might be executing those campaigns online or offline, or in combination. And, based on the complexity of the campaign and your resources, you can use Salesforce to assist the execution of parts of your campaign.

Delivering an online campaign

If you send out e-mail campaigns as part of your marketing strategy, you can use Salesforce for elements of the execution. Those elements might include

- Exporting an e-mail list from Salesforce for delivery to your e-mail execution vendor or internal resource.

- Building an automated Web form to capture leads as part of your e-mail or Webinar campaign. (See the section "Capturing leads from Web forms," later in this chapter, for details on building Web-to-Lead forms.)

- Using standard e-mail templates with merge fields so you can control the look and feel of your messaging.

You can use Salesforce to deliver and track mass e-mails, but Salesforce wasn't designed or intended to be used for large-scale mass e-mail marketing. Some Salesforce customers use the mass e-mail tool for small campaigns. Depending on which edition of Salesforce you have, you can send 100 (Professional), 500 (Enterprise), or 1,000 (Unlimited) e-mails per mass mailing. Your company is always limited to 1,000 e-mails a day through this feature.

Several e-mail vendors have integrated their campaign execution tools with Salesforce. With this integration, marketing managers can more seamlessly deliver e-mail campaigns from Salesforce. The costs and functionality vary across the e-mail marketing vendors, so check out the options on the AppExchange directory at www.appexchange.com. Search under the Email Marketing category.

Executing an offline campaign

If you execute offline campaigns, you can also use Salesforce in a variety of ways to simplify the process. How you use Salesforce depends on the type of campaign, but here are some suggestions:

- ✔ If you're sponsoring a conference, set up a Web registration form for your booth computers to capture information on attendees who visit your booth.

- ✔ If you're sending out direct mail pieces, use Salesforce to generate lists for your fulfillment vendor.

Tracking Responses

After you launch a campaign, you can use Salesforce to track responses. In Salesforce, you have three basic types of tracking mechanisms, which we describe in the following sections.

To track responses on a campaign, you need to be able to view the Campaign related list on lead and contact records. If you can't view this list, see Chapter 20 on customizing page layouts or see your system administrator for help.

Capturing leads from Web forms

Whenever we help clients with using Salesforce, we take a look at their Contact Us Web page. If it's filled with a bunch of e-mail addresses, we immediately recommend they get Web-to-Lead up and running. A company with a Web site using Salesforce in this day and age should take advantage of capturing information via an online form. Web-to-Lead is a Salesforce feature that enables your company to easily capture leads from your Web sites and automatically generate new leads in Salesforce. With Web-to-Lead, you can collect information from your Web sites and generate up to 500 new leads a day. You might already have a registration or a lead form on your public Web site. With Salesforce, you can, in minutes, generate HTML code that your Webmaster can apply to your existing form. Then, when people fill out the form on your Web site, the information is routed instantaneously to users in Salesforce. By using Web-to-Lead, your reps can follow up on leads in a timely manner.

Specifically for campaign tracking, you can also create forms for Web pages designed for a unique campaign to capture information on a campaign member who responds.

Before you can capture leads from an external Web page, you need to enable Web-to-Lead, add any additional custom fields to your lead record, generate the HTML code, and add the code into a Web page.

All Salesforce customers can capture leads from Web forms. First, you need to turn it on for your company.

To enable Web-to-Lead, log in to Salesforce and follow these steps:

1. **Go to Setup⇨Customize⇨Leads⇨Web-to-Lead.**

   The Capturing Leads from Your Web Site instructions page appears. Under the Steps to Capturing Leads from Your Web Site heading, look to see if Web-to-Lead is already enabled. If so, you're done with these steps.

2. **If Web-to-Lead isn't enabled, click the Enable Web-to-Lead link.**

3. **Fill out the page.**

   Salesforce provides three fields:

   - **Web-to-Lead Enabled:** Select this check box.

   - **Default Lead Creator:** Use the Lookup icon to select the default creator for when a lead is generated from a Web form. You usually select the user who manages marketing campaigns for your organization.

   - **Default Response Template:** Select a default e-mail response template. (See the Bonus Chapter on this book's Web site on creating e-mail templates, and see Chapter 8 for details on lead assignment rules.)

4. **When you're done, click Save.**

   The Capturing Leads from Your Web Site page reappears.

Generating HTML

You can use a tool in Salesforce that takes the guesswork out of generating HTML code for your Web forms.

To generate a general or a campaign-specific Web-to-Lead form, log in to Salesforce and follow these steps:

1. **Go to Setup⇨Customize⇨Leads⇨Web-to-Lead.**

   A Capturing Leads from Your Web Site page appears.

2. **Click the Create Web-to-Lead Form button in the middle of the page.**

   The Web-to-Lead Setup page appears.

3. **In the Create a Web-to-Lead Form section, customize which fields you want to include on your Web-to-Lead form.**

   Click a field name in the Available Fields column, and then click the Add arrow button to add that field from the Available Fields column to the Selected Fields column. Also, you may remove fields from the Selected Fields column by similarly clicking on a field name in the Selected Fields column, and then clicking the Remove arrow.

4. **In the URL field, enter a return URL, if known, and then click the Generate button at the bottom of the page.**

   The return URL corresponds to the landing page that appears after the lead has submitted his or her information online. When you click the Generate button, a page appears with HTML code inserted in a box.

   If you're creating a Web form specific to a campaign, create the campaign first and make sure that you've selected the Active check box for that campaign record. By doing this, you can select the fields for Campaign and Campaign Member Status, which enables you to track the specific campaign.

5. **Copy and paste the HTML code into a text file and send it to your Webmaster.**

6. **Click Finished when done.**

You are returned to the Web-to-Lead Setup page.

Viewing and testing the form

You can view and test the HTML code as an actual form by using your favorite Web publishing application and a browser.

To view and test the form, follow these steps:

1. **Open a new file in your favorite Web publishing program.**

   Popular programs include FrontPage, Dreamweaver, or HomeSite.

2. **Copy and paste the HTML code in the HTML mode.**

3. **Save the Web page on your computer.**

4. **Open a browser and choose File⇨Open to open the Web page.**

   A Web form appears with the lead fields that you selected. The form is relatively unformatted, but your Webmaster can apply code to make the form fit with your desired look and feel.

5. **Fill out the basic form and click the Submit button.**

   If you inserted a return URL, that page appears. If not, a page appears that displays the information that was sent to Salesforce.

6. **Log in to Salesforce and click the Leads tab.**

7. **Select Today's Leads from the Views drop-down list.**

   The leads list for today appears. If the test lead isn't listed, click the Refresh button on your browser until the test lead appears.

8. **Click the test lead's link under the Name column to validate the information from your test lead.**

   The lead record appears and displays the information that you submitted.

9. **Scroll down to the Campaign related list.**

   You should see a link to the campaign and the default member status. If you selected the Campaign Member Status field when generating the HTML code, you can apply a member status to all leads derived from the Web form.

Manually updating member statuses

If your campaign is designed to have recipients respond by phone or e-mail, your reps can manually update records as they interact with campaign members. Reps might have to create lead or contact records first if you didn't build your target list from Salesforce. For example, if you rent a third-party list for an e-mail campaign, the respondent might not yet be recorded in Salesforce.

To manually update a lead or contact responding to a campaign, follow these steps:

1. **In the sidebar Search, search for the lead or contact.**

   See Chapter 2 for details on using Search.

2. **If you can't find the lead or contact record, create it.**

   See Chapters 5 and 8 for details on creating contact and lead records, respectively. If you find the record, skip this step.

3. **Go to the specific lead or contact record page.**

4. **Click the Edit button to make any changes to the record, and then click Save.**

   For example, you might use the fields to type in additional information supplied by the respondent.

5. **Use the related lists to log any related information or future activities.**

Adding a member to a campaign

In those circumstances when your target list was built externally, reps should add the member to the campaign.

To manually add a member to a campaign, go to the lead or contact record and follow these steps:

1. **On the Campaign History related list, click the Add Campaign button.**

   The Add Campaign page appears.

2. **Select the appropriate campaign from the Campaign Name drop-down list and click Next.**

   The Add Campaign page reappears.

3. **Select the appropriate member status from the Status drop-down list and click Save.**

   The lead or contact record reappears.

Updating the status of a current member

If the lead or contact is already linked to the campaign in Salesforce, you'll want to update the member status when he or she responds.

To update member status manually, go the lead or contact record and follow these steps:

1. **On the Campaign History related list, click the Edit button next to the relevant Campaign Name.**

   The Add Campaign page appears.

2. **Use the Status drop-down list to change the status and click Save.**

Mass updating campaign statuses

If leads or contacts that are part of a campaign respond in a batch, you can do a mass update of campaign members. For example, if you sent out a direct mail campaign to existing contacts, and you received a batch of business reply cards, you could perform a mass update. The following sections tell you two ways to update statuses.

Mass updating all member statuses in a campaign

To mass update campaign statuses for all contacts or all leads in a campaign, log in to Salesforce and follow these steps:

1. **Click the Campaigns tab and select the specific Campaign whose members statuses you'd like to update.**

2. **Click the Manage Members button.**

   The Manage Members: *Campaign Name* page appears, allowing you to select a specific campaign.

3. **Click the Update Status — Existing Contacts (or Leads) link, as appropriate.**

   In our example, we'll choose to update leads. The Update Members Status from a List of Leads page appears.

4. **Confirm the campaign whose members you want to update.**

   Use the Lookup icon to search for a different campaign.

5. **Confirm the new member status.**

   Use the Lookup icon to search for a different campaign.

6. **Click Next to continue.**

   Step 2 of the wizard appears.

7. **Choose a view and select members to be updated for this campaign.**

   You may select up to 250 members to update.

8. **Click Update Statuses to apply the new statuses to your selected members.**

   A status bar displays the results of the operation. You may continue updating by selecting new views, or click Done when finished.

Mass updating all member statuses in a report

To update the status of several members at once, follow these steps:

1. **Click the Reports tab and scroll down to the Campaigns Reports heading.**

2. **Click the Campaign Call Down Report link.**

   A page appears, allowing you to select a specific campaign.

3. **Use the Lookup icon to choose a campaign and click the Run Report button.**

   A Campaign Call Down Report for your campaign appears.

4. **Click the Add to Campaign button.**

   The Add Members Wizard opens.

5. **Confirm the campaign in the Campaign field. Use the Lookup icon to search for your match.**

6. **After a campaign is selected, choose the appropriate status from the Member Status drop-down list.**

7. **Use the radio buttons to toggle whether you want the existing member statuses to be overridden by this member status.**

   The default is to not override existing member statuses. However, if your goal is to update all statuses of members in this report, choose to override the status.

8. **Click Add to Campaign to continue.**

   Step 2 of the wizard appears with a status message of your attempt.

9. **Click Done when information has been verified.**

   You're returned to your view page.

You may also mass update campaign statuses for contacts or leads in a campaign by updating the information in a .csv file first and then importing it. For example, a tradeshow exhibitor may give you a file of all show attendees that you can cross-reference with leads that you invited. Once you know which of your invitees actually attended, you may import this file into Salesforce. Just make sure you've added and edited a column for Member Status (unless all records will use the default status) and have a column for Lead or Contact ID. Then, click the Manage Members button, as mentioned in previous sections, click the Update Status — Import File link, and follow the guidelines to update the campaign history.

Chapter 13

Building Your Internet Marketing Channel

In This Chapter

▶ Understanding Internet marketing

▶ Perfecting search engine marketing

▶ Introducing Google AdWords

▶ Tracking your Google AdWords campaigns

Search engines help you navigate the vastness of the Internet by directing you to certain Web sites when you're not sure which sites may have what you're looking for. Very rarely, however, does a business have the name recognition to garner the top search result spot. What do you do if your business and its Web site aren't a destination yet? How will people ever hear of your business when they're looking on the Internet for what you're selling?

Enter Google, the 500-pound gorilla in the search engine space. Consumers go to Google for accurate and fast search results. And when they get accurate and helpful results, users come back to Google. More eyeballs on Google and its search results means that the importance of advertising on Google's site (or on any search engine, for that matter) becomes critical for any business, of any size. If your company's not showing up high on that search result's first page, you're missing out on a huge amount of potential traffic to your site.

Google AdWords allows marketing managers to easily advertise on Google. AdWords ads are displayed alongside search results, giving your business exposure to a huge audience. Tracking these AdWords ad campaigns and analyzing which ones were more effective than others is now more important than ever.

In this chapter, we begin with a short intermission from Salesforce and provide an overview of Internet and search engine marketing. Rest assured, all this background is highly relevant when we explain how Google AdWords plays a key role. We culminate this chapter with showing you how to track your Google AdWords campaigns directly in Salesforce, so you can take advantage of the activity tracking and reporting strengths of the platform.

Understanding Internet Marketing

Internet marketing (or *online marketing*) refers to any marketing of your products or services done over the Internet. Sounds obvious, right? Well, underneath that rather broad phrase lie several key terms that you should know as a marketing manager:

- ✔ **Keyword:** A word or phrase that a user enters into a search engine

- ✔ **Search engine results page (SERP):** The pages of results a user gets after he or she enters a keyword into a search engine

- ✔ **Organic search:** When a user finds a Web site by clicking links in the SERP that are naturally listed by the search engine, as opposed to a sponsored listing purchased by an advertiser

- ✔ **Sponsored link:** A link that was paid for by an advertiser

- ✔ **Search engine marketing (SEM):** A subset of Internet marketing that aims to promote a business's products and services by increasing its Web site's visibility in SERPs

Search engine marketing (SEM) is a rapidly evolving field and job function that focuses on marketing to potential customers by making sure relevant keyword searches return your company's Web site higher on the list than that of your competition and through paid advertising on search engine Web sites.

Paid placement advertising for your business

Even if you've done your best to get your Web site search-engine optimized, you're still not going to be guaranteed a top position in an organic search result. Maybe you're in a business with high competition for certain keywords, or maybe a change in the search engine's algorithm suddenly bumps you from the top spot. To increase the probability of a company appearing in an organic search listing, many companies also purchase paid placement ads on search listing pages.

This means that marketing managers (or advertisers) bid on keywords that they think their target audience will use when looking for a similar product or service. When a user types in that keyword, he or she may see that ad on the SERP, identified as a Sponsored Link. Advertisers have to pay their bid amounts only when a user clicks on that link.

Where do marketing managers go to place these bids? They head to various ad networks, one of which is run by Google. The program that advertisers use to create ads and bid for keywords on Google is called Google AdWords.

For more in-depth discussion about paid advertising, check out Peter Kent's *Pay Per Click Search Engine Marketing For Dummies* (Wiley Publishing, Inc.). To find out more about Google AdWords, pick up a copy of Howie Jacobson's *AdWords For Dummies* (Wiley).

Introducing Salesforce for Google AdWords

So, you've started advertising your business on Google. People have been clicking your ads. You've taken them to a landing page with a clearly defined call to action. Now they're hopefully filling out a form. These leads need to be captured somewhere, and you can capture them within Salesforce. Fortunately, the hard part of integrating Google AdWords and Salesforce so your online ads can be directly tied to your closed sales has been done. Your part is easy.

To see the Salesforce for Google AdWords tab set, log in to Salesforce and go to the AppExchange drop-down list in the upper-right corner of your browser window. Make sure the drop-down list has Google AdWords selected.

Clicking the Google AdWords Setup tab takes you to the page that lets you associate your Google AdWords account to your Salesforce account, as shown in Figure 13-1.

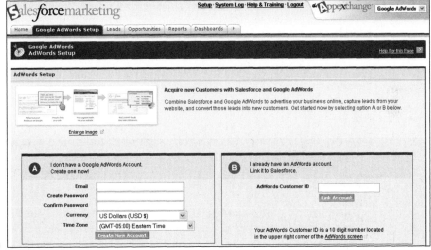

Figure 13-1: The AdWords Setup screen in Salesforce.

Signing up for a Google AdWords account

If your organization doesn't already have a Google AdWords account, you can sign up for one from the Google AdWords Setup screen. To create an AdWords account, perform the following steps:

1. **Enter the e-mail address that you want associated with your company's AdWords marketing.**

   This could be the e-mail address of the search engine marketing manager, or you can use an alias, as long as it routes to the SEM manager.

2. **Create a password and confirm it by re-entering it in the proper field.**

   For security purposes, the password must be a minimum of seven characters and a combination of letters and numbers.

3. **Confirm the currency you'll be using to make your keyword bids.**

   The default is set to U.S. dollars.

4. **Confirm your time zone.**

   This comes in handy later when determining when ads go live.

5. **Click the Create New Account button.**

   Salesforce for Google AdWords automatically creates your new AdWords account, shows you a confirmation screen, and e-mails you a confirmation request. Follow the instructions on that e-mail to activate your new AdWords account before using AdWords for the first time or click the Sign In and Activate Your New Account button on the confirmation page.

At any time, you're able to disconnect the connection between your Salesforce account and your Google AdWords account. You'll have to be logged in both sites at the same time. See "Disconnecting Your Google AdWords Account" in Salesforce's online help for more detailed information.

Linking your Google AdWords account

If you already have a Google AdWords account, perform the following steps to link your AdWords and Salesforce accounts:

1. **Get the AdWords Customer ID number. From the AdWords Setup tab, go to Box B to enter your AdWords account number.**

   To find your AdWords Customer ID, log in to Google AdWords and look at the upper-right portion of the screen.

2. **Click the Link Account button.**

   The linking could take a few hours. Wait for a confirmation e-mail to inform you when the link has been made.

3. **After you receive the confirmation e-mail, go back to the AdWords Setup tab and click the Log Into AdWords and Approve button to approve the linkage between the two sites.**

4. **Log in again to Google AdWords, and you'll see a dialog box displayed on the AdWords Campaign Management tab.**

It's basically informing you that Salesforce now has access to your AdWords account, and Google is asking you for approval of this action.

5. **Confirm that the radio button for the Yes option is selected and click the Submit Decision button.**

Once your Google AdWords account and your Salesforce account are linked together, the AdWords Setup tab becomes the Google AdWords Account Summary page.

You may associate one, and only one, Salesforce account to one Google AdWords account. If you're already linked to one Salesforce account and want to associate your AdWords account with a different Salesforce account, you'll have to sever the existing link and create a new one. See "Disconnecting Your Google AdWords Account" in Salesforce's online help for more detailed information on disconnecting a linkage between your Salesforce and AdWords accounts.

Integrating Lead Tracking with Google AdWords

After you link your Google AdWords account to your Salesforce account, you're ready to dive in and start counting the leads flowing in, right? Almost. Your administrator needs to complete a few steps.

Creating a Web-to-Lead form

You publish an ad on a search engine so that a user will click your link. That link should lead to a particular landing page that describes the call to action. Usually, this action requires the user to provide some of his or her information to get something of yours that he or she desires (like viewing a Webinar, whitepaper, or submitting a tradeshow registration). To set up a Web-to-Lead form that's integrated with Google AdWords, do the following:

1. **From the Google AdWords Setup tab, go to the AdWords Lead Tracking section and click the Set Up Lead Tracking button.**

2. **Click the Create Web-to-Lead Form button.**

3. **Select the fields that you want to capture from your leads.**

4. **Enter the return URL of the page you want to display after the lead submits the form.**

5. **Click the Generate button.**

6. **Copy the HTML code that's generated and provide it to your Webmaster.**

7. **Click Finished to return to the Google AdWords Setup tab.**

For more information on Web-to-Lead forms, check out Chapter 12.

Adding the tracking code to your Web pages

Work with your Web site administrator to add some tracking code to each of your Web pages so you can better track your Web-generated lead sources.

The tracking code looks like this:

```
<!- Begin Salesforce Tracking Code, place immediately before closing </BODY> tag
        -->
<SCRIPT type="text/javascript" src="https://lct.salesforce.com/sfga.js"></
        SCRIPT>
<SCRIPT type="text/javascript">__sfga();</SCRIPT>
<!- End Salesforce Tracking Code, place immediately before closing </BODY> tag
        -->
```

The code will be able to tell if a lead came to your landing page via a Google ad, for example. Don't worry, it's not as scary as it looks. Many Web site administrators today have worked with Web site tracking tags for other applications, such as Google Analytics or RightMedia.

The code is JavaScript. Here are some tips on where to put it:

✔ Place the code at the bottom of your pages. Usually, you do this in the footer template. Put it before the last `</BODY>` tag.

✔ Make sure the tracking tag isn't embedded within any other elements (such as `<TABLE>`, `<TR>`, `<SPAN>`, or `<DIV>` tags).

Confirming your Web site setup

Once your Web site administrator has embedded the tracking code into your Web site pages, it's time to confirm that Salesforce is successfully seeing it. To confirm your tracking code setup, follow these steps:

1. From the Lead Tracking Setup page, under the Google AdWords Setup tab, click the Test Your Setup button.

2. Enter the URLs of pages on your site that have the tracking code.

   Enter the URL of one of your landing pages.

3. If the URL contains a Web-to-Lead form, make sure the Web-to-Lead Form? check box is marked.

4. Click the Run Test button and follow any additional instructions to resolve any outstanding issues.

Viewing Tracked Leads

Once your tracking code has been embedded, you can start automatically tracking your online lead generation statuses. The Google AdWords Setup tab's home page now reveals the Google AdWords Account Summary. The Account Summary displays the number of leads from the following online sources:

- **Google AdWords:** The lead came from an AdWords ad.

- **Organic Search:** The lead came from an organic search.

- **Web Referral:** The lead came from a link that referred to your site.

- **Web Direct:** The lead came directly to your landing page.

Reviewing the lead source detail

Because Salesforce for Google AdWords integrates your AdWords campaigns directly to your lead generation efforts, you'll be able to see exactly what search terms and which AdWords ad brought a lead to you. On a lead record, look in the Activity History related list for a Lead Source Detail task. Click this task to see detailed information in the body of the task about what keywords the searcher used and which ad they clicked.

Working your leads

Once your leads come into Salesforce, you should work them just as you would any other prospect. See Chapter 8 for more detailed information on managing leads and converting them into viable business opportunities.

Analyzing results with analytics

A powerful benefit of Salesforce for Google AdWords is the standard set of lead generation and sales reports that come with the product, as well as the Google AdWords dashboard that provides you with visual feedback on your campaign efforts.

To access your Google AdWords reports, click the Reports tab and select Google AdWords Reports from the folder drop-down list. For more information on customizing reports, see Chapter 17.

To access your Google AdWords dashboard, go to the Google AdWords Account Summary page and click the Google AdWords Dashboard link. For more information on customizing dashboards, see Chapter 18.

Chapter 14

Driving Sales Effectiveness with Document Management

*I*f you, as a sales or marketing manager, expect to get the most out of your sales reps, you have to put the best tools at their fingertips. Aside from a desk, chair, phone, and some caffeine, reps need accurate and compelling documentation: sell sheets, whitepapers, case studies, and so on. All too often, however, sales documents reside in multiple places: network drives, e-mails, desktops, and so on.

If your reps are losing business because they can't access the right documents, take advantage of the Salesforce Document Library, which you can use to store the latest sales collateral in easy-to-use, organized folders. And so long as you have an Internet connection, reps can access the Document Library, even if they're sitting in an airport in Omaha, Nebraska.

What does an easily accessible library mean for you? If you're a sales rep or manager, this means spending more time in front of your customers and less time chasing information. If you're in marketing or product management, you can better control the message to customers with the confidence that sales reps are providing customers the most up-to-date information available. And, regardless of your role, you can individually store documents in your own personal folder.

For companies that need to organize a large amount of current documents, Salesforce Content also lets you share content. (Salesforce Content is available for an additional fee.) Its additional capabilities allow you to search document contents, notify you when content is updated, and track user feedback. All these features help to further increase your sales and marketing teams' productivity.

In this chapter, we show you how to use the Document Library and search for documents so that your reps can put them to work to sell more effectively. We also discuss the various ways to use Salesforce Content and when you might prefer a specific option.

Understanding the Document Library

The Document Library is much like a network drive that you use to store critical reference documents. You can create folders to organize sales documents and index those documents so that they're easily retrievable by sales teams. Non-sales departments, such as Human Resources, may also maintain copies of their latest documents here, so remote workers know where to go for the most up-to-date versions.

Depending on your desire for document control, you can store your documents directly in Salesforce or simply use Web links if you prefer that your documents be maintained internally. Whichever method you decide to use, the point is that you want to make reference information quickly accessible to your sales people wherever they are and whenever they need it.

A document record comes standard with a set of fields that help you find, retrieve, and maintain your documents.

Building Folders in the Document Library

If you want documents to be a highly effective sales tool for your staff, you have to organize your documents so that people can easily find them. By using folders, you can sort documents into logical groupings.

We've seen many different and effective approaches to organizing document folders in Salesforce. Some companies like to separate documents by product family; others prefer to take a vertical approach. The only right answer is the one that works for your company, so make sure you spend some time deciding on a naming convention for your folders. The Folder drop-down list on the Documents home page will grow along with your folders, so a clean and intuitive naming convention will help prevent a cluttered appearance. The following is a list of common folders that work for many organizations:

- ✔ Sell sheets
- ✔ Sales presentations
- ✔ Product data sheets
- ✔ Proposal templates
- ✔ Press releases
- ✔ Case studies
- ✔ General marketing
- ✔ Salesforce training

To create a document folder, you must first have the Manage Public Documents permission. (If you're not sure, you can quickly find out by seeing if you get past Step 1 in the following list. If you're not able to get past Step 1, ask your administrator to help.) To continue, go to the Documents home page and follow these steps:

1. **Click the Create New Folder link under the Document Folders heading.**

   A New Document Folder page appears.

2. **Type a name for the folder in the Document Folder field.**

3. **Use the Public Folder Access drop-down list to select the access rights.**

4. **Click the radio buttons to select who should have access to the folder.**

5. **When you're done, click Save.**

   The *Folder Name* Documents page appears, and you may begin adding new documents to your new folder.

As you plan out your document strategy, keep in mind that not all sales documents need to be in the Document Library. Some might be better suited as attachments on an account record; others you might not even want in Salesforce. As a general rule, documents that might be re-useable or have wide applicability are good for the Library. Documents that relate to a specific account are typically more relevant as attachments to Account detail pages.

Adding Documents

Before reps can begin using documents in Salesforce, you or someone in your company must first add the documents to the Document Library.

You basically have two options for adding documents to the Library: uploading the actual file or creating a link that points to where the document is stored on your network or intranet. You can do both, depending on which approach is appropriate for a particular file. In this section, we show you how to upload a document.

If you're not overly concerned with storage, you might prefer to upload your files into Salesforce. The huge advantage of the upload option is that users can access the actual documents anywhere and at anytime, as long as they can connect to the Internet.

When uploading files, the file size limit on any individual file is 5MB. For some companies, this might be the average size of a PowerPoint presentation or a PDF file with graphics, so plan accordingly.

When setting up your Document Library, create folders before adding documents so that you don't have to re-file documents later.

To add a document and upload its file, log in to Salesforce and follow these steps:

1. **Select Document from the Create New drop-down list on the sidebar.**

   An Upload New Document page appears.

   If you don't see the New Document link, see your system administrator about whether you have the Edit Documents permission.

2. **Type a name for the file in the Document Name field.**

   You don't have to make it the actual name of the file, but you should use a name that's obvious to you and your users.

   If you want the document name to be an exact match of the filename, leave this field blank. After you select the file, the filename automatically populates the empty Document Name field.

3. **Select the For Internal Use Only check box only if you want this document to be confidential.**

   If you select this check box, you don't alter its access, but you flag your end users not to send the file outside the company.

4. **Select the Externally Available Image check box only if you're uploading an image that you'll be sending in HTML e-mail templates to people that should view it without having to log in to Salesforce to see it.**

   For example, logos or letterhead footers should have this box checked.

5. **Use the Folder drop-down list to select a folder.**

   If you haven't yet created the appropriate folder, or you don't have read-write access to the correct folder, you can first store the file in the My Personal Documents folder and re-file the document later.

6. **In the Description field, type a brief description of the document.**

7. **In the Keywords field, type keywords that'll help your end users find the document.**

   Salesforce provides a Find Documents search tool on the Documents home page, so you should select keywords that you think your users will enter.

   For example, if you're adding a case study, you might enter keywords that include relevant products, customer names, challenges, and so on that sales reps could use for cross-referencing.

8. **Under the Select the File step, the Enter the Path radio button is selected by default, so you just need to click the Browse button to select the desired file.**

   A Choose File dialog box appears.

9. **Select a file from the folders on your computer and click Open.**

   The dialog box closes, and the document path is entered in the File to Upload field.

10. **When you're done, click Save.**

    A pop-up window appears, showing progress on the upload. When the upload is completed, the document record page reappears in Saved mode with information on the document and a link to view the document.

Using Documents

After you create documents in Salesforce, you can use various tools to search and use documents in the course of your selling. In the following sections, we show you how to use the Documents home page to search for documents with the Document Folders drop-down list and the Find Documents search box. Then we cover the simple practice of attaching a document to an e-mail before sending it to a customer from Salesforce.

Searching for documents

You can search for documents with keywords from the search box located on the Documents home page. To perform this action, click the Documents tab to go to the Documents home page and follow these steps:

1. **In the Find Document search box, type search terms, as shown in Figure 14-1.**

   Salesforce doesn't search the actual contents of the document itself, just the Document Name, Type, Keywords, and Description fields. So it's important to enter good keywords and descriptions to enable good searches.

Figure 14-1: Searching for a document.

> **Documents Home**   Tell me more! | Help for this Page [?]
>
> Enter keywords to find matching documents.
>
> web form   [Find Document]

2. **Click the Find Document button.**

   A Document Search page appears with a list of documents based on your search. The results are ordered by closest matches, as shown in Figure 14-2. Salesforce uses Document Name and Keywords fields to rank the closest matches.

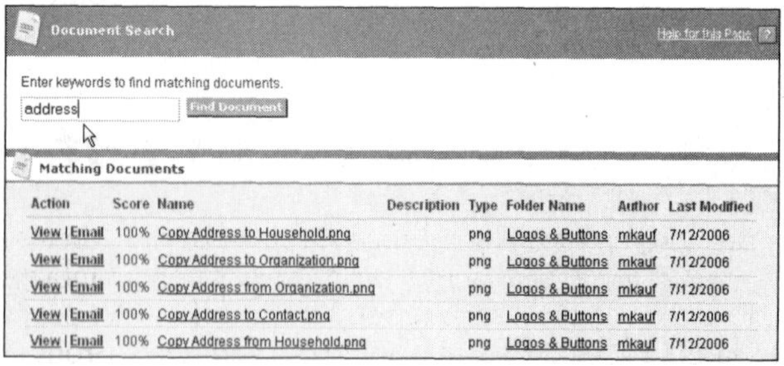

Figure 14-2: Viewing document search results.

> **Document Search**   Help for this Page [?]
>
> Enter keywords to find matching documents.
>
> address   [Find Document]
>
> **Matching Documents**
>
> | Action | Score | Name | Description | Type | Folder Name | Author | Last Modified |
> |--------|-------|------|-------------|------|-------------|--------|---------------|
> | View \| Email | 100% | Copy Address to Household.png | | png | Logos & Buttons | mkauf | 7/12/2006 |
> | View \| Email | 100% | Copy Address to Organization.png | | png | Logos & Buttons | mkauf | 7/12/2006 |
> | View \| Email | 100% | Copy Address from Organization.png | | png | Logos & Buttons | mkauf | 7/12/2006 |
> | View \| Email | 100% | Copy Address to Contact.png | | png | Logos & Buttons | mkauf | 7/12/2006 |
> | View \| Email | 100% | Copy Address from Household.png | | png | Logos & Buttons | mkauf | 7/12/2006 |

3. **Click a View link in the Action column if you want to make sure that you've found the correct document.**

   A window opens with your selected document.

Sending documents by e-mail

If you're focusing on a specific document and you want to send it out to people, you can save a lot of time and effort. For example, if marketing prepares a new product launch and announces that a new product sheet is available, you might want to go directly to the document list or detail page and e-mail the document to a set of customers.

To send an e-mail with a document attached, go to a document list or the Document detail page and follow these steps:

1. **Click the Email link from a document list or click the Email Document button from a record.**

   The result is the same. A Send an Email page appears. You can see that your document is attached by scrolling down to the Attachments related list.

2. **Fill out your e-mail as you would normally.**

3. **When you're done, click Send.**

   The document page that you initiated the e-mail from reappears. You can view a record of the e-mail and the document sent from the Activity History related lists of the records that you linked in the e-mail. For example, if you send a document and e-mail to a contact, you can view the e-mail under the Activity History related list on the Contact detail page.

When you send an e-mail with an attachment, Salesforce doesn't store a copy of the attachment with the e-mail record, but Salesforce does reference the name of the file sent. By doing this, you conserve your storage space, but you have to go back to the document if you want to review its content.

Understanding Salesforce Content

Anyone who has ever managed a document repository for themselves or their company can tell you that repositories need to be maintained to remain effective. If you sell a variety of products, for example, your product sheets need to be updated as specs change, deleted if you retire products, and added as you release new products.

Though Salesforce provides easy-to-use tools to help you manage the workload of document control, keeping a large amount of documents up to date can still be a daunting task. At some point, you may need a true content management system (CMS) to . . . well, manage your content.

If your company is committed to using Salesforce as the central repository for every department's content, you may want to consider using Salesforce Content for the following reasons: increased collaboration, document tagging, a deeper search, and notification of content changes.

As of this printing, Salesforce Content isn't available for organizations using the Partner Portal (see Chapter 11) or the Customer Portal (see Chapter 16).

Setting up Salesforce Content

Check with your Salesforce account executive to provision Salesforce Content, and then make sure the users you want to help set up content in your system are enabled. Go to Setup➪Administration Setup➪Manage Users➪Users, and then edit the users that you want maintaining your content management system. Make sure the Salesforce Content User check box is selected for those users. You'll then be able to see a set of tabs under the Content app in the AppExchange drop-down picklist.

A *workspace* is more than just a folder for your content. It's a repository that allows your content to be fully searchable, including the content within your documents. Also, with workspaces, a document can be shared across various workspaces. For example, in some contexts, you may have a legal document in a Sales workspace. But that same legal document could also be referenced in a Legal workspace. Instead of making you choose one location or another for the file, Salesforce Content lets you reference this file from several workspaces.

As of this writing, an automated migration path of documents from the standard Salesforce Documents folder to Salesforce Content doesn't yet exist. Migrating data will require some manual re-entry, but consider this a perfect time to review everything in your old directory to see what needs to be moved over and what doesn't need to make the trip.

Creating workspace permissions

Before you create a workspace and add certain users in your organization, you first need to define what those users can do in the workspace. Go to Setup➪App Setup➪Customize➪Salesforce Content➪Workspace Permissions and click the Add Workspace Permissions button. In Figure 14-3, you can see the various permission options you can grant when creating a new workspace permission.

In our example, we create a permission for someone to view and add comments, and add tags to the workspace. Click Save when you finish creating your workspace permission.

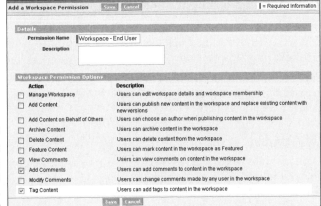

Creating a workspace and adding members

To create a workspace, simply go to the Workspaces tab in the Content app and do the following:

1. **In the My Workspaces section of the Workspaces tab, click New.**

    The New Workspace Wizard appears.

2. **Fill out the name of the workspace.**

    You can add a description so others won't need your help in figuring out what the workspace is for.

    Click the Save and Add Members button. Step 2 of the wizard appears.

3. **Select which users or public groups you want as part of this workspace. Click Next to continue.**

    Use the Add and Remove buttons to add users you want into the column on the right.

4. **Assign a workspace permission to each member by using the picklist.**

    Once you've saved these mappings, you're taken to that workspace's home page.

To quickly switch workspace home pages, use the Switch Workplace dropdown list on the right of your workspace area. You can use this list to navigate with a minimum amount of clicks.

Creating content types

Content types are similar to traditional Salesforce object layout templates (see Chapter 20 for more on page layouts). These pages appear when you're uploading content. As with other Salesforce objects, you can add custom fields to capture whatever information you want about your content:

✔ To create custom content fields, go to Setup⇨App Setup⇨Customize⇨ Salesforce Content⇨Fields. Click the New button in the Content Custom Fields & Relationships section.

✔ To create a new content type, go to Setup⇨App Setup⇨Customize⇨ Salesforce Content⇨Content Types. Click the New button to create essentially a new page layout for content.

Contributing content

Uploading content into a workspace is known as contributing content. To upload a new document, follow these steps:

1. **Click the Contribute tab in the Content app and hit the Upload a New File button.**

   You can add a Website Link if you want to refer people to an online video or to information stored in your intranet.

   The Contribute Content pop-up window appears.

2. **Browse your hard drive for the document that you want to upload.**

   Salesforce Content will automatically upload the document you select.

   Once Salesforce Content uploads your document, it asks you to describe and publish your content.

3. **Give your content a descriptive title.**

   Follow standard naming conventions within your company.

4. **Associate a workspace with your document.**

5. **(Optional) Add tags to this document if you want to identify it with words that may not be used in the standard workspace definitions.**

   Separate words with commas.

6. **Click Publish when you're done.**

To associate content with more than one workspace, follow these steps:

1. **Return to the Workspaces home page.**

2. **Select a document from the Top Content section.**

3. **In the Content Details page, select the Share to Another Workspace option in the Workspace Actions drop-down list.**

4. **Choose more workspaces to share this document.**

Managing content

End users that belong to one or more workspaces can perform the following actions in Salesforce Content:

- ✔ **Search for content.** Use the Content tab to search for documents. Salesforce Content not only lets you search content details, it also looks inside the content to see if any words match up. You can also search for more popular content by going to the Workspaces tab and looking at the Popular Tags section.

- ✔ **Subscribe to content.** Click the little orange icon to the right of the content type logo to subscribe to a piece of content. This means that anytime changes are made to the document, you'll be notified of it.

- ✔ **Tag content.** When looking in the Content Details page of a document, add tags to help you remember this document. The more specific the term you use for the tag, the better.

- ✔ **Comment on content.** In the Content Details page, you can write comments to provide specific written feedback to the content creators. You can even vote on whether you like the content by clicking the thumbs up or thumbs down buttons. This helps bridge the gap that often exists between the groups that create the documents and those that actually have to use them.

Chapter 15

Performing Fast and Accurate Support

Salesforce Service & Support is more than just a simple customer support application to track and resolve cases.

With Salesforce Service & Support, you have all the tools at your fingertips to efficiently deliver excellent customer service while managing the costs of operations. In days and weeks, versus months and years, you can start and manage a fully integrated customer service strategy that supports the many channels that customers use to communicate with you.

In this chapter, we help support reps understand how to use Salesforce Service & Support. We first discuss basic support rep processes for handling new cases, and then we cover how to manage the growing caseload within Salesforce Service & Support.

Walking through a Day in the Life of a Sales Rep

Salesforce Service & Support follows a general process when it comes to managing cases. Support reps commonly perform these tasks on any given day. The specific tasks may be different in your company, but you probably see some similarities:

✔ Responding to inbound e-mails and calls

✔ Taking down new cases from assigned queues

✔ Validating that the inquiry is coming from an authorized contact

✔ Creating a case to begin tracking efforts to resolve the issue

✔ Working the caseload, including researching solutions

✔ Resolving issues

✔ Communicating the resolution to the customer

At its core, service and support is all about accepting questions and answering them in a timely and consistent manner. How you handle your responses — and the scale on which you handle them — are more complicated issues.

High-volume call centers can take advantage of Salesforce's customer management and reporting capabilities by using Salesforce Call Center. Salesforce Call Center integrates Salesforce with third-party computer-telephony integration (CTI) systems. This allows your call center agents to do cool stuff such as dial and receive calls right from their computers and see what contact records or cases are related to the calls.

Understanding the Case Record

With Salesforce Service & Support, the secret is the integrated relationship between two objects: cases and solutions. A *case* is a record of a customer service inquiry (you may call them *tickets*), as shown in Figure 15-1. Just like other common records, such as accounts and contacts, you can track all interactions on a case from a single detail page. And to manage all your cases, Salesforce Service & Support comes out of the box with all the tools that you need for routing, queuing, and escalating cases, plus complying with service level agreements (SLAs), if that applies to your company.

A case record comes preconfigured with standard fields and two icons commonly used for case management. Most of the standard fields are self-explanatory, but in the following list, we highlight key fields that are less obvious:

✔ **Status:** This field defines the important statuses in your case process. It comes preconfigured with a basic process, but you should modify the values to fit your process. If you're an Enterprise or Unlimited Edition user, you can use this field to distinguish multiple support processes appropriate to the different kinds of cases you want to track.

✔ **Case Number:** When you create a case, Salesforce Service & Support automatically assigns a sequential number used for tracking.

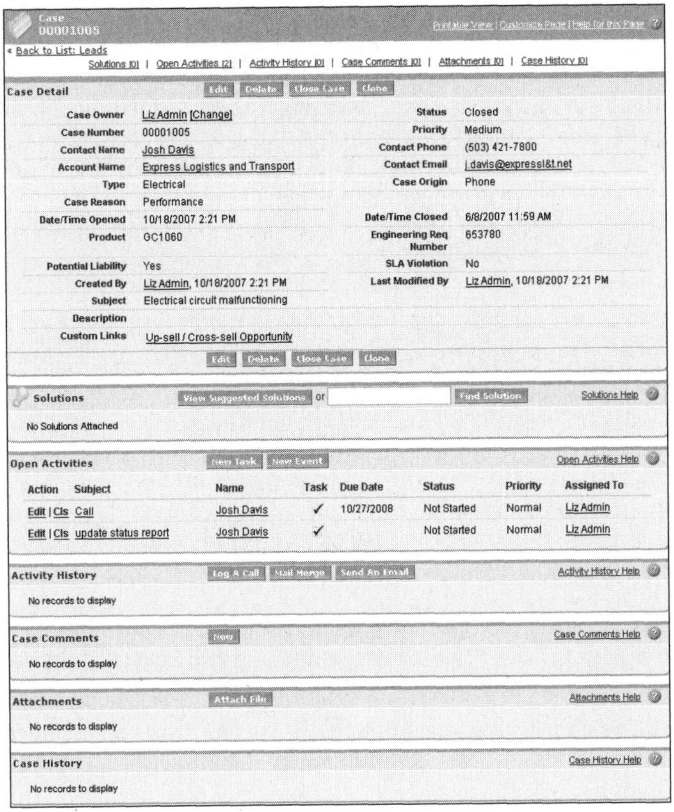

Figure 15-1:
Introducing
the case
record.

✔ **Type:** Use this picklist field to define the type of case. Salesforce Service & Support presets this list with selections that include Problem and Question, but you can modify the picklist to match your categories.

✔ **Reason:** Use this picklist field to specify the reason the case was opened. Many companies track this field to identify areas of customer service that they can improve. Of course, you can also modify this list to suit your needs.

✔ **Case Origin:** Use this field to record from which channel the case originated — for example, by phone, e-mail, or Web. Many companies report on this field to understand and improve the methods by which customers interact with service and support agents.

✔ **Internal Comments**: Use this field to jot brief comments on this case to communicate internal messages, as needed. Comments that are marked Public may be viewed by clients in the Self-Service Portal, if you have it enabled.

Creating a Case

One of the main responsibilities of an agent is handling new inbound inquiries. Writing notes on little sticky notes that you attach to your monitor may not be the best way to track information, especially if you have terrible handwriting. In the following sections, we discuss how to begin the case management process in Salesforce Service & Support, so the right information is tracked for the right customers.

Validating the contact

The first step in creating a case is validating the company and contact information to see if any special circumstances or service level agreements (SLAs) exist. Can't have just any random person taking up your precious time, can we? This information should reside in custom fields on the account record. For example, to do this in response to an inbound call, log in to Salesforce Service & Support and follow these steps:

1. **Type the company name (or account number — whatever your company uses to identify its customers) into the Search field on the sidebar on your Home page and click the Go button.**

   The Search Results page appears. Hopefully, you see the account name listed.

2. **Click the Account Name.**

   The Account record appears. Verify information on this record that helps you identify that you're allowed to support this company.

3. **Look at the Contact detail list to locate the person with the problem.**

   Again, depending on your company's policies, you may or may not have specific customer contacts authorized to call you for support.

4. **Click the Contact Name.**

   The Contact record appears. Verify information on this record that helps you identify that this person is permitted to call for support. If the contact record doesn't already exist, create a new contact record. For more information, refer to Chapter 5.

Entering new cases

After you've qualified the customer, you have to associate a case to each new issue you receive. Because cases are associated with contacts, the best, most reliable way to create case records is by starting from the relevant Contact detail page. From the Contact detail page, you can add a case using either the Create New drop-down list on the sidebar or the New button on the Cases related list. The result is the same in both situations, and you automatically pre-fill the Contact lookup field. By doing this, you can always find your case, and your case activities will be listed on the overall Contact detail page.

To create cases by using the best practice, follow these steps:

1. **From the Contact detail page, click the New button on the Cases related list.**

   The Edit mode of a new case appears.

2. **Fill in the fields as much as you can or as required.**

   Notice that the Contact field is pre-filled with the contact you were working from.

3. **When you're done, click one of the following buttons:**

   • **Save:** After you click the Save button, the Case detail page appears.

   • **Save & Close:** Clicking this button saves the current case info and automatically takes you to the Close Case detail page, where you select the appropriate closed case status and add additional details. Use this if you quickly resolve an issue.

   • **Save & New:** Clicking this button saves the current contact info and automatically opens a new, blank contact record.

   • **Check Spelling:** Clicking this checks the spelling of the contents of the Description field.

To clone a case, click the Clone button at the top or bottom of the case record. This is similar behavior across other records in the Salesforce family.

Managing Cases

As a service or support agent, one of your key goals is to address and resolve many customer issues as quickly as possible. Ideally, the need for speed is balanced with some defined processes to ensure a sense of order. Over time, your caseload will build up as different cases take different lengths of time to resolve. In the following sections, we describe how to efficiently update a case as you work it, and then we discuss how to manage your growing caseload.

Updating case fields

As you work your cases, you may need to modify case information. To update a case, follow these steps:

1. **Type the case number in the Search tool and click Go.**

   A Search results page appears.

2. **Click the desired Case Number link.**

   The Case detail page appears.

3. **Click the Edit button at the top of the case record.**

   The case record appears in Edit mode.

4. **Update the fields, as necessary, and click Save.**

   The case detail page reappears. Notice that the fields you edited have been changed.

Case comments can't have their own related list on the case detail record and are meant to record any short internal conversations that agents may review at a glance. If you have the Self-Service Portal set up, agents may optionally share certain comments with contacts on a case.

Reassigning case ownership

You might find that after you create cases in Salesforce, you need to transfer them to the right people. These may be people who become responsible for case resolution after it's been escalated, for example.

To reassign a case, go to the case record and follow these steps:

1. **Next to the Case Owner field, click the Change link.**

   The link is in square brackets. The Change Case Owner page appears.

2. **Select the user you're assigning the case to.**

   By clicking the check box on the page, you can choose to notify the recipient with an e-mail.

3. **When you're done, click Save.**

   The case record reappears. Notice that the Case Owner field has changed to the assigned user.

Getting a clue on views and queues

Case views and case queues are accessed from the same location — the Case View drop-down list.

A *case view* is a list of cases that match certain criteria. When you select a view, you're basically specifying criteria to filter the results that you get back. The advantage of using a view, versus searching, is that you can use the view over and over again.

If your company has several agents resolving cases for a variety of products and services, your administrator may set up *case queues* to automatically funnel cases to the right pairs of eyeballs. For example, you may use your Web site to collect both product and billing inquiries. Case queues would allow support agents to grab new cases from the product queue, while accounts receivable staff monitor the billing queue.

To try out a predefined view, do the following:

1. **On the Cases home page, open the Cases Views drop-down list.**

   The four default options appear and maybe some other choices that have already been created for you.

2. **Select the My Open Cases option.**

   The My Open Cases list opens, as shown in Figure 15-2.

   Notice that Salesforce lays the list out with seven standard columns that correspond to commonly used case fields, plus an Action column so you can quickly modify a record.

3. **Click a column header to re-sort the list page.**

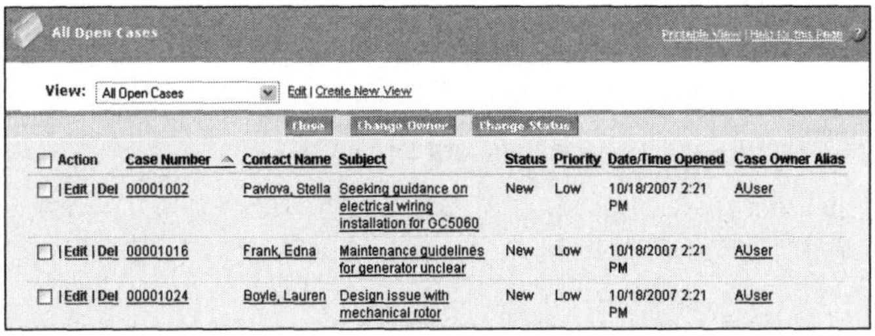

Figure 15-2:
Viewing
a preset
case list.

4. **Open the record for any case by clicking a link in the Case Number column.**

   A Case detail page appears.

5. **Click the Back button on your browser, and then click the Edit button on the same row as the contact you just clicked.**

   The case record appears in Edit mode, and you can make changes to the data.

6. **Check the boxes on certain rows if you'd like to close, change ownership, or change the case status en masse. Then, click the corresponding button to perform the group action.**

   The case record appears in Edit mode for that action, and you can make changes, as appropriate.

Queues ensure that everyone has an equal chance at the latest cases.

To choose a case from a queue, follow these steps:

1. **From the Cases home page, select the view that corresponds to a queue you're supposed to monitor.**

   The list page appears, as shown in Figure 15-3.

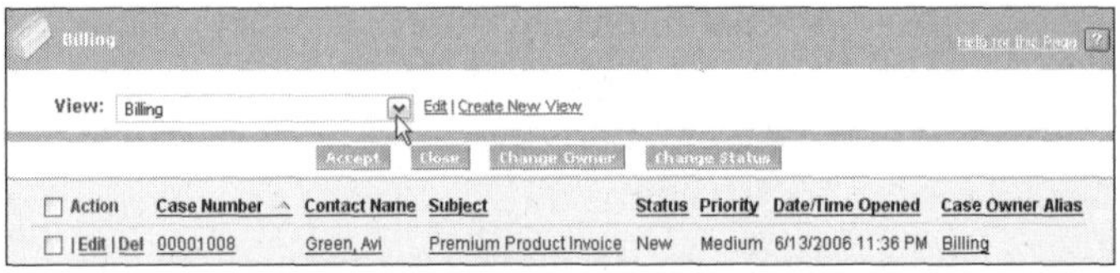

Figure 15-3:
Viewing cases in a case queue.

2. **In the Action column of the case list, select the check boxes for the case records that you want to accept and begin working on.**

3. **Click the Accept button to take ownership of these cases.**

   You've now claimed these cases from the general pool of new cases.

Creating custom case views

If you want special lists for the way that you track your cases, we recommend building custom views. For most objects with tabs in Salesforce, you can create a custom view. See Chapter 4 to find out how to generally create a custom view.

Researching and Resolving Cases

Now that you have your set of assigned cases, the next milestone is to resolve the customer's issue. In general, case resolution means finding a solution to the issue and doing it efficiently so you minimize time spent on repetitive tasks. For example, typing out the same explanation to "Where's the any key (when the manual says to hit any key)?" can tend to get stale after a while.

Understanding solutions

A *solution* is an answer to a commonly asked question. As you resolve cases, service reps can both apply existing solutions from your knowledge base and create new ones that your teams can use in the future. Using solutions helps new agents ramp-up more quickly and makes any agent on your team proficient on a wider range of topics. The following list describes additional terms used when discussing solutions:

- A solution has a related list that indicates all the cases that use the solution. This association is the key to a feature called *Suggested Solutions,* which substantially reduces the amount of time it takes to get answers to cases. In essence, it finds similar cases and suggests solutions that have answered those cases.

- *Solution Categories* group similar solutions together. One solution may belong to one or more categories.

- Your collection of solutions is often referred to as the *knowledge base* and can populate both a Self-Service Portal and a searchable FAQ for a public Web site.

Finding solutions

From the Case record, look for solutions by using the method described in this section.

If this feature is enabled, you'll see a View Suggested Solutions button on the Solutions related list, as shown in Figure 15-4. Click the View Suggested Solutions button to view relevant solutions. We generally recommend that you only associate reviewed solutions with cases.

To look for solutions by using the Search box in the Solutions related list, follow these steps:

1. **In the Search box of the Solutions related list, enter keywords related to a possible solution.**

   Once you get more familiar with solutions and their unique IDs, you may even look up a solution by part of its solution number.

2. **If your company uses solution categories, select a category in which to search.**

3. **Click Find Solution.**

   The Find Solution for Case *Number* page appears. If Solutions Categories are enabled, search results are first shown by category and subcategory groupings.

Attaching solutions to a case

Once you're viewing the relevant solutions, you want to find the appropriate solution(s) and associate it (or them) to your case. You may do this in two ways:

- ✔ From the reviewed list of relevant solutions, click the Select link next to a reviewed solution.

- ✔ If you need to confirm the details of the solution first, click the Solution Title link, and then click the Select button on the Solution detail page when you're sure of the right solution.

After either method, you're returned to the Case record page. In the Solutions related list, you see the solution you just attached. You may add more than one solution to a case — simply repeat the steps for finding solutions and associate them to your case, as appropriate.

Attaching a solution to a case counts as a solution being "used" in Salesforce Service & Support. This tally can later be analyzed in reports so support executives and product managers can see which problems or questions are being reported the most (which, in turn, warrant the use of certain solutions). By getting measurable feedback on issues, the support and product teams can work more closely to address the actual issue before cases need to be logged.

Communicating the Solution

After you've researched your case and found the right solutions for it, you now must communicate this resolution to your customer before you officially mark the case closed. Make sure your administrator has created appropriate case resolution e-mails for your support team.

See Chapter 7 for details on how to create e-mail templates.

Responding with standard e-mail templates

Standard e-mail templates allow you to merge your attached solutions into the body of an e-mail template, which you then send to your customer. This increases the efficiency with which the support team can answer questions. To provide a response to a customer using an e-mail template, refer to Chapter 7 for details.

Closing a case

Once you've resolved your case and successfully notified your customer, it's time to close the case and move on to the next one. One of the key advantages of Salesforce Service & Support is its easy-to-use reporting system (more about that in Chapter 16). Additional information is collected once you're closing a case, so support executives can use the collective feedback to continuously improve the customer experience.

To close a case, follow these steps:

1. **From the Case record, click the Close Case button.**

   Alternatively, if you're in the edit page for the case record, click Save & Close. The Close Case page appears in Edit mode.

2. **Select the appropriate closed case status and add any internal comments, if needed.**

   Other fields are shown based on your company's customizations. If you're a Professional, Enterprise, or Unlimited Edition user, you'll also see an additional section allowing you to create a solution from this case.

3. **Edit the solution title as needed so the solution may be applicable for all customers.**

4. **Check the Submit to Knowledge Base check box to submit the solution for review by your team's designated solution managers.**

   This will also link the case to your new solution.

5. **Click Save when finished.**

Part V
Delivering Excellent Customer Service

The 5th Wave   By Rich Tennant

"I wouldn't qualify this one too long."

In this part . . .

Ask any professional sports coach, and he or she can tell you one single truth: "Although offense gets you in the game, defense wins championships."

You can say the same thing about your customer relationship management (CRM) strategy. If sales are the offense that puts revenue on the board, service and support are the keys to lasting success with your customers. You take a big step toward beating your competitors by keeping the customer satisfied.

And customer service success means that you have to do more than just deliver excellent service. Any good manager knows that to succeed you have to focus equally on managing costs, creating efficiencies, and addressing your customers with consistency across multiple communication channels.

To meet those demands, Salesforce Service & Support gives you capabilities to deliver excellent service efficiently across multiple channels, with all the advantages of the on-demand model, including easy deployment, rapid customization, and real-time reporting. If you're not a support executive or a system administrator, you can still breeze through this part, dog-ear some of the pages, and send the book over to your support pal with a note reading, "Thinking of you."

Chapter 16

Managing Your Customer Service Solution

*T*he heart of any successful customer service application is case management, and Salesforce Service & Support provides a fully integrated solution to track, resolve, and manage all customer interactions, regardless of the point of entry.

Your support team can log in and begin using cases and solutions immediately; but they'll be much more successful if you invest some time upfront to customize the program to the team's exact needs.

In this chapter, we guide the support executive or administrator on setting up case processes and customizing cases. Next, we review how to configure a scalable knowledge base with your collection of solutions. Then, we cover the different methods for automating customer service processes to improve agent efficiency.

Preparing Your Salesforce Service & Support Strategy

As a support executive, if you want to get Salesforce Service & Support working for you, you need to do some careful upfront planning. After you think through your processes, you can customize cases either by yourself or with your Salesforce Service & Support administrator. Here are some tips to think about before you get started:

- ✔ **Define and prioritize your service and support objectives.**

- ✔ **Identify and acknowledge your key challenges.** Try to identify the biggest ones first.

- ✔ **Start with the end in mind.** The best way to customize your application is to decide what you want to measure first.

- ✔ **Map out your key processes.** If you're a Visio whiz, use that tool. If not, grab a marker and diagram your key processes out on a whiteboard or flip chart. For different types of support issues, think about the similar and different types of information that you want your reps to capture.

- ✔ **Figure out the best approach for your business.** You have many different ways to tackle a business issue with Salesforce Service & Support — some of these approaches work better than others.

- ✔ **Assess how much of your support efforts you and your team can share with your customers.** If your users would welcome this sort of change, you may want to set up the Self-Service Portal or the Customer Portal.

- ✔ **Keep it simple.** Don't sacrifice your objectives just to keep things simple. The more complexity you build, the greater the risk that people won't use the application, however.

For cases, as with other objects, Salesforce Service & Support provides some common design elements that let you customize the record. As you consider customizing cases, keep in mind that you should be striving for ease of use, relevance, and data that can help you manage your support executive job while allowing your agents to efficiently manage theirs. (See Chapter 20 for the how-to details on adding new fields, customizing page layouts, adding record types, and other design tricks.)

Automating Case Management

As a support executive or system administrator with the right permissions, one of your biggest challenges will be managing and administering a growing collection of cases. And because support centers need to maintain customer satisfaction, efficiently opening and resolving cases and keeping customers happy are paramount to your bottom line.

Salesforce Service & Support provides built-in tools to help efficiently queue, route, and escalate cases according to your support needs. By distributing and managing case workload more effectively, you ensure that the right agents address the right cases to comply with internal or external SLAs.

Adding case queues

To set up a case queue, choose Setup⇨Customize⇨Cases⇨Queues, and then follow these steps:

1. **From the Case Queues page, click the New button.**

2. **Complete the required fields for Queue Name and Queue Email.**

   The e-mail address will be used for notifications, such as when a new case has been added to the queue. The e-mail can be for an individual or point to a distribution list.

3. **Move Available Members into the Selected Members column to add them to the queue.**

4. **When you're finished, click Save.**

   The Case Queues page reappears with your new queue displayed.

Using assignment rules for routing

Assignment rules are the key to efficient and timely routing of new cases. Your team can apply these assignment rules when adding or editing cases, or when customers submit cases themselves through your Web site, e-mail, the Self-Service Portal, or the Customer Portal (see later sections for more on supporting multiple channels). These rules allow cases to route directly to users or queues.

For assignments, escalations, and other support automation tools, don't forget to set up e-mail templates for notifications — both internal and external. See Chapter 7 for tips on customizing e-mail templates.

To set up assignment rules, choose Setup⇨Customize⇨Cases⇨Assignment Rules, and then follow these steps:

1. **From the Case Assignment Rule page, click the New button.**

   A New Case Assignment Rule page appears.

   If you haven't yet selected a Default Case Owner or Automated Case User, you'll be prompted to make those selections first. A *default case owner* is the person whom the buck stops at — the person to whom the case routes when the assignment rules can't seem to find anyone else. *Automated case users* are the owners of cases that are created by Salesforce Service & Support, as opposed to a manual creation by a human being.

2. **Type a rule name and select the check box if you want this to be the active rule; then click Save.**

   Typically, you have one case assignment rule to serve all your case assignment purposes. So, for example, you may have an active assignment rule called US Standard Support and another called US Holiday Support that you activate only when your holiday schedule is running.

   The Case Assignment Rules page appears with your rule listed.

3. **Click the rule name for the assignment rule you just created.**

   The Case Assignment Rule page for your rule appears.

4. **Click New under the Rule Entries related list.**

   A Rule Entry Edit page appears.

5. **In Step 1 of the Rule Entry Edit page, enter a number for the order of the entry you're about to make.**

   Note that Salesforce Service & Support evaluates these rule entries until it finds a match and then stops. The first successful match satisfies the rule, and an assignment is made accordingly.

6. **In Step 2 of the Rule Entry Edit page, enter criteria for the rule entry.**

   For example, if your company provides a different support team for partner inquiries, you might enter a criterion of **Account: Type Equals Partner** to denote cases that relate to partners.

7. **In Step 3 of the Rule Entry Edit page, select the user or queue to assign the case to and the notification template that goes to the new owner.**

8. **When you're finished, click Save, or Save & New to set up another rule entry.**

   When completed, the Case Assignment Rule page for your assignment rule appears with the related list of rule entries.

Automating case escalation

To make sure that no case is ever overlooked and proper attention is paid to priority cases, you can apply escalation rules. Escalation rules prevent Chicken Little-type overreactions — so you don't unnecessarily run around telling your team that the sky is falling . . . unless it really is. Instead, these rules allow you to create automated actions when cases with certain criteria are still open or untouched after a set duration. When escalating, you set up rule entries (similar to assignment rule entries) to notify users, re-assign the case, or both.

To establish escalation rules, click Setup⇨Customize⇨Cases⇨Escalation Rules, and then follow these steps:

1. **From the Case Escalation Rules page, click the New button.**

2. **Type a name, select the check box if you want this to be the active rule, and click Save.**

   As with case assignment rules mentioned in the preceding section, only one case escalation rule may be in effect at one time.

   A Case Escalation Rules page appears with your rule listed.

3. **Click the rule name for the escalation rule you just created.**

   The Case Escalation Rule page for your rule appears.

4. **Click New under the Rule Entries related list.**

   The Rule Entry Edit page appears.

5. **Complete the rule entry fields, following these guidelines:**

   • See Steps 5 through 7 in the preceding section for tips on completing Step 2 of the rule entry fields.

   • In Step 3, check the Ignore Business Hours box only if you want the escalation rules to be in effect at all times (this means weekends and holidays, folks).

   • In Step 4, select a radio button to determine how you want escalation times to be set.

6. **When you're finished, click Save, or click Save & New to repeat the process for additional rule entries.**

   The Rule Entry Edit page reappears with a related list for Escalation Actions.

7. **Click the New button on the Escalation Actions related list.**

   An Escalation Action Edit page appears.

8. **In Step 1, specify the time criteria in the Age Over (Business Hours) field to trigger the escalation rule.**

   Notice that you can set escalations to occur after 30 minute intervals.

9. **In Step 2, select the user or queue that will be re-assigned ownership of the escalated case.**

   You may also select a notification template for the recipient.

10. **In Step 3, select a user to notify once an escalation occurs.**

    You must also select a notification template for the recipient.

11. **Checking the Notify Case Owner box ensures that the case owner will be notified when one of his or her cases escalates.**

12. **Use the Additional Emails box to type in up to five e-mail addresses that you want notified of this escalation, as shown in Figure 16-1.**

    These addresses don't have to belong to Salesforce Service & Support users.

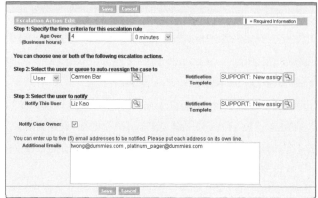

Figure 16-1: Specifying actions related to an escalation rule entry.

13. **When you're finished, click Save.**

    The Rule Entry Edit page reappears.

    Repeat Steps 8 through 13 as often as needed to add your escalation rule entries, plus corresponding actions.

Another way to automate assigning tasks and sending e-mail alerts within your organization is through workflow rules. Workflow is available to Enterprise and Unlimited Edition customers only; for details, see Chapter 20.

Building the Knowledge Base

Consider the amount of information and expertise each person in your company holds. Salesforce Service & Support's knowledge base feature helps you build a central repository of that valuable information so your customer service agents can tap into it at any time.

Solutions properly collected over time create a *knowledge base* in which the wisdom of product experts is retained and shared for both internal and external audiences. New agents can get up to speed quickly, and the support team can follow a process that standardizes solutions handling, which both

contribute to speedier case resolution and more consistent responses. A
public knowledge base is one searchable by customers from your Web
site. In the following sections, we quickly highlight the ideal review process
for ensuring the highest quality and most accurate solutions for your
knowledge base.

Defining the review process

To make sure the most appropriate solutions are clearly and concisely
written for your knowledge base, your support team should adhere to a
solutions review process. Generally, this involves drafting a solution; having
someone review it for accuracy, grammar, spelling, and all that other English-
class stuff; and then finally approving the solution for use.

Determine who may submit a solution for review, and then decide who
should review it. The *solution manager* can be one or more members of your
support team that will be in charge of reviewing, modifying, and publishing
solutions to the knowledge base.

Defining categories

By identifying solution categories, you can substantially improve the chances
that agents and customers can get to the right answer quickly as your knowledge base grows.

Customizing solutions

You can customize the solutions record much the same way you customize
other records in Salesforce. (See Chapter 20 for details.) But before diving in
to add fields and change picklist values, take some time to evaluate what's
out there so far.

Writing solutions

After a member of your support team has verified that a solution is needed
for a specific inquiry and doesn't already exist, he or she should write a draft
solution for review. No, the solution shouldn't be a manifesto or a college
essay, but it should meet certain guidelines in language, structure, search-
ability, accuracy, and categorization.

Reviewing solutions

To maintain a consistent and high level of quality for your knowledge base, we recommend solution managers follow these general guidelines during the solution review process:

- ✔ **Check for duplicate solutions.**
- ✔ **Update the solution status.** After reviewing the solution, edit the record and update the Status field, as appropriate.
- ✔ **Publish the solution.** Check the Published and Visible in Public Knowledge Base fields to make the solution available to customers.

Publishing your knowledge base

You know what customers' common questions are. You can significantly reduce related cases and first-call issues if you make the answers accessible and searchable to them by adding a special search box and button to your Web site that allows customers to search your solutions knowledge base without having to contact your support center.

Capturing and Associating Cases Efficiently

In addition to using the phone, customers want to access support in two other common ways: directly from the Web and via e-mail. You can have your customers use a Web-based form or let them send an e-mail to your support organization. For either method, Salesforce Service & Support can enable these additional channels and make it easy for your agents to follow up. In this section, we describe the various options you can use to begin collecting this information from your Web site.

Where do customers go when they have problems? Many customers would be happy if they could simply log the problem and be assured of a prompt response. With Web-to-Case, you can quickly generate an HTML form that captures cases submitted from your Web site. Then, by using case assignment rules, new cases can route directly to the agents or queues responsible for handling these inquiries. (See "Using assignment rules for routing," earlier in this chapter, for information on automating assignments.)

To automate Web-to-Case, choose Setup⇨Customize⇨Self-Service⇨Web-to-Case and follow these steps:

1. **From the Capturing Cases from Your Web Site page, review the general outline, and then click the Generate the HTML link.**

   The Capturing Cases from Your Web Site: Capture Cases page appears.

2. **Type a return URL where the users will end up after submitting their cases, choose if you want the form to be visible in the Self-Service Portal so customers can submit new cases while monitoring existing ones (more on that later), select the case fields to include on the form, and click Generate.**

   The return URL you specify usually leads to a thank-you page or your support home page. After you click Generate, a new page appears with the HTML code in a box.

3. **Copy and paste the HTML code into a page hosted on your Web server. Click Finished when done.**

   You'll want to review the notes at the top of the HTML, but this step is pretty simple. If such a review seems foreign to you, simply copy and paste the HTML into an e-mail and send it to your Webmaster for help with this step. He or she knows what to do.

   Once you click Finished, you'll return to the Capturing Cases from Your Web Site page.

When the Web page with your case-capturing form is live, fill out the form, like the unformatted sample in Figure 16-2, and test it to make sure the case routes to the right resource.

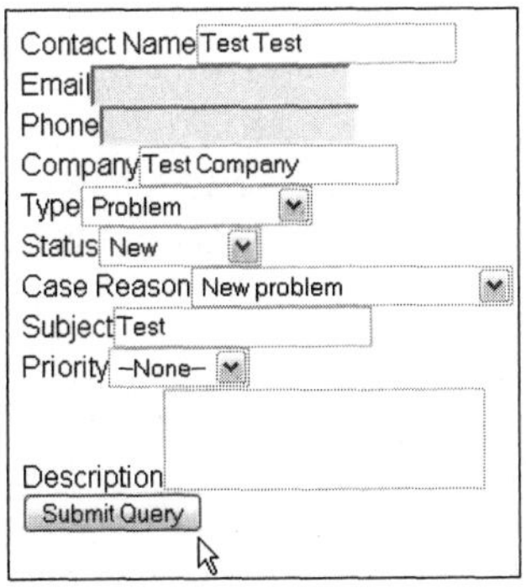

Figure 16-2:
Testing an unformatted sample Web-to-Case form.

When customers have issues, they often want to send an e-mail to your support team and expect a timely response. With Email-to-Case, customers can send e-mail messages to aliases you create, which route new cases directly to the assigned resources and populate relevant case fields. Even attachments stay attached to the original e-mail message. Setting this up does require an installation of an Email-to-Case agent, which is a Java toolkit available on the Force.com Developer Tools page at `https://wiki.apexdevnet.com/index.php/Tools`. Under the Email Tools section, click the Email to Case Toolkit link for more information.

Salesforce Service & Support can also route responses to your customers after they've submitted a case by using the Web or e-mail. This response informs the customer that your company has gotten his or her submission, and it can explain support policies, too. As long as you have those e-mail templates defined (see Chapter 7), you can assign them to use when responding to cases from Web-to-Case, Email-to-Case, or even the Self-Service Portal or Customer Portal. Choose Setup➪Configure➪Cases➪Auto-Response Rules to configure this.

Helping Customers Help Themselves

You'd be surprised by how many customers would like to get the answers themselves (if they knew where to go), rather than call you. If you're creating a knowledge base already, you can actually take the next step in providing a Self-Service Portal to your customers. With the Self-Service Portal, customers can find solutions from the public knowledge base, submit cases (with attachments and comments), collaborate with your support agents, and track the status of their cases. In the following sections, we show you how to jump-start the launch of the portal and allow your customers to get on board.

Before implementing the customer Self-Service Portal, make sure your internal knowledge base is up to snuff. That is, your knowledge base must be populated with answers to many common customer inquiries, and the solutions must be well written and appropriate for public consumption.

Launching a Self-Service Portal

No matter what size support organization you run, by creating a secure, authenticated portal for your customers, you can have a professional online presence in minutes. With the Self-Service Portal solution, you have a means of providing real-time insight into the steps being taken to resolve cases. You also deflect inquiries that customers can answer on their own, while still maintaining high levels of quality service.

Make sure your corporate logo is saved in the Document Library before you upload it into the portal header.

To jump-start your Self-Service Portal, choose Setup⇨Customize⇨Self-Service⇨Self-Service Portal⇨Settings, and then follow these steps:

1. **From the Self-Service Setup page, click Jump Start.**

   A Setup Your Organization's Self-Service Portal introduction page appears.

2. **Review the benefits and click Continue.**

   The Setup page appears in Edit mode.

3. **Complete the fields, as shown in the example in Figure 16-3, to determine your portal's look and feel, and then click Save.**

   Most of the fields are self evident; they control the basic look and feel of tabs and page headers.

4. **From the Self-Service Jump Start page, click the various buttons to test out your portal.**

   Here are some tips to test out your portal:

   - Click Generate if you need a demo username and password to log in to the portal.
   - Click Access the Self-Service Portal if you'd like to access the portal immediately.
   - Click Invite if you'd like to grant access to other users to test out the portal.
   - Copy and paste the URL highlighted in red into a browser to view the login page.

   Remember to send the URL to your Webmaster so that he or she can create a link from your Web sites.

5. **Click Done when finished.**

   The Self-Service Setup page appears with related lists for Portal Page Sections, Pages, and Top Solutions.

6. **Click the Action links on the related lists to further customize parts of the portal.**

   The Edit and Preview links in the Action column are obvious, but click Page Layout if you wish to customize the Case page layout. (See Chapter 20 for details on modifying page layouts.)

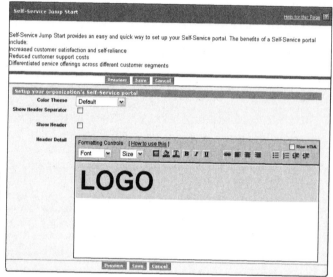

Figure 16-3:
Jump-
starting a
Self-Service
Portal.

The Add links in the Top Solutions section allow you to select up to five solutions to display at the top of the Self-Service Portal. Use this to provide answers to frequently asked questions.

7. **Click the Self-Service Setup button if you want to further modify settings.**

A Self-Service Setup Edit page appears.

Managing Self-Service users

After you thoroughly test your Self-Service Portal, you want to make it available to customers.

To add, edit, or reset users, choose Setup➪Customize➪Self-Service➪Self-Service Portal➪Users, and then follow these tips:

- ✔ Click Edit next to a User Name if you want to modify a user's information.

- ✔ Select multiple users with the check box column; then, click either Edit User(s) or Reset Password(s) to perform those actions.

- ✔ Click Enable New User(s) if you want to grant access to the Portal to new users.

Another way to add users is to go to a Contact detail page and click the Enable Self Service button at the top of the contact record.

Launching a customized Customer Portal

Think of the Customer Portal as the Self-Service Portal on steroids. If your business deals with several types of customers, each requiring a customized Portal interface, you can create them. For example, maybe your platinum customers need Portal access to report on very specific information captured in custom fields that don't apply to your regular customer base. Or maybe you're dealing with a large set of customers testing out the newest version of your product, and you need them to provide specific feedback that isn't normally captured for your current products. You can also use a Customer Portal if your company has built or downloaded some additional custom objects that you want your customers to access.

Organizations that use either the Customer or Partner Portal can also enable Salesforce Ideas, which allows your community of customers or partners to create, vote for, and comment on ideas related to any topic on which you want to gather community feedback.

You can use the Customer Portal for an additional charge. For more specific information on setting this up, make sure you organize your knowledge base and solutions, and then go to the Help & Training section in the top-right area of the application and search for the Salesforce Customer Portal Implementation Guide for the latest information on rolling this out.

Improving Team Productivity

For those of you who may operate a support center in which you handle a high volume of support issues, you may have a strong desire to make your agents' time as productive as possible. What information can you put at their fingertips to help them resolve that case that much faster? In the following sections, we review a time-saving option that may be a good fit for your team.

Using the Salesforce Console

High-volume call center agents need access to a lot of information at once. Fewer keystrokes mean resolving a customer's issue takes less time. From a single Web page, the Salesforce Console allows an agent to view all of his or her cases, handle a single case, and see all the records — including accounts, contacts, and opportunities — that relate to a case. The Salesforce Console lays out an interface within a tab in Salesforce, designed to be a one-stop desktop for your agents.

Setting up the Salesforce Console

We highlight the basic steps you need to take to get the Salesforce Console up and running in the following sections. Try to walk through a scenario in which an agent handles a new case and sees it to closure from within that Console. Check out the Help & Training section in Salesforce, under Console, for more details on the following summaries.

Creating your Console layouts

Go to Setup⇨App Setup⇨Console⇨Console Layouts to create a new layout that defines which objects your agents will see in the console.

See Chapter 21 for more information on layouts and assignment rules.

Customizing your mini-view

Mini-views are summary previews of a record that you can see when you hover your mouse over the record name. Before you tell Salesforce what fields in a record comprise a mini-view, you'll have to choose those objects. Once you've selected these objects, then you define their layouts — that is, which fields appear where in the preview. Finally, you assign user profiles to console layouts so the right Salesforce users in your organization can see what they need to see in the console.

Adding the Console tab

The final step is adding the tab to your users' view. Decide which set of apps in your AppExchange drop-down list will contain this tab.

Chapter 17

Analyzing Data with Reports

. . . .

. . . .

*H*ow much time do you waste every week trying to prepare reports for your manager, your team, or yourself? You have to chase the information down, get it into a useful format, and then hopefully make sense of the data. By the time you've done all this, the information is probably already outdated, despite your best efforts. Have you ever felt less than confident of the details or the totals?

If this sounds like a familiar problem, you can use reports in Salesforce to generate up-to-the-moment data analysis to help you measure your business. As long as you and your teams regularly use Salesforce to manage your accounts, opportunities, and other customer-related information, you don't have to waste time wondering where to find the data and how to consolidate it — instead, Salesforce does that work for you.

And unlike other applications where the business users often have to spend precious time relying on more technical people to build their custom reports, you can do this all by yourself in minutes, with no geeky programming. With an easy-to-use reporting wizard, you can customize existing reports or build them from scratch.

This chapter includes looking over the standard reports provided by Salesforce, building reports from scratch, and modifying existing reports to make them your own. Within a report, we take you through the different ways you can limit the report to get just the information that's necessary for creating a clearer picture of your business. Finally, be sure to check out our suggestions on how to keep your reports organized in easy-to-find folders as your universe of reports expands.

Discovering Reports

With reports, you can present your data in different formats, select a seemingly infinite number of columns, filter your data, subtotal information, use color to highlight when certain conditions are met, and embed formulas, just to name a few features. And like other pages in Salesforce, you can quickly find the details. So, for example, you can go from the Reports home page to a lead report to a lead record simply by clicking links.

Navigating the Reports home page

When you click the Reports tab, you'll see a search bar, a Report Folders drop-down list, a subtab that lists all your available reports, and another subtab that shows recently run reports. Salesforce has functionality on the Reports home page to help you more easily navigate through a large set of reports. Salesforce comes standard with a set of predefined reports and folders that are commonly used for measuring sales, marketing, support, and other functions.

You can't save a custom report in a standard folder. If you're an administrator, consider creating custom folders for your important functional areas that ultimately replace these standard folders.

From this page, you can do the following:

- ✔ Type keywords into the custom reports search bar and click Find Report to return matching reports based on the report name description fields.

- ✔ Unless you have Group Edition, use the Report Folders drop-down list to quickly navigate to a set of reports in a particular folder.

- ✔ If you're an administrator, click the Create New Folder link to create new report folders to house custom reports.

- ✔ Click the Collapse All or Expand All link on the right side of the All Reports and Recent Reports subtabs to hide or show all reports in all folders.

- ✔ To reorder folders up or down on the page, click the Reorder Folders link to the right of the All Reports and Recent Reports subtabs.

- ✔ To view recent reports, click the Recent Reports subtab and use the drop-down list to match the criteria of what reports you want to see.

- ✔ To display the report, click a report title. Either the report appears or you see a wizard that you need to follow to generate the report.

✔ On custom reports, click the Edit, Del, or Export links to edit or delete a report or export its data to Excel.

✔ Click the Create New Custom Report button to start the Report Wizard.

✔ If you have permission to manage public reports, click the Report Manager button to organize reports.

Displaying a report

When you click a report title or run a report from the wizard, a report page appears based on the criteria that was set. For example, under the Opportunity Reports folder, click the Opportunity Pipeline link. The Opportunity Pipeline report appears, as shown in the example in Figure 17-1. This report is one of the most-used standard reports in Salesforce.

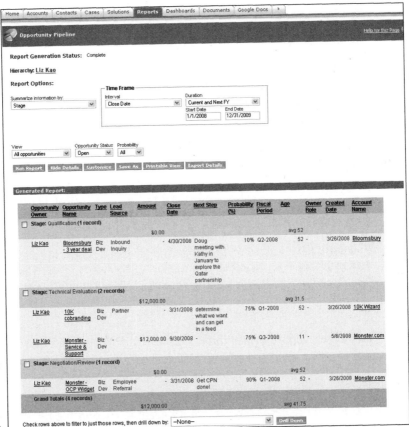

Figure 17-1:
Displaying a report.

A basic report page in Salesforce is broken up into two or three parts:

- ✓ **Org Drill Down:** You can use this area at the top of the page to quickly limit results based on role hierarchy. See Chapter 19 for steps on setting up the role hierarchy.

- ✓ **Report Options:** This section is at the top of the page, just below the Org Drill Down. You can use it to filter and perform other operations on a report. For details on report options, see the section "Filtering on a Report," later in this chapter.

- ✓ **Generated Report:** This section shows the report itself. What's visible depends on the construction of the report and what you have permission to see in Salesforce. See Chapter 19 for more details on sharing.

In the Generated Report section, you can click a column heading to quickly re-sort your report by the selected column.

Developing Reports with the Wizard

Salesforce comes with a huge menu of useful reports, and yet they might not be exactly what you're looking for. For example, if your company has added custom fields on the account record that are unique to your customer, a standard New Accounts report doesn't show you all the information you want to see on recent accounts.

The next time you need a custom report, don't pester the IT geeks. Instead, use the Report Wizard to build a new report or customize an existing one.

Building a report from scratch

You don't have to be a technical guru to create a report in Salesforce. Just make sure you can articulate a question that you're trying to answer, and then Salesforce's Report Wizard will guide you through the steps for creating a custom report that will help you answer the question. Anyone who can view the Reports tab can create a custom report.

To create a report from scratch, click the Reports tab and follow these steps:

1. **Click the Create New Custom Report button.**

   The Report Wizard page appears.

2. **Select the data type you want to report on, and then click Next.**

You do this by first selecting the basic type of data from the drop-down list and then being more specific in the dependent list box, as shown in Figure 17-2. When you click Next, Step 1 of the wizard appears.

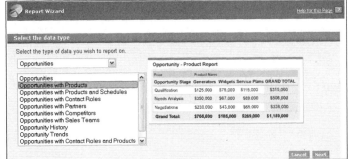

Figure 17-2:
Defining the
data type for
the report.

3. **Select the radio button for the type of report that you want.**

   You have three options:

   - **Tabular Reports** provide the most basic way to look at your data in a tabular format.

   - **Summary Reports** allow you to view your data with subtotals and other summary information.

   - **Matrix Reports** enable you to create reports in grids against both horizontal and vertical categories. This type of report is particularly helpful for comparing related totals, especially if you're trying to summarize large amounts of data.

4. **When you're done, select the Select Columns option from the Jump to Step drop-down list in the top-right corner.**

   The Select the Report Columns page appears.

   The report type that you select dictates how many of the seven possible Report Wizard steps you see and the order that they're presented in the wizard. And at any time, you can use the Jump to Step drop-down list to skip around the wizard.

5. **Select the check boxes for the columns that you want in your report.**

   Depending on the data type you chose, the Select the Report Columns page displays standard and then custom fields divided into sections.

6. **When you're done, select the Select Columns to Total option from the Jump to Step drop-down list.**

A wizard page appears with the columns that can be totaled (such as currencies, amounts, and percentages) based on the columns you selected in Step 5 of this list.

7. Select check boxes for columns that you want summarized and how you want them summarized.

Salesforce provides you options for summing, averaging, and choosing highest or lowest values. For example, on an opportunity report, you could use averaging to measure the average amount of an opportunity.

8. When you're done, select the Order Columns option from the Jump to Step drop-down list.

The wizard page appears.

9. Click the directional arrows to order the columns.

This is how columns will appear on the report, from left to right, if you're showing all details.

10. When you're done, select the Select Criteria option from the Jump to Step drop-down list.

The wizard page appears.

11. Use the criteria filters to limit results on your report.

The standard filters will vary based on the data type you chose. For advanced filters, select fields and operators by using the drop-down lists, and then enter values, similar to creating custom views.

With advanced And/Or filters, you can create precise reports that might include complex conditions. For example, if you define strategic accounts as companies that did either over $1 billion in annual revenue or had over 500 employees plus $500 million in annual revenue, you can now generate this report. To do this, enter your advanced filters as before, and then click the Advanced Options link at the bottom of the Advanced Filters section. When the page reappears, click the Tips link located next to the Advanced Filter Conditions field. Modify your Conditions as recommended before clicking the Run Report button. (You must have Professional, Enterprise, or Unlimited Edition.)

12. When you're done, select the Select Groupings option from the Jump to Step drop-down list.

The wizard page appears.

13. Select the columns by which your report will be grouped.

For example, if you want to measure the number of opportunities owned by rep and subtotaled by close month, use an opportunity summary report. First sort by Opportunity Owner, and then by Close Month.

14. **When you're done, select the Select Chart & Highlights option from the Jump to Step drop-down list.**

    The wizard page appears.

15. **Complete the fields to build a chart, and then click the Run Report button.**

    Many users include this step if they need to generate a specific chart or graph, or use colors to highlight certain conditions to support the report. (See the section "Adding conditional highlighting," later in this chapter, and Chapter 18 for more details on using color and building charts in dashboards or reports.) When you click the Run Report button, the actual report data displays under the Generated Report heading.

16. **If you want to save the report, click the Save As button.**

    A New Custom Report page appears.

17. **Complete the fields and click the Save As button.**

    Here are pointers for completing the fields:

    - Enter a title for the report in the Report Name field.

    - Type a question or sentence in the Report Question field that will help you remember the purpose of the report.

    - If you have permissions to manage public folders, select a folder for the report.

    After clicking the Save As button, the Reports home page appears with a link to the report under the selected folder.

Customizing existing reports

A fast and easy way to generate reports is to customize from an existing report. For example, if you like the standard Pipeline Report, but you want to modify the columns, you can simplify work from the existing report.

To customize an existing report, go to the Reports tab and follow these steps:

1. **Click a link for an existing report.**

   The report appears.

2. **Click the Customize button.**

   A page from the Report Wizard appears.

3. **Based on what you want to customize, select a step from the Jump to Step drop-down list.**

   The wizard page appears based on what you selected.

Creating custom report types

The Report Wizard is pretty darn thorough. At the same time, your company's quant jocks may want to perform even more advanced reporting than what's offered in the standard Report Wizard. Or you may want to simplify the number of fields that your report users see when they go through the wizard. Professional, Enterprise, and Unlimited Edition administrators can create custom report types (CRTs) to address both of these needs.

For more advanced reporting capabilities, in techno-speak, CRTs let you change the joins on the table. So if you have a Projects object and want to report on all accounts with projects and project team members, you can create a CRT and determine which fields show up in your Select Columns to Total step. For more information on setting up CRTs, go to the Help & Training section within Salesforce and search for Setting Up Custom Report Types.

4. **Modify the fields within that step to customize your report.**

   For example, if you want an opportunity report with only forecasted opportunities, select the Select Criteria option from the Jump to Step drop-down list. Then add an advanced filter, such as Forecast Category Equals Commit. (Forecast Category is the field, Equals is the operator, and Commit is the value.)

5. **Continue jumping to steps until you're satisfied, and then click the Run Report button.**

   The report appears modified based on your settings from the wizard.

6. **When you're done, click Save or Save As.**

   The Save button replaces the prior custom report. The Save As button saves a new one. In either case, a page appears to save the report.

7. **Complete the fields and click Save.**

   The Reports home page appears.

Building custom summary formulas

Salesforce provides pre-built functionality that calculates the sum, average, highest value, and lowest value of certain fields you select for your reports. However, some of you need to see additional summary information based on calculations unique to your business. For example, your business may want to see win rate percentages or coverage ratios on your reports. Salesforce allows the addition of custom formula calculations for your reports (and dashboards). This means you can take summary information from other fields and mash them together to come up with a new calculation and corresponding result. It doesn't matter if you know old math or new math, Salesforce can derive these values for you using Excel-like commands.

To create a new custom summary formula, follow these steps:

1. **Click a link for an existing report.**

   The report appears.

2. **Click the Customize button.**

   A page from the Report Wizard appears.

3. **Select the Select Columns to Total value from the Jump to Step drop-down list.**

   The wizard page appears.

4. **Scrolling down the page, you see the Custom Summary Formulas section. Click New.**

   A pop-up window showing the Formula Builder page appears.

5. **Complete the fields, as required:**

   • In the Label field, enter a unique name for your formula as it'll appear on the report.

   • Optionally, type in a description. Ideally, this helps explain the math formula in regular-person terms.

   • With the Format drop-down list, select the type of format you want your results to be in. For example, if you want to calculate the revenue per item of all your products in the pipeline this year, you'll want your result to be Currency.

   • From the Decimal Places drop-down list, select the number of decimal places to display for your selected data type.

6. **Now, build your formula in the Formula section:**

   a. **Select one of the fields listed in the Select Field drop-down list.**

      This field's value is used in your formula. In our example, we select Amount.

   b. **Select the kind of summary type to use in your formula.**

      You've seen these before in the standard summary section of your Report Wizard: sum, average, highest value, and lowest value.

   c. **Click Insert.**

Salesforce enters the corresponding part of the formula into the formula box.

d. Click the appropriate operator icons to the right.

In our example, we select the / button.

e. Repeat these steps, as needed, to build your formula.

7. Click Validate Syntax to check your formula for errors (see Figure 17-3).

Syntax which contains errors is automatically highlighted by the cursor.

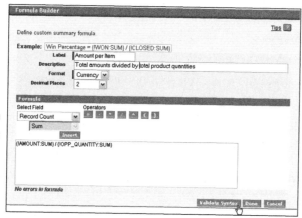

Figure 17-3:
Validating
a custom
summary
formula.

8. Click Done when finished.

The pop-up window closes, and you're back at the Report Wizard.

9. Optionally, you can uncheck the Display box for this summary if you want to associate it with the report but not display it.

The custom summary formula isn't saved until you save the report. Clicking Done just includes it in this step of the Report Wizard. Make sure you save the report.

10. After saving the report, click the report name to run it and verify that you see the new column showing your custom summary formula.

To see all the different types of operators and functions available for use with custom summary formulas, go to the Help & Training link and search for Operators and Functions in the Help section. You'll find a comprehensive list of what you can use, with descriptions for each.

Adding conditional highlighting

You can apply conditional highlighting to summarize matrix reports and help you easily highlight values that might deserve more of your attention. You can use this with custom summary formulas to highlight high or low percentages, averages, and ratios. There are a lot of syllables in this feature, but what conditional highlighting translates into is setting thresholds for certain key numerical values and color-coding them to show when a threshold has been surpassed (or not).

To use conditional highlighting on a summary report, follow these steps:

1. **Click a link for an existing report.**

   The report appears.

2. **Click the Customize button.**

   A page from the Report Wizard appears.

3. **Select the Select Chart & Highlights option from the Jump to Step drop-down list.**

   The wizard page appears.

4. **Scroll to the Conditional Highlighting section at the bottom of the page and choose up to three summaries in the drop-down list to highlight.**

   In our example, we'd like to highlight any extraordinary pipeline that a sales rep is carrying — perhaps that means his or her territory is a bit plump and needs to be better split up. We select Sum of Amount, as shown in Figure 17-4.

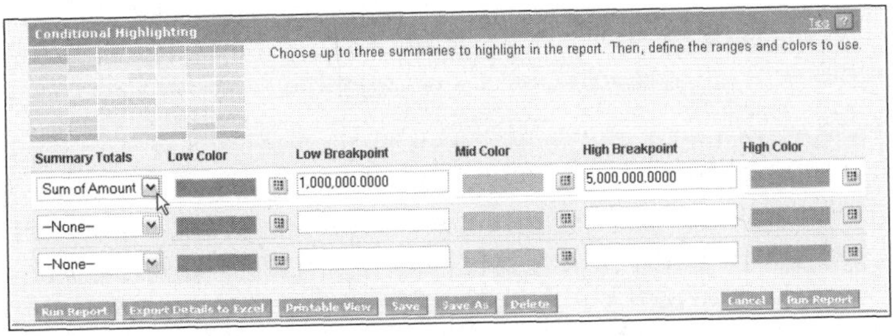

Figure 17-4: Selecting summary totals.

5. **Enter either a Low Breakpoint value, High Breakpoint value, or both.**

   Thus, if the summary value is higher than your high breakpoint value, it'll be highlighted in the high color, which defaults to green. If the summary value is lower than your low breakpoint value, it'll be highlighted in the low color, which defaults to red. Any value in between will be highlighted in dark yellow.

If you wish to change the colors, click the Choose a Color icon next to any of the color bars.

If you don't want a certain range to be highlighted with a color, click the Choose a Color icon for that range and select the white color.

6. Click Save to save the report.

The wizard page appears.

7. Run the report to verify that the highlighting is in effect.

In our example, we can quickly tell one rep is faring a bit worse than the other with the red and green highlighting, as shown in Figure 17-5.

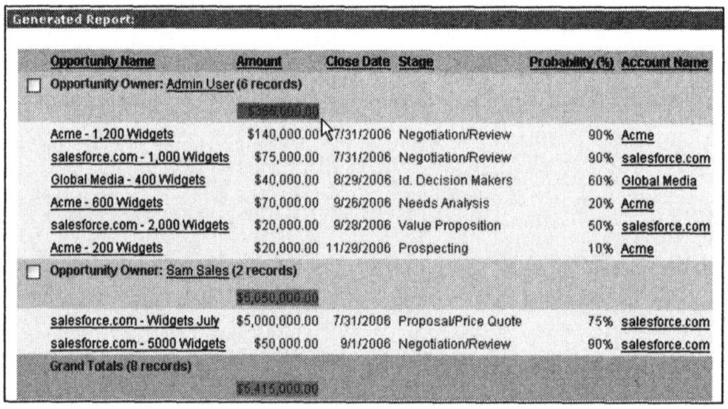

Figure 17-5:
Highlighting
summary
values.

Filtering on a Report

Over time, you'll develop core reports that have the columns that you want in a format that makes sense to you. One of the huge benefits of reporting in Salesforce is that you can use existing reports on the fly and apply report options to limit or reorder the report results.

All those options and more are possible in seconds without having to use the Customize button. In the following sections, we show you how to filter your reports with tools and enhanced drill down and break out options.

Using the Report Options section

When you open a report, it appears with a variety of filters in the Report Options section at the top of the page. By using the filters in the Report Options section, you can look at your data from multiple angles. The available standard filters depend on the type of report that you selected.

To try out the standard filters in the Report Options section by using the Opportunity Pipeline report as an example, first go to the Reports home page and click the Opportunity Pipeline link. The report appears. From the report, you can do the following with the filters in the Report Options section:

- ✔ From the **Summarize Information By drop-down list,** select a field that determines how your information is summarized. For example, if you want to look at your opportunities by rep, select Opportunity Owner.

- ✔ From the **Interval drop-down list,** first select a date field, and then in the drop-down list to the right, select a standard interval or create a custom range. For example, if you want to look at all opportunities created from 2006 to the present, you'd first select Created Date, and then define the interval.

- ✔ From the **Relationship to Opportunity drop-down list,** select the scope.

- ✔ Use the **Opportunity Status drop-down list** if you want open and/or closed records.

- ✔ Use the **Probability drop-down list** if you want to limit the results by probability.

At any particular time, click the Run Report button to apply your selected filters. The report reappears based on the filters you defined.

If you ultimately want to save the report, click the Save or Save As button, and then save the report as usual. (Refer to the section "Building a report from scratch," earlier in this chapter, for details on saving.)

Hiding and showing details

To see a collapsed or expanded view of your report data, use the Hide/Show Details button in the Report Options section. For example, from the Reports home page, click the Sales by Account report under Sales Reports. When the report appears, click the Hide Details button. The report reappears in a collapsed view, and the Hide Details button has morphed into the Show Details button. Now click the Show Details button, and the report expands again. By using Hide Details, you can easily view headings, subtotals, and totals, especially for matrix reports.

Filtering with the drill down menu

Reports in Salesforce have a drill down function that you can use to select rows within a report and instantly break them down by a different field. For example, if you're reviewing an Opportunity by Rep report, you might want to select a specific rep and then sort the rep's opportunities by stage. With enhanced drill down and break out options, you can do this in just a few quick clicks.

To use the drill down and break out options (using Sales by Rep as the example), follow these steps:

1. **From the Reports home page, click the Sales by Rep link under the Sales Reports folder.**

   The report appears.

2. **In the left column of the Generated Report section, select check boxes for records you want to view.**

   If you don't see check boxes, and you know you've closed opportunities in Salesforce, select an interval in the Report Options section to see all your historical opportunities and click Run Report to view more records.

3. **At the bottom of the page, select a field from the Drill Down By drop-down list to summarize the information, if desired, and then click the Drill Down button.**

   The report reappears based on your selections. For example, if you chose the Close Month option from the Drill Down By drop-down list, your selected opportunities would be sorted by close month.

4. **If you want to use the report in the future, click Save As, and then follow the normal directions for saving reports.**

   See the section "Building a report from scratch," earlier in this chapter, for saving details.

Clearing filters

If you have reports with advanced filters, you can easily view and clear the filters to expand the results. For example, if you created and saved the test report in the preceding section, you might want to clear the filter on the selected rep(s) to see all closed opportunities by close month for all reps. The advanced filters, if any, appear just below the Generated Report header on a report page.

To clear a filter, follow these steps:

1. **Click the link for a report that you've applied filters to.**

   The report appears, and your criteria filters are listed under the Filtered By header directly below the Generated Report header.

2. **Right below the Filtered By header, click the Clear link to remove a filter.**

   The report reappears, displaying a potentially wider universe of data.

3. **Be sure to click the Save or Save As buttons if you want to save this report.**

You can quickly modify advanced filters by clicking the Edit link next to the Filtered By header. The Select Criteria page of the Report Wizard appears.

Exporting Reports to Excel

Ideally, you want to run your reports right out of the application, getting rid of that mad scramble of collecting data before your next big meeting. However, sometimes you'll want to generate a report and then export it to Excel. Maybe you need to run some complex spreadsheet calculations, or you need to plug numbers into an existing macro template. No problem. You can do that with the click of a button.

To export a report, click the Reports tab and follow these steps:

1. **Click the link to a report.**

   The report appears. You can bypass this step if you see an Export link next to a report title on the Reports home page.

2. **Click the Export Details to Excel button.**

   A page appears to define your settings for exporting the file.

3. **Complete the fields and click the Export button.**

   A window appears, prompting you to open or save the file.

4. **Follow the steps, as desired.**

   When the file opens, the report data appears in Excel.

5. **Click Done to return to your Salesforce report.**

   The report page reappears.

Some companies get nervous about certain users having the ability to export company data. If this is a concern, and you have Enterprise or Unlimited Edition, you can take one precaution by using custom profiles to eliminate the ability of some users to export to Excel. See Chapter 19 for more details on creating custom profiles.

Organizing Your Reports

A word to the wise: Reports start multiplying like rabbits as you become addicted to reporting in Salesforce. Do yourself a favor: Organize them from day one and lay out a process for maintaining and deleting reports.

Creating new folders

Nothing is worse than seeing a kazillion reports under the Unfiled Public Reports folder. You start wasting a ridiculous amount of time just identifying which one is the report you want. If you have permission to manage public folders, avoid the headache by creating new report folders.

To create a new report folder, click the Reports tab and follow these steps:

1. **Click the Create New Folder link to the right of the Folder View drop-down list.**

   A New Report Folder page appears.

2. **Type a name for the folder in the Report Folder field.**

   For example, if you want a folder for operational reports, you might name it Sales Ops Reports.

3. **Use the Public Folder Access drop-down list to determine read versus read/write privileges to the folder.**

   For example, if you select Read/Write, a user with access to the folder could save over the original report.

4. **Use the two list boxes and the Add/Remove buttons to select reports in the Unfiled Public Reports folder and move them to the new folder.**

5. **Use the radio buttons to select who should have access to the folder.**

   As with other Salesforce folder tools, your choices amount to all, none, and selective.

6. **If you chose the Selective option in Step 5, use the two list boxes and Add/Remove buttons to highlight groups or roles and move them to the Shared To list box.**

7. **When you're done, click Save.**

   The Reports Home Page reappears, and your folder is added to the Folder menu.

Maintaining your report library

Actually, what's worse than a kazillion reports under Unfiled Public Reports is a universe of reports, some of which are valuable, others of which are useless. Creating public report folders is a good first step, but you might want to apply some of these additional hints on a periodic basis:

- ✔ **Accurately name your reports.** You and your users can't know what's behind a report link unless you name it clearly and precisely.

- ✔ **Consider using report numbers within your report names.** For instance, 1.1 Latin America Pipeline. By doing this, managers can refer to report numbers so that everyone's looking at the same report.

- ✔ **Delete unnecessary reports.** If multiple people in your company have permission to manage public reports, you might want to survey them before accidentally deleting a report. Unnecessary or redundant reports just make it harder for everyone to find what they want. And in case you mistakenly delete a report (you'll find out soon enough), you have up to 30 days to rescue it from the Recycle Bin.

- ✔ **Hide folders, as necessary.** If you're an administrator, you can do this globally by clicking the Edit link next to the appropriate Folder drop-down list selection. If you're a user, you can use the little arrows on the Reports home page to hide folder's contents.

- ✔ **Update existing reports as needs arise.** For example, if you created an Opportunity Product Report and used an advanced filter such as Product Family Equals Software, make sure that you update the report if the product family name changes. Otherwise, your reports will be off.

- ✔ **Use clear report questions.** For example, you might use the Report Question field to summarize certain filters to your report.

Part VI
Measuring Overall Business Performance

The 5th Wave   By Rich Tennant

SALES PICNIC

"Get names!"

In this part . . .

*Y*ou stand a better chance of achieving and surpassing your sales and customer support goals if you know exactly where you are and how fast you're going. By using reports and dashboards in Salesforce, you can get real-time insight into your sales and support teams, customers, and overall business. Manual reporting will be a thing of the past. Sound too good to be true? It's not. As long as you and other users are updating records in Salesforce, the data is at your fingertips.

In this part, we explain everything you need to know about reports and dashboards. We show you how to use the standard reports and create your own custom ones by using the Salesforce report wizard. If for some reason you still need to work with your data in spreadsheets, we show you just how simple it is to export your data into Excel. And you discover how to build powerful dashboards to visually depict key parts of your business.

Chapter 18

Seeing the Big Picture with Dashboards

Dashboards are visual representations of custom reports that you create in Salesforce. You can use dashboards to measure key performance indicators (KPIs) and other metrics important to your business. A metric is simply something you want to measure (for example, sales by rep, leads by source, opportunities by partner, cases by agent, and so on).

What does this mean for you? If you're a sales or service rep, you can track your daily progress against attainment of goals. If you're a manager, you can easily see how reps are stacking up against each other and where you need to get involved to hit the numbers. And if you're on the executive team, you have actionable charts and graphs for strategic decision making to improve the business.

In this chapter, first we share with you some tips on planning out your strategy, and then we show you how to create dashboards. We walk you through updating dashboard properties and components. You also discover how to organize dashboards and their related reports so that you know you're looking at the right information.

Figuring Out Dashboards

Dashboards are pages in Salesforce that are made up of tables and charts designed to help you understand important aspects of your business. Because dashboards are so critical, the following sections help you understand some basic concepts and consider your strategy before you start unleashing them on your organization.

Breaking down basic elements

You can build a dashboard with as many as 20 individual charts, tables, metrics, or gauges (each of these items is referred to as a *dashboard component*). Similar to building charts with the Report Wizard, components are based on reports that you create. In fact, you can click a component on a dashboard to make the underlying report appear. Here's a quick summary of the components available to you:

- **Horizontal or Vertical Bar Charts** are great when you want to depict a simple measurement with an x and y axis. For example, use bar charts if you want to create a component that displays pipeline by stage.

- **Horizontal or Vertical Stacked Bar Charts** work well when you want grouping within a bar. For example, use stacked bar charts if you want to create a chart that shows cases by status and then by type (such as problems versus feature requests).

- **Horizontal or Vertical Stacked to 100% Bar Charts** are excellent when you're more interested in percentages than amounts. If you're comparing new versus existing business, stacked to 100% charts can help you understand what percentage of each stage was new business versus existing business.

- **Pie Charts** work just like the standard bar charts, but the data are shown as a pie. (Not recommended if you're on a diet.)

- **Line Charts** are helpful if you're trying to express trends, particularly when time is part of the measurement. For example, use a line chart if you want to analyze the number of newly created opportunities by month for your entire company.

- **Line Group Charts** add a layer of complexity. For example, a line group chart could help you express the number of newly created opportunities by month broken out by region or unit.

- **Tables** create simple but powerful two-column tables. For example, use tables if you want your dashboard to show the top ten forecasted deals in the quarter in descending value. You can create tables in dashboards but not in the charting tool of the Report Wizard.

✔ **Metrics** insert the grand total of a report at the end of a dashboard label that you customize. Metrics are compelling when you want to tell a story that might require a bit more explanation. Metrics tend to work well in concert with other components. For example, if you use a pie chart to summarize opportunity by stage, you could add a metric to summarize total pipeline.

✔ **Gauges** are useful when you have a specific measurable objective and you want to track your progress. A gauge applies the grand total of a report as a point on a scale that you define. For example, use a gauge if you want to measure actual quarterly new bookings against a quota that you define.

✔ **Custom S-controls** let you create your own, or download other people's, custom dashboard components. Even if you're just interested in a snazzier graphic element, go to `www.appexchange.com` and click the Components category to see what others have created.

If you're an administrator or a user with permission to manage dashboards, you can create, edit, and organize them. Even if you don't have such permissions, you can still view them.

Planning useful dashboards

We always say that the best way to build a system is to envision what you want to ultimately measure. Do you want to know who your top sales reps are? Would you like to understand what your best accounts are buying from you and how much? Do you wonder how long it takes to close a case? This method of starting with the business questions you want to answer applies to your building of reports and is true of dashboards. If you're an administrator or part of the team responsible for deploying Salesforce, consider these tips as you develop your dashboards:

✔ **Focus on your end users.** Meet with sales, marketing, and support management and have them define their key performance indicators (KPIs) for their teams and business. Knowing this helps you customize Salesforce and construct useful dashboards.

✔ **Create a common set of components to reflect a universal way to look at business health.** This is especially true if your company has multiple sales teams. For example, after you determine the key sales metrics for your company's overall dashboard, you can replicate the dashboard and then customize other dashboards for each sales team. By doing this, everyone in the company is speaking a common language.

Building Dashboards

To build a dashboard, you need to create your custom reports first. You also need to create public folders for your dashboard reports if you want dashboards to be viewable for other users. See Chapter 17 for all the details on creating custom reports and organizing them in folders.

Only system administrators and users with permission to manage dashboards can add, edit, and delete dashboards.

In the following sections, we show you how to create a sample dashboard and how to clone a dashboard, and finally, we cover the steps to build a dashboard from scratch.

Generating a sample dashboard

One of the best ways to get your feet wet with dashboards is to generate a sample dashboard. Salesforce not only creates the dashboard for you, but also builds the underlying sample reports to generate the components.

To generate a sample dashboard, follow these steps:

1. **Click the Dashboards tab.**

   Either the last dashboard that you viewed or an introduction page appears. If this is your first visit to the Dashboards tab, the most recently created dashboard appears.

   If you're having trouble accessing dashboards, you might not have the proper permissions. In this circumstance, consult with your administrator.

2. **If a dashboard appears, click the Go to Dashboard List link at the top-left of the page.**

   A folder's list page appears.

3. **Click the Add Sample Dashboard button.**

   The list page reappears with a link to a sample dashboard entitled Company Performance Dashboard.

4. **Click the Company Performance Dashboard link.**

   The dashboard appears, as shown in the example in Figure 18-1.

5. **Click the Closed Sales to Date gauge.**

   A sample report appears entitled Closed Sales. Click the Back button on your browser to return to the dashboard.

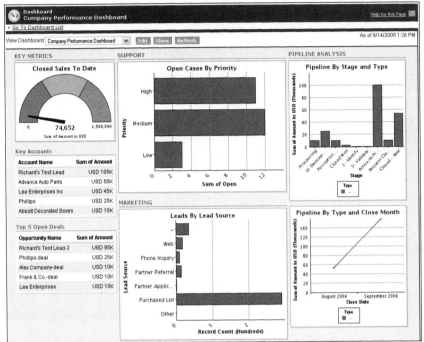

Cloning a dashboard

You can generate a dashboard by cloning an existing one. If you envision creating multiple dashboards for different sales units with common components, you can use this shortcut and then modify the associated reports.

To clone a dashboard, follow these steps:

1. **Click the Dashboards tab.**

   A dashboard appears.

2. **Use the View Dashboard drop-down list to select a dashboard you want to clone.**

   In this example, choose the sample dashboard entitled Company Performance Dashboard.

   The dashboard appears.

3. **Click the Clone button.**

   A New Dashboard page appears.

4. **Complete the required settings, paying close attention to the following:**

   - Change the **Title** of the dashboard.

   - Select the **Dashboard Layout Style.**

   - Modify the **Security Settings,** if necessary. The *Running User* is the user whose security settings will apply to the dashboard. So, any user that can view the dashboard will see what that Running User sees.

   - Alter the **Default Chart Settings,** if desired.

5. **When you're done, click Save.**

   The new dashboard appears.

When you clone a dashboard, you don't clone another set of identical reports. Instead, the newly cloned dashboard references the same custom reports that the original dashboard references. If you want the new dashboard to refer to different reports, see the "Editing a component" section, later in this chapter.

Developing a dashboard from scratch

In preceding sections, you test the waters and even generate some sample custom reports. In this section, you find out how to develop a dashboard from scratch.

To build a new dashboard, follow these steps:

1. **Click the Reports tab.**

   The Reports home page appears. You need to build your custom reports before you can develop a dashing new dashboard.

2. **Build your custom reports and save them to a public folder.**

   Dashboards that you want others to see can't use reports in your My Personal Reports folder. For purposes of this exercise, go to the My Personal Reports folder (commonly located at the top of your Reports home page) and click the following reports:

   - **Sample Report: Sales Pipeline by Stage:** Modify the Report Options to summarize information by Opportunity Owner and then Stage. Then save the report as Pipe by Rep and Stage to a public folder.

   - **Sample Report: Top Accounts:** Under Report Options, change Opportunity Status to Closed Won. Then, save the report as Top Revenue Customers to a public folder.

REMEMBER

You must be an administrator or a user with permission to manage public reports if you want to add report folders.

3. **Click the Dashboard tab.**

   A dashboard appears.

4. **Click the Go to Dashboard List link.**

   A folder's list page appears.

5. **Click the New Dashboard button.**

   The New Dashboard page appears.

6. **Complete the settings and click Save.**

   The dashboard appears in Edit mode. See the preceding section for tips on completing the settings.

7. **In the left column, click the Add Component link.**

   A New Dashboard Component page appears in Edit mode.

8. **Complete the fields, as shown in the example in Figure 18-2:**

   • Click a radio button to select a component type. See the section "Breaking down basic elements," earlier in this chapter, for details on the components. In the example, stay with chart. The steps will differ, depending on which component type you select.

   • Enter a header, footer, and/or title. In the example, name the header **PIPELINE METRICS** and enter the title **Pipe by Rep and Stage**.

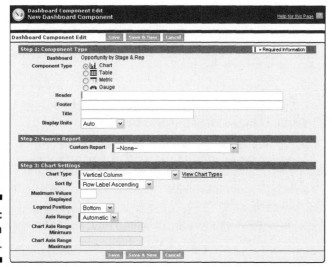

Figure 18-2: Adding a component.

- Use the Display Units drop-down list to select the unit of measurement.

- From the Custom Report drop-down list, select the correct report. In this example, select Pipe by Rep and Stage.

- For chart components, use the Chart Type menu in Step 3 to select a chart. In the example, choose Horizontal Bar – Stacked.

- For table and chart components, use the Sort By drop-down list to select the order of sorting. For example, if you want to rank the reps from biggest to smallest pipeline, choose Row *Value* Descending. You may also sort the row labels if you wanted to rank the reps by their names.

- If you want, enter a number under Maximum Values Displayed.

- For charts, select an option from the Legend Position drop-down list.

- For bar or line charts, select an option from the Axis Range drop-down list. If you select Manual, the next two fields (Chart Axis Range Minimum and Chart Axis Range Maximum) become available for input.

- For tables, metrics, and gauges, set up to two Breakpoint Values to separate different range colors from each other. Select Range Colors to represent a range of data, separated by the breakpoint values. (See Chapter 17 for more information on conditional highlighting.)

- If you chose metric as your component type, enter a Metric Label to describe the value displayed. A metric displays the grand total of a custom report following your label for that value.

- For gauges, set your Minimum and Maximum Values to represent the lowest and highest values on the gauge.

9. **When you're done, click Save.**

   The dashboard reappears in Edit mode with the component displayed based on your settings.

10. **In the middle column, click the Add Component link.**

    Repeat the basic instructions from Step 8, but this time

    - Select Table for Component Type.

    - Name the header **SALES METRICS** and enter the title **Top 10 Customers by Revenue**.

    - Select the Custom Report called Top Revenue Customers.

- Sort by Row Value Descending.
- Set the Maximum Values Displayed at 10.
- Optionally, set indicator colors to conditionally highlight certain breakpoints.

11. **When you're done, click Save.**

    The dashboard reappears in Edit mode with a table in the middle column.

12. **When you're satisfied, click Done.**

    The dashboard appears in Saved mode.

Updating Dashboards

Over time, you might have to make changes to your dashboards, whether for cosmetic reasons or to make substantive updates. We can come up with a dozen common edits, but the good news is that updating is easy.

Editing dashboard properties

If you need to change the basic settings of a dashboard, you need to edit dashboard properties. To edit properties, follow these steps:

1. **Click the Dashboards tab.**

   A dashboard appears.

2. **Select a desired dashboard from the View Dashboard drop-down list.**

   The dashboard appears.

3. **Click the Edit button at the top of the dashboard page.**

   The dashboard appears in Edit mode.

4. **Click the Edit Properties button.**

   The Settings page of the dashboard appears.

5. **Modify the settings, as needed, and click Save.**

   When you click Save, the dashboard reappears in Edit mode, and your setting changes are applied.

Editing a component

You might want to add or change an existing component. To edit a component, follow these steps:

1. **Go to a dashboard and click the Edit button.**

   The dashboard appears in Edit mode.

2. **Click the Edit link above a component that you want to modify.**

   The Dashboard Component Edit page appears.

3. **Modify the fields, as necessary, and then click Save.**

   The dashboard reappears in Edit mode with the changes you applied to the component.

Modifying the layout

If you need to modify the dashboard layout, you can also perform this while in Edit mode, as shown in Figure 18-3.

Go to a dashboard, click the Edit button, and alter the layout. You can

- ✔ **Modify a column size.** Click the Narrow, Medium, or Wide links at the top of the column. All the components in the column change in size based on your setting.

- ✔ **Add a component.** Click the Add Component link at the top of the column and follow the steps in the section "Developing a dashboard from scratch," earlier in this chapter.

- ✔ **Delete a component.** Click the Delete link located above a component. A pop-up window appears to confirm the deletion. When you click OK, the pop-up closes, and the dashboard reappears, minus the deleted component.

- ✔ **Rearrange components.** Click the directional arrows above a component.

When you're satisfied with your changes, remember to click the Done button. The dashboard then reappears with your modifications.

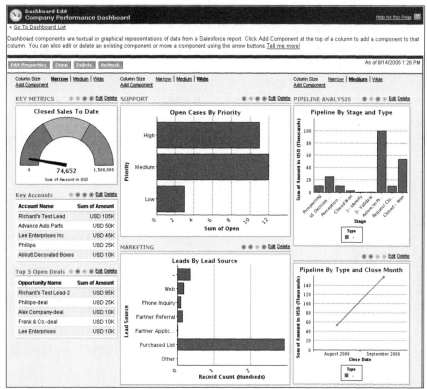

Refreshing the dashboard

Click any dashboard from your dashboard list. In the top-right corner of the dashboard, you see a timestamp starting with As Of. You can use this to let you know the last time your dashboard data was updated.

Several times a day, Salesforce automatically updates your dashboards with the most current information available. Sometimes, you can even see the page components reappearing, and a Refreshing Dashboard notification in red font appears in the top-right corner of the page. The fact that Salesforce does this for you is quite refreshing, but if you want to update your dashboard data on your own, simply click the Refresh button at the top of the dashboard page, whether it's in Saved or Edit mode. The components reappear one by one, and when the refresh is completed, a new timestamp appears.

Organizing Your Dashboards

You can organize your company's dashboards in folders and define the proper security access for users if you have permissions to manage dashboards, manage public reports, and view all data. By organizing dashboards, you can make sure that the right people are focusing on the right metrics to manage their business.

Viewing dashboard lists

Unlike most other tabs in Salesforce, clicking the Dashboard tab doesn't take you to its home page. Instead, the last dashboard that you viewed appears.

To access your viewable dashboards, simply follow these steps:

1. **Click the Go To Dashboard List link at the top-left corner of any dashboard.**

   A dashboard folder's list page appears.

2. **Use the Folder drop-down list to select a desired folder.**

   The page for the selected folder appears with a list of available dashboards.

3. **From this list page, users with the permissions mentioned in the preceding section can perform a variety of functions that include**

   - Clicking a column header to re-sort a dashboard list. (See Chapter 2 for more details on navigating list pages.)

   - Clicking a title name to view a dashboard.

   - Clicking the Edit link next to a dashboard to modify it.

   - Clicking the Del link next to a dashboard to delete it.

   - Clicking the New Dashboard or Add Sample Dashboard buttons to build dashboards. (See the section "Developing a dashboard from scratch," earlier in this chapter.)

Building dashboard folders

From a list page, you can also create and edit folders. Editing a folder is easy when you understand how to create one.

To create a folder, follow these steps:

1. **Click the Create New Folder link next to the Folder drop-down list.**

   A New Dashboard Folder page appears.

2. **Type a name for the folder in the Dashboard Folder field.**

   For example, if you want a folder for only senior management, you might name it Executive Dashboards.

3. **Use the Public Folder Access field to determine read versus read/write privileges to the folder.**

4. **Use the radio buttons to select who should have access to the folder.**

   Your choices amount to all, none, and selective.

5. **If you chose selective in Step 4 (the third radio button), highlight groups or roles in the Available for Sharing list box and add them to the Shared To list box.**

6. **When you're done, click Save.**

   The folder's list page reappears, and now you can add dashboards or move existing dashboards to the new folder, which we explain in the section "Editing dashboard properties," earlier in this chapter.

When naming folders, dashboards, and dashboard reports, consider using a standard numbering convention. You could name the senior management folder 1.0 Executive Dashboards. Then the executive sales dashboard might be 1.1 versus the executive marketing dashboard of 1.2. By using a standard numbering methodology, you can more efficiently create, clone, and organize dashboards and dashboard reports.

Chapter 19

Fine-Tuning the Configuration

*I*n earlier chapters, you can discover how to add custom fields, define pick-lists, and create standard templates so that Salesforce looks like it was made exactly for your business. If you're starting to think about additional ways to tweak the system so that each user sees only information pertinent to him or her, you've come to the right chapter.

For administrators or members of your customer relationship management (CRM) project team with the right privileges, Salesforce allows you to easily configure your system so that users can access and share information according to your goals. Regardless of which Salesforce edition your company has chosen, you have a variety of ways to control access and sharing of data, from system-wide sharing rules to assigning profiles. And, if you have Enterprise or Unlimited Edition, you have industrial-strength flexibility, even to the point of field-level security.

In this chapter, we show you all the steps you can take (or should consider) for configuring Salesforce, including creating the role hierarchy, assigning profiles, determining field-level security, creating users, setting up your sharing rules, and managing groups. We also show you other methods for controlling security, which include password policies, session settings, audit trails, and delegating administrative privileges.

Figuring Out Configuration

All the things that you can change can be conveniently accessed from the Setup menu of Salesforce. If you have administrative permissions, log in to Salesforce and follow these steps:

1. **Go to Setup⇨Administration Setup.**

   The Administration Setup page appears with a page title that includes the edition (or version) of Salesforce that you're using.

2. **In the sidebar, click the + buttons to expand the first three folders under Administration Setup: Manage Users, Company Profile, and Security Controls.**

   These are your basic options and the first things that you should use when configuring Salesforce.

Breaking down basic elements

Before jumping into the guts of system configuration, it's helpful to review four basic configuration elements:

- ✔ **Users:** The specific people who use your Salesforce system.

- ✔ **Roles:** Control a user's level of visibility to information in Salesforce — what records you can and can't see. For example, if you're a manager of a team of sales reps, you'll have read and write access to the information owned by the reps reporting to you in the role hierarchy. Each user should have an assigned role within your defined role hierarchy.

- ✔ **Profiles:** Control a user's permissions to perform different functions within a record in Salesforce. For example, service reps will find some fields on an account record more relevant than other fields. To make their view of the account record less confusing, you could hide certain irrelevant fields from their view. You must assign a profile to each user.

- ✔ **Sharing model and rules:** Defines the general access that users have to each other's data.

You use these four elements as the primary levers to deliver the proper level of access and control for your company in Salesforce.

Planning configuration to achieve success

Put the major stakeholders of your Salesforce solution in a room and ask them one question: "How do you envision people sharing information in Salesforce?" More often than not, you'll get blank stares.

Discuss sharing issues with your CRM project team after you've heard about their current CRM processes. Current business processes, explained without any Salesforce jargon from the team, can often help you formulate an opinion based on what you believe would be best for your company. Take into consideration the culture, size, and type of sales organization at your company. Use this opinion to guide the specific nature of your questions.

Now, you _should_ ask that question, but we suggest following it up with scenarios. Here are a couple of ideas to get you started:

- ✔ Should a telemarketer be able see what the CEO sees?

- ✔ Should a sales rep be able to view data from other reps? Should one sales rep be allowed to edit another's lead record?

- ✔ Do certain groups need wider access than others? For example, does a call center team that supports all customers need more or less access than a team of sales reps?

- ✔ Does a manager require different permissions than a rep?

- ✔ Do multiple people commonly work on the same account or opportunity?

- ✔ Do you have any concerns with a fully open or completely private sharing model?

Use these types of questions and their answers to guide your configuration.

Verifying Your Company Profile

In your Company Profile folder, you can modify many basic settings for your organization that include default time zone, language, currencies, and fiscal year. If you're the administrator, you can also use this section to monitor and anticipate your future needs relative to user seats.

This is an easy but important step. If you're an administrator beginning your implementation, get this done before you even think of adding a new user.

To update your company information, click the Setup link in the top-right corner of Salesforce and follow these steps:

1. **Go to Administration Setup⇨Company Profile⇨Company Information.**

   The Company Information page appears.

2. **Click the Edit button.**

   The Edit Organization Profile page appears. Review all the fields. Pay closest attention to verifying the accuracy of the three or four required fields in the Locale Settings section, as shown in Figure 19-1:

   • Use the Default Locale drop-down list to select your company's primary geographic locale. This setting affects the format of date and time fields (for example, 09/30/2007 versus 30/09/2007).

   • Select an option from the Default Language drop-down list.

   • Verify that the Default Time Zone drop-down list is correctly set.

   • Choose the proper location from the Currency Locale drop-down list in the event that you use a single currency. This affects the corporate currency. (You won't see this field if you set up multi-currencies.)

   Don't worry, users can still modify their individual locale settings in the future.

3. **When you're done, click Save.**

   The Company Information page reappears with any changes you made.

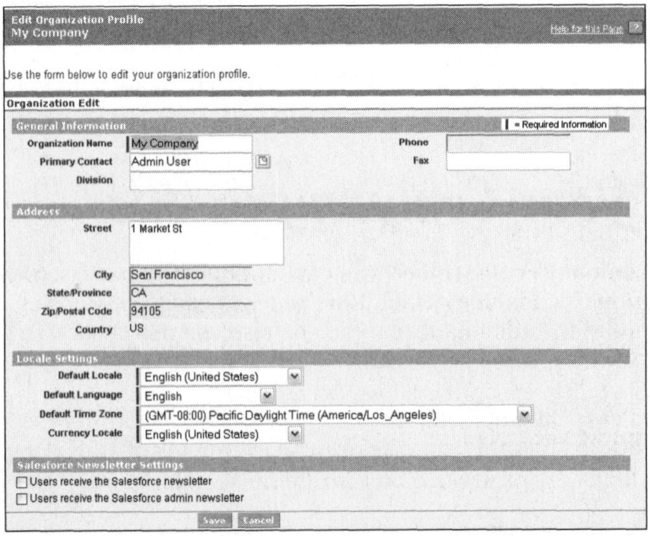

Figure 19-1:
Updating locale settings on the company profile.

Edit Organization Profile
My Company

Help for this Page

Use the form below to edit your organization profile.

Organization Edit

General Information

= Required Information

Organization Name My Company   Phone
Primary Contact   Admin User   Fax
Division

Address

Street   1 Market St
City   San Francisco
State/Province CA
Zip/Postal Code 94105
Country   US

Locale Settings

Default Locale   English (United States)
Default Language   English
Default Time Zone   (GMT-08:00) Pacific Daylight Time (America/Los_Angeles)
Currency Locale   English (United States)

Salesforce Newsletter Settings

☐ Users receive the Salesforce newsletter
☐ Users receive the Salesforce admin newsletter

Save   Cancel

Defining the Role Hierarchy

Think of a role hierarchy as the Salesforce system's data-access trickle-down org chart: If you're assigned to the role at the top of the chart, you have full access to your own data, and that privilege trickles down to the data of everyone below you in the hierarchy — and life is good.

When you're constructing your hierarchy, don't confuse your actual company org chart with the role hierarchy. Role hierarchy is all about access to data to perform your duties in Salesforce and how you want to organize certain sales-related reports. As such, hierarchies often have fewer layers than a typical org chart. For example, if your executive team will be users, you might simply create a role called Executive Team, assuming that many of those users will have similar trickle-down viewing and editing privileges.

You can use the role hierarchy in Salesforce as a primary method to control a user's visibility and access to other users' data. After you assign a role to a user, that user has owner-like access to all records owned by or shared with subordinate users in the hierarchy. For example, if you set up a hierarchy with a Sales Rep role subordinate to a Sales Manager role, users assigned to Sales Manager would have read and write access to records owned by or shared with users in the Sales Rep role.

To set up your company's role hierarchy, click the Setup link in the top-right corner and follow these steps:

1. **Go to Administration Setup⇨Manage Users⇨Roles.**

   The Understanding Roles page appears, and you see a sample hierarchy.

2. **Use the View Other Sample Role Hierarchies drop-down list if you want to select a different sample hierarchy.**

3. **Click the Set Up Roles button.**

   The Creating the Role Hierarchy page appears.

4. **Use the drop-down list on the right side of the page if you want to select a different view of the hierarchy.**

   Salesforce provides three standard views for displaying the role hierarchy: a tree view, a list view, and a sorted list view.

5. **In the tree hierarchy view, click the Add Role button.**

   A Role Edit page appears for the new role.

6. **Complete the fields.**

   The fields are pretty obvious, but here are some tips:

- Use the This Role Reports To lookup field to define the role's place in the hierarchy. Because the lookup field is based on roles you've already created, add roles by starting at the top of your hierarchy and then working your way down.

- Select the Contact, Opportunity, and Case Access options that fit your company's objectives. (You may not see these fields if you have a very public sharing model — more on that in the following section.) You can provide an account owner with read/write access to related opportunities or cases that she doesn't own, view-only access, or no access at all. This flexibility comes in handy in heavily regulated industries, in which you might have to prevent an account executive from knowing about certain deals or issues going on with her account.

7. **When you're done, click the Save button or the Save & New button.**

   If you click Save, the Role: *Role Name* page appears, displaying the detail information you just entered and listing any users in this role. From the Users in *Role Name* Role detail list, you may also assign existing users to this role or create new users with this role (check out the section "Adding Users to Salesforce," later in this chapter).

   If you click the Save & New button, a New Role page appears, and you can continue building the hierarchy. Repeat Steps 3 through 6 until your hierarchy is done.

Defining Your Sharing Model

As an administrator or member of your CRM project team, one of your biggest decisions in Salesforce is how users will share information. A *sharing model* controls the level of access that users have across an organization's information, not just up and down the chain. You can use the sharing model with the role hierarchy, public groups, personal groups, and the default access for each role to get pretty specific about what you want people to view or change. You use the organization-wide sharing model, and if necessary, public groups and expanded sharing rules in Salesforce to configure your sharing model.

When in doubt, start with an open, collaborative sharing model, as opposed to a secretive sharing model in which no one knows what anyone else is doing. (A secretive sharing model sounds like any oxymoron, right? Well it can be because, if you don't carefully think about ramifications, you could be back to where you started with giant heaps of information.) If collaboration is one of your goals, a more restrictive sharing model can have a greater potential negative impact on end user adoption. You can always change the sharing model in the future if people scream loudly enough. But nine out of ten times, the value of collaboration overcomes the initial concerns with users viewing other users' data.

Setting organization-wide defaults

The organization-wide defaults set the default sharing access that users have to each other's data. Sharing access determines how data created by users in a certain role or public group are viewed by users within another role or public group. For example, you many want your Sales Operations team to see the dollar value of won opportunities so that they can calculate commissions. But you probably don't want them editing the amount of that opportunity. If any role or public group possesses data that at least one other role or group shouldn't see, then your sharing model must be private; all other levels of openness must be granted as an exception via groups (more on that later). No matter which defaults you set to the sharing model, users will still have access to all data owned by or shared with users below them in the role hierarchy.

To configure the organization-wide defaults, click the Setup link and follow these steps:

1. **Go to Administration Setup⇨Security Controls⇨Sharing Settings.**

   The Sharing Settings page appears.

2. **Click the Edit button on the Organization Wide Defaults list.**

   The Organization Sharing Edit page appears.

3. **Select the desired settings.**

   Click some picklists to see the different options. The options are generally Private, Public Read Only, Public Read/Write. For example, if you want the most restrictive model, choose the following as your defaults: Private for the major records and Hide Details for Calendar.

   A Private sharing setting on an object still assumes that people with a role above yours in the role hierarchy can see and report on those records. Salesforce always respects the hierarchy structure — sharing settings determine only how peers and those outside your typical chain of command see your data.

4. **When you're done, click Save.**

   The Sharing Settings page reappears with your settings listed under the Organization Wide Defaults list.

Creating groups

You can create public and personal groups in Salesforce to extend greater sharing privileges. Groups comprise users, roles, or even other groups. So, if your organization-wide default is geared towards a private sharing model, use groups to create exceptions.

Public groups work in combination with sharing rules to expand sharing access to information beyond the organization-wide defaults. You can access public groups from the Manage Users heading or the Security Controls heading on the sidebar on the Personal Setup page.

To create a public group, click the Setup link in the top-right corner and follow these steps:

1. **Go to Administration Setup⇨Manage Users⇨Public Groups.**

   The Public Groups page appears.

2. **Click the New button.**

   A Group Membership page appears.

3. **Enter a name for the group in the Group Name field, and then highlight users, roles, or other groups in the Available Members list box and add them to the Selected Members list box.**

4. **When you're done, click Save.**

   The Public Groups page reappears with groups that you added listed.

Granting greater access with sharing rules

By using public groups, roles, or roles and subordinates, you can create sharing rules to extend access above and beyond the organization-wide defaults. For example, if your default sharing model is read-only, but you want a group of call center agents to have edit privileges on account records, you could do this with a custom sharing rule.

To add a sharing rule and apply it to your data, click the Setup link and follow these steps:

1. **Click the Sharing Settings link under the Security Controls heading on the sidebar.**

   The Sharing Settings page appears.

2. **Scroll down and click the New button next to any of the standard or custom object Sharing Rules lists.**

   All lists operate much the same but relate to different records. A sharing rule page appears for your selected record.

3. **Use the drop-down lists to define the data you want to share and the related roles or groups that you want to share that data with.**

For example, you might create a public group for your call center team and then grant them read/write privileges to data owned by members of the Entire Organization group.

4. **When you're done, click Save.**

   The Sharing Settings page reappears with your new rule listed under the appropriate related list.

When you add a new sharing rule, Salesforce automatically re-evaluates the sharing rules to apply the changes. If your modifications are substantial, you'll be warned with a dialog box that the operation could take significant time. When you click OK, the dialog box closes and the Sharing Settings page reappears. Use the Recalculate button on the appropriate related list to manually apply the changes when you've made modifications to groups, roles, or territories.

Setting Up Profiles

You can use profiles to control a user's permission to perform many functions in Salesforce. Roles and sharing rules determine which objects a person sees, and a profile determines what a person sees on that object. Depending on which edition you're using, you can use profiles to

- ✔ Define which page layouts a user will see.
- ✔ Control field-level access.
- ✔ Determine the apps viewed by a user.
- ✔ Alter the tabs displayed to users.
- ✔ Make record types available to certain users.
- ✔ Secure certain login settings.

Reviewing the standard profiles

Most editions of Salesforce come with five or six standard profiles, which can't be altered except for tab settings. Many large organizations can stick to these standard profiles and address the majority of their company's requirements related to user permissions. If you have Team or Professional Edition, you can't actually view the settings on the standard profiles.

If you have Enterprise or Unlimited Edition, go to Setup⇨Administration Setup⇨ Manage Users⇨ Profiles to see your profiles. Otherwise, here's a brief explanation of the standard profiles and how they're typically applied:

- ✓ **System Administrators** have full permissions and access across all Salesforce functions that don't require a separate license. You'd typically grant this level of control only to users administering the system or who play a critical part in configuring and customizing Salesforce.

- ✓ **Standard Users** can create and edit most record types, run reports, and view but not modify many areas of the administration setup. If you can't create custom profiles, you'd probably choose to assign sales reps to the standard user profile.

- ✓ **Solution Managers** have all the rights of standard users and can review and publish solutions.

- ✓ **Marketing Users** have all the rights of standard users and can perform a variety of marketing-related functions, including importing leads and managing public documents and e-mail templates. If your Salesforce edition has campaigns, marketing users can also administer campaigns.

- ✓ **Contract Managers** can add, edit, approve, and activate contracts. They can also delete non-activated contracts.

- ✓ **Read Only** is just what its name implies. Users assigned to this profile can view data and export reports, but can't edit anything.

Profiles never conflict with your organization's sharing model or role hierarchy. For example, a Standard User profile allows a user to create, edit, or delete leads, but if your sharing model is read-only for leads, then the Standard User won't be able to delete leads owned by others.

Creating custom profiles

If you have Enterprise or Unlimited Edition, you can build custom profiles that provide you greater flexibility over standard permissions that can be granted to users and the layouts that they see. For example, you may want to create a custom profile for your Sales Operations team, so only users with that profile can edit check boxes on the opportunity that track if certain signed forms have been submitted when you've closed a deal. See Chapter 20 for details on creating custom layouts, business processes, and record types.

To create a custom profile, you can start from scratch, but we suggest cloning and modifying an existing profile by following these steps:

1. **Go to Setup⇨Administration Setup⇨Manage Users⇨Profiles.**

   The User Profiles page appears.

2. **Click the Standard User link in the Profile Name list.**

   The Profile: Standard User page appears. In practice, you can clone from any of the profiles, but by starting from the Standard User profile, you can simply add or remove permissions.

3. **Click the Clone button.**

   The Clone Profile page appears.

4. **Type a title in the Profile Name field and then click Save.**

   The Profile page for your new profile appears.

5. **Click the Edit button to modify the permissions.**

   The Profile Edit page appears.

   Salesforce packs a plethora of possible permissions into a profile page. Some of those permissions aren't obvious; others are dependent on your selecting other permissions. If you have questions as you're working through the Profile Edit page, you can click the Help for This Page link in the upper-right of the page to go directly to the relevant Help documentation. If you place your cursor over the *i* icons, located next to certain Administrative Permissions on the Profile Edit page, rollover text appears with tips on other settings required.

6. **Under the Custom App Setting section, determine which standard and custom apps are visible for a profile and which one is the default.**

   This determines the content of the AppExchange app drop-down list.

7. **Under the Tab Settings section, use the drop-down lists to determine the tab settings for your new profile.**

   Choose from the three possible options:

   - Stay with Default On if you want a tab to be displayed.

   - Select Default Off if you want a tab not to appear while still allowing a user assigned to the profile the choice to turn the tab back on. For example, if you created a profile for sales reps, and you wanted to hide the Contracts tab but give the rep the option to display it, you'd select Default Off on the Contracts field.

   - Select Tab Hidden if you want the tab to be hidden without an option to the user to turn the tab back on. For example, if your company isn't going to use cases, you might decide to hide the tab.

   Making a tab hidden in a user's profile doesn't prevent the user from accessing those records (in reports, for example). To prevent a user from accessing a particular type of record altogether, remove the Read permission on that type of data.

8. **Select the Overwrite Users' Personal Tab Customizations check box if you want to overwrite the user's current personal customization settings with the settings for the new profile that you're applying.**

9. **Under the Administrative Permissions header, select or deselect check boxes to modify administrative permissions from the profile.**

   Most of these settings are designed for administrators, but some of these might be important, depending on your goals for a custom profile. For example, if you want to build a manager's profile, you might retain permissions such as Manage Public Reports and Manage Public List Views so that managers can create public reports and list views for their teams.

10. **Under the General User Permissions header, select or deselect check boxes to modify common user permissions from the profile.**

    For example, if you don't want sales reps to be able to export customer data to a file, you could create a custom profile for reps and remove the Export Reports setting.

11. **Under the Standard Object and Custom Object Permissions headers, select or deselect check boxes to modify standard or custom object permissions from the profile.**

    For example, if you don't want support reps to be able to modify opportunities, you could create a custom profile for support reps and check just the Read box in the row for opportunities.

12. **When you're done, click Save.**

    The Profile page reappears for your new profile.

13. **Click the View Users button if you want to assign users to the profile.**

    A Custom: *Custom Profile Name* list page appears in which you can view, add, or reset passwords for users in the profile. See the following section to add users to Salesforce.

Adding Users to Salesforce

When Salesforce supplies user licenses for your organization, administrators can add users into Salesforce. (See the "Setting Up Profiles" section, earlier in this chapter, for the scoop on viewing and modifying your company profile.) You don't have to create the roles and profiles before you add users, but we recommend doing so because Role and Profile are required fields when you're creating a user record.

To add users, click the Setup link and follow these steps:

1. **Click the Users link under the Manage Users heading on the sidebar.**

   A users list page appears.

2. **Use the View drop-down list if you want to select from standard or custom list views of your users.**

   Salesforce presets your views with three standard options: All Users, Active Users, and Admin Users.

3. **Click the New User button if you want to add users one at a time.**

   A New User page appears in Edit mode.

4. **Complete the fields, paying close attention to selecting appropriate Role and Profile values.**

   You can select the last check box at the bottom of the New User page if you want to notify the user immediately. If you're in the midst of an implementation, we recommend unchecking this box and doling out passwords when you're good and ready.

5. **When you're done, click Save.**

   After you click Save, the User detail page appears.

Using Other Security Controls

Beyond the major configuration settings, such as roles, profiles, and sharing model, as an administrator, you have other settings for managing the use and security of your data in Salesforce. Those features are located under Setup⇨Administration Setup⇨ Security Controls.

In the following sections, we discuss how to manage field-level access and delegate a subset of administration to others.

Setting field-level security

If you have Enterprise or Unlimited Edition, you have three primary ways to control access and editing on specific fields: profiles (which we discuss earlier in this chapter), page layouts (Chapter 20 covers these), and field-level settings (stay right here for the details). With field-level security, you can further restrict users' access to fields by setting whether those fields are visible, editable, or read-only.

To view and administer field-level security, click the Setup link and follow these steps:

1. **Go to Administration Setup⇨Security Controls⇨Field Accessibility.**

   The Field Accessibility page appears.

2. **Click the link for the type of record for which you want to view and manage field-level security.**

   A Field Accessibility page for the selected record type appears. For example, click the Account link if you want to review the security settings on account fields.

3. **Under the Choose Your View header, click the View by Fields link.**

   The Field Accessibility page for the record type reappears with a Field drop-down list. If you want to see a different view of this information, in which you get to see one profile and the security levels for all the fields for the selected data type, click the View by Profile link.

4. **Select a field from the Field drop-down list.**

   The page reappears with a table displaying your company's profiles and the profiles' accessibility to the selected field.

5. **In the Field Access column, click a link to edit the profile's field access.**

   An Access Settings page for the selected profile and selected field appears, as shown in Figure 19-2.

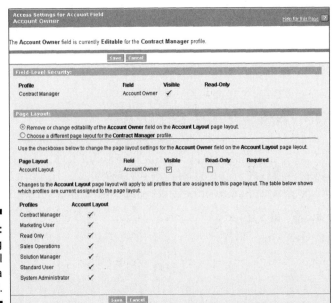

Figure 19-2: Modifying field-level access on a profile.

6. **Select the check boxes to modify the field-level settings, and then click Save.**

   The Field Accessibility page for the selected record type reappears.

Delegating administration

As an administrator for your growing world of Salesforce users within your company, you hold the key to who accesses your Salesforce instance. You shouldn't try to cut corners by making everyone system administrators just because you're annoyed each time they're bugging you to add a new user. Salesforce allows you to delegate some administrative duties to non-administrators. Delegated administrators can help you create and edit users in roles you specify, reset passwords for those users, assign users to certain profiles, and manage custom objects. For example, if your marketing department is growing quickly, you may want to allow a manager in the Marketing Manager role to create and edit users in the Marketing Manager role and all subordinate roles.

To delegate administration, you must first define the groups of users that you want to delegate these new privileges to. Then you have to specify what you want those newly delegated administrators to do. To define delegated administrators, follow these steps:

1. **Go to Setup➪Administration Setup➪Security Controls➪Delegated Administration.**

   The Manage Delegated Groups page appears.

2. **Click New.**

   The Edit Delegated Group page for the new delegated group appears.

3. **Type in the Delegated Group Name.**

   In our example, we selected Sales Operations.

4. **Click Save when done.**

   The Delegated Group page for your new group appears.

5. **Click the Add button on the Delegated Administrators related list to specify which users will belong in this group.**

   The Delegated Administrators page appears.

6. **Use the Lookup icons to find and add users to this group.**

7. **Click Save when done.**

   The Delegated Group page for your group reappears.

8. **To specify which roles and subordinate roles a delegated administrator can manage, click the Add button on the User Administration related list.**

   The Roles and Subordinates page appears.

9. **Use the Lookup icons to find and add roles that your delegated group may manage.**

10. **Click Save when done.**

    The Delegated Group page for your group reappears.

11. **Click Add in the Assignable Profiles related list to specify which profiles these delegated administrators may assign to users.**

    The Assignable Profiles page appears.

12. **Use the Lookup icons to find and add profiles that your delegated group may assign.**

13. **Click Save when done.**

    The Delegated Group page for your group reappears.

14. **Click Add in the Custom Object Administration related list to specify which custom objects and related tabs a delegated administrator may manage.**

    The Custom Object Administration page appears.

15. **Use the Lookup icons to find and add custom objects that your delegated group may assign.**

16. **Click Save when done.**

    The Delegated Group page for your group reappears.

Part VII
Designing the Salesforce Solution

"For 30 years I've put a hat and coat on to make sales calls and I'm not changing now just because I'm doing it on the Web in my living room."

In this part . . .

*B*ack in the day, using a CRM system required a lot of time invested with big-name tech consulting firms, and you weren't always guaranteed to get what you wanted. Even today, configuring data or editing reports in many other systems means getting in line and waiting for someone more technical than you to help. Customers of Salesforce, however, rave about how easy it is for end users to use. But what's equally (if not more) amazing is how simple it is to fine-tune Salesforce to suit the unique needs of your company . . . as long as you understand the basic elements of the Setup, that is.

As an administrator, the Setup options available to you are extensive, regardless of what Salesforce edition you have. In this part, we focus on the four main areas of Setup that are necessary to successfully implement and then administer Salesforce for your end users: configuring the system, customizing the default records for CRM, building new records (or getting them from someone else), and migrating and maintaining your data. With system configuration, we show you how you can modify Salesforce for the way that you want users to have privilege to data. You then discover how you can easily customize the pages by adding fields, defining processes, changing layouts, and more. We next discuss using Salesforce as a platform to build new pages and optionally share them with others. Finally, we show you ways to maintain your data so it's fresh and useful for your users.

The details in these chapters are simple enough for anyone to follow but sophisticated enough for even the largest organizations.

Chapter 20

Customizing Salesforce

. . . .

. . . .

*I*f you're just beginning your implementation, Salesforce comes preconfigured with a number of common fields in simple layouts for each of the
tabs. You could buy your licenses, log in, and without any customization,
start using it to track your customers. So why is it that with over 40,000 customers and growing, no two instances of Salesforce are likely to be identical?

The answer is a key ingredient to your success: The more Salesforce is customized to your business, the more likely your company will use it effectively
and productively.

If you're an administrator or a user with permission to customize Salesforce,
you have a universe of tools to design Salesforce to fit the way you do business. And you don't need to be a technical wizard to make these changes.
With common sense and a little help from this book, you can customize
Salesforce on your own.

Salesforce has many customization features. We could write another book
if we tried to address each feature. So instead, in this chapter, we show you
how to perform all the core customization options, including creating fields,
building in your standard processes, adding Web links, and rearranging
layouts. Then, for companies that have Enterprise or Unlimited Edition and
possess complex needs, we show you how to develop custom page layouts,
multiple business processes, and record types that link to custom profiles.

Discovering Customization

All your customization tools are conveniently accessible from the Customize menu located under the App Setup heading of Setup in Salesforce. Navigating the Customize menu is simple when you understand some basics. If you have administrative permissions, log in to Salesforce and do this now:

1. **Go to Setup⇨App Setup⇨Customize.**

   The Customize page of Setup appears, and the sidebar expands to display headings for the various tabs that can be customized. Under the Customize heading on the sidebar, you see a few select headings for other areas of Salesforce (such as Call Center and Self-Service), which can also be customized.

2. **Click the + buttons or headings that correspond to the major tabs, such as Accounts, Contacts, and Leads.**

   The sidebar expands with the different customization features available under each heading. These are all the basic things you can do when customizing a standard tab. Notice that although certain headings have more features, most of the headings have links to common customization features, such as Fields, Page Layouts, Search Layouts, Buttons and Links, and in certain editions, Record Types and Processes.

3. **Click the Fields link under a tab-related heading on the sidebar.**

   A Fields page appears based on the selected tab heading. This easy and consistent navigation will help you through the customization.

Breaking down basic elements

When diving into customization, it's helpful to keep five basic concepts in mind:

- **Records** are the high-level data elements (such as accounts, contacts, and opportunities) that are stored in the Salesforce database. Each of the tabs corresponds to a type of record. Records consist of fields.

- **Page layouts** is a feature that allows you to control the way a page is displayed to users.

- **Search layouts** is a feature that allows you to control the way search results are displayed to users. Search layouts correspond to the organization of columns that are displayed on a search results page, lookup dialog page, or record home page in Salesforce.

✔ **Processes** is an option that allows you to build various sales, marketing, and service processes in Salesforce that you want your reps to follow.

✔ **Record Types** is a feature that allows you to offer certain business processes and subsets of drop-down lists to users based on their profiles. Not to be confused with a type of record (such as an account or contact), a record type, when used with page layouts and profiles, can make only some of the drop-down list values available to users within a profile.

Customizing for relevance

Prior to customizing Salesforce, your CRM project team should conduct a series of business process reviews with functional representatives or stakeholders of the teams that will be using Salesforce. In those meetings, not only should you map out current and desired processes, but you should ask sets of leading questions that will impact the design of fields, records, layouts, and more. Key questions should include

✔ How do you define your customer?

✔ What information do you want to collect on a contact?

✔ How do you know you have a qualified lead?

✔ What do you want to know about an opportunity?

Use the answers to construct a list of standard and custom fields per record that you believe should be in Salesforce. That spreadsheet should include columns for field name, field type, field values, justification, and so on, and you should review it with your project team prior to customization.

 When customizing, keep it simple at the beginning. Don't add or keep a field unless you ultimately believe that you or someone else will use it. You can always build additional fields in the future, especially if you build momentum based on early user adoption success.

Building and Editing Fields

Maybe you've heard the adage from the movie *Field of Dreams:* "If you build it, they will come." Well, when it comes to customizing Salesforce fields, the "it" stands for "something useful and easy." The more relevant you make the record fields to your actual business, the better the user adoption batting average and the higher the likelihood of hitting a usefulness home run.

Adding fields

All editions of Salesforce let you add fields, but some versions let you add significantly more fields than others. For example, if you have Team Edition, you can add 100 custom fields per record; with Enterprise and Unlimited Edition, you can create up to 500 per record.

To add a field, click the Setup link in the top-right corner of Salesforce and follow these steps:

1. **Click any tab-related heading under the Customize heading on the sidebar.**

   The options under the selected heading appear.

2. **Click the Fields link under the heading.**

   The Fields page for the tab appears, displaying a list of standard fields at the top and a list of custom fields and relationships at the bottom.

3. **Click New on the Custom Fields & Relationships related list.**

   Step 1 of the New Custom Field Wizard appears. Data types with descriptions of each of them appear in a list.

4. **Select a radio button matching the type of field you want to create and then click Next.**

   Step 2 of the wizard appears. A *field label* is what's displayed on page layouts, in reports, and to end users' eyes. A *field name* may be the exact same as a field label but may use an underline ('_') as a substitute for a space character. Field names are used as an internal reference by Salesforce and are key for integration.

5. **Enter the details and click Next.**

   Step 3 of the wizard appears. The details page varies based on the field type you selected. For example, the settings for a Text Area field are different than for a Currency field.

6. **For Enterprise or Unlimited Edition, use the check boxes to select the field level security access and edit rights per profile and then click Next.**

   Step 4 of the wizard appears.

7. **For Enterprise or Unlimited Edition, use the check boxes to select the page layouts that should include this field and then click Save.**

   The Fields page for the selected record reappears.

Viewing and updating fields

On an ongoing basis, situations come up in which you might need to update the properties of a field.

To view and update your fields, go to Setup⇨App Setup⇨Customize. Then click the Fields link under a tab heading under the Customize heading on the sidebar. The Fields page for the selected tab appears, displaying lists of standard and custom fields. From this page, you can do the following:

✔ Click the Edit link if you want to update a field.

✔ If you want to change the field type on a field, first click the Edit link, and then click the Change Type of This Field button at the bottom of the Step 2 page. Step 1 of the wizard appears, and you can follow the steps in the preceding section.

✔ Click a link in the Field Label column to view the field and its properties.

✔ Click the Del link next to a custom field if you want to delete it.

✔ If you want to add values to a drop-down list, first click the link in the Label column, and then click the New button on the Picklist Values list.

✔ If you want to replace values on a drop-down list, click the Replace link next to a field. A Find and Replace Picklist page appears. Make sure you've added the new value before trying to replace.

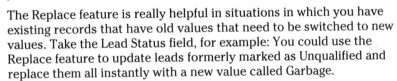

The Replace feature is really helpful in situations in which you have existing records that have old values that need to be switched to new values. Take the Lead Status field, for example: You could use the Replace feature to update leads formerly marked as Unqualified and replace them all instantly with a new value called Garbage.

✔ If you want to reorder values on a drop-down list, first click the link in the Label column, and then click the Reorder button on the Picklist Values list.

Replicating your key standard processes

On certain standard records in Salesforce, you use a standard drop-down list to map your business processes.

You'll probably want to put some careful thought into handling each type of record. To define your standard business processes, do the following:

1. **Expand the Customize menu until you see the Fields links for various records (under the Activities heading, refer to the Task Fields link).**

2. **Click a Fields link under one of the records mentioned in Step 1.**

   The Fields page appears with Standard Fields and Custom Fields & Relationships related lists.

3. **Depending on the record you chose, look on the Standard Fields related list and click the Status or Stage link to modify the corresponding processes.**

   In each circumstance, a field page appears with a Picklist Values related list, listing all of the values within the process.

4. **On the Picklist Values related list, adjust your process, as necessary.**

   See the preceding section for details on updating picklist fields.

Understanding custom formula fields

Now that you've got the hang of adding custom fields, you might want to explore some additional cool things you can do with them.

Custom formula fields are a custom field type that automatically calculate their values based on the content of other values or fields. For example, if you charge your customers a shipping and handling fee based on the total quantity of a product listed in an opportunity, create a custom formula field called S&H that multiplies your total quantity amount with a predefined value.

To create a custom formula field, first define the task at hand. What is it you want to calculate? Then follow up to Step 3 of the numbered list in the section "Adding fields," earlier in this chapter, and choose to add Formula field. Then continue with these steps:

1. **At Step 2 of creating your new custom field, provide a field label and field name.**

2. **Use the radio buttons to select the format that your returned value will take and click Next.**

   Depending on your selection, Salesforce may ask you how many decimal spaces you want your returned value to display.

3. **Type out your formula in Step 3 (as shown in Figure 20-1).**

   Salesforce displays two subtabs — Simple Formula and Advanced Formula:

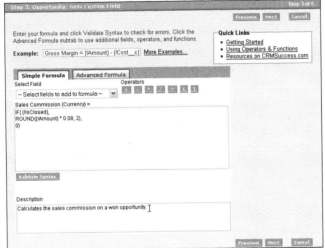

Figure 20-1:
Creating a
custom
formula.

- The Simple Formula subtab reveals a subset of merge fields to add to your formula, along with standard math operators.

- The Advanced Formula subtab reveals all possible merge fields for your record, provides more operators, and shows you a set of Excel-like function categories that you can use to plug into your formula.

4. **Click Validate when complete to make sure your formula is up to snuff.**

   If you get an error message, go back and check your formula. If no errors are found, click Next to continue.

5. **On Step 4, confirm field-level security for your new field and click Next.**

   Since it derives its content automatically, the field will be a read-only field. You just have to confirm who can see it.

6. **On Step 5, confirm which page layout you want to add this new field to. Click Save when finished.**

   The Fields page for the record reappears.

You don't have to be a math or Excel whiz to benefit from custom formula fields, though that sure can help you master it faster. If you're like the rest of us and would rather not even figure out the tip on your dinner tab, make sure you go to the Successforce Web site at www.successforce.com and download the *100 Ways to Use Custom Formula Fields* guide for a ton of suggestions on how your organization can benefit from pre-built formulas.

Adding images to records

Someone once said that a picture is worth a thousand words — image fields in Salesforce can help users identify information faster than they can read those words. Image fields are a type of custom formula field that allows you to display an image that resides in your documents folder or elsewhere. For example, image fields can be used to insert an employee photo into a user record, or they can point to a traffic light that changes based on certain conditions defined in your formula.

To create an image field, follow the instructions to create a custom formula field described in the section "Understanding custom formula fields," in this chapter, that returns text as a value and uses the IMAGE function from the Advanced Formula subtab's function list. For some tips and samples, go to www.successforce. com and search for Image Fields.

Using Custom Buttons and Links

Many sales, marketing, and support teams rely on Web sites and secure Web applications to perform their jobs. For example, your company might use a research Web site for market intelligence. By building powerful custom links that connect to important Web sites, users can use Salesforce more efficiently without having to manually open another browser window.

Salesforce lets you create custom buttons to represent your links or to perform actions that would usually take several mouse clicks to complete, such as escalating a case.

To build a custom button or link, click the Setup link in the top-right corner and follow these steps:

1. **Click any record heading under the Customize heading on the sidebar.**

   The selected heading expands.

2. **Click the Buttons & Links link under the record heading.**

   The Buttons & Links page for the selected record appears.

3. **Click the New button on the Custom Buttons and Links list.**

   The Custom Link page appears in Edit mode. Complete the fields as explained, telling Salesforce whether you're creating a button or link, and what action should occur when you click it.

4. **Click Save when finished.**

   The Custom Link page reappears.

This book doesn't go into any detail about the Force.com platform or S-controls. What you should know about S-controls is the following: If your company has specific business processes not currently addressed by Salesforce, you can use the procedural language of S-control technology to build your own application in Salesforce. S-controls combine HTML with browser-based technologies such as Java and Active-X, so you'll need to recruit some techie geeks, if this sounds foreign. But how much time could your company save if, for example, your reps could click a custom link on an opportunity page and immediately populate an order form in Salesforce? You could do that. For additional information on S-controls, go to www.salesforce.com/developer.

To display your custom links to users, you must add the new links to the appropriate page layout. See the section "Modifying a page layout," later in this chapter.

Customizing Page and Search Layouts

Wouldn't it be great if you could take the fields on a record and rearrange them like jigsaw puzzle pieces on a page until they fit just right? Sounds too good to be true, but with Salesforce, you can do just that and more.

Use page layouts to modify the position of fields, custom links, and related lists on Record detail pages and Edit pages. While you're modifying a page layout, you can also edit field properties to determine which fields should be required or read-only.

And with Enterprise and Unlimited Editions, you can create multiple page layouts and assign them to profiles. By doing this, you can ensure that different users are viewing just the right information to do their jobs.

Modifying a page layout

If you have permission to customize Salesforce, you can modify page layouts at any time. We typically recommend that you create some or the majority of your proposed custom fields first before rearranging them on the layout.

To edit a page layout, click the Setup link in the top-right corner of any Salesforce page and follow these steps:

1. **Click any tab heading under the Customize heading on the sidebar.**

   The selected heading expands with links to customization options.

2. **Click the Page Layouts link under the tab heading.**

   The Page Layout page for the selected tab appears.

3. **Click the Edit link next to a page layout that you want to modify.**

   An Edit Page Layout page appears. Choose from the following options to edit the layout:

   • To arrange fields, links, or related lists, select an option from the View drop-down list on the right-side menu, and then click and drag fields to desired locations on the layout.

   • To modify field properties, click one or multiple fields on the layout, and then click the Edit Field Properties button.

   • In the pop-up window that appears, use the check boxes to modify Read Only and Required settings and then click OK.

   • To organize the record with sections, click the Edit link on a section or click the Create New Section button.

   • In the pop-up window that appears, type a name for the section, use the drop-down lists to adjust basic settings such as columns and click OK.

      For example, on an account page layout, you might want to build a section named Strategic Account Planning to organize fields for account planning. When you click OK, the window closes.

   • To preview the layout, click the Preview button.

      A window appears with sample data displayed in the layout as you've currently modified it. In the preview window that opens, review the layout and click Close.

4. **When you're satisfied with your layout changes, click Save.**

   The Page Layout page for your selected record reappears.

Assigning layouts to profiles

After you create custom page layouts, you can assign your layouts to profiles. By doing this, users will view detail pages based on their profile and associated page layout.

To assign layouts to profiles, click the Setup link in the top-right corner of any Salesforce page and follow these steps:

1. **Click any tab heading under the Customize heading on the sidebar.**

   The selected heading expands with a menu of options.

2. **Click the Page Layouts link under the tab heading.**

   The Page Layouts page for the selected tab appears.

3. **Click the Page Layout Assignment button at the top of the Page Layouts list.**

   A Page Layout Assignment page appears with a list of current assignments.

4. **Click the Edit Assignment button.**

   The page reappears in Edit mode.

5. **In the Page Layout column, highlight one or multiple cells by clicking the links.**

   Use Ctrl+click or Shift+click to select multiple cells.

6. **From the Page Layout to Use drop-down list, choose the page layout that you want to assign to the selected profiles.**

7. **When you're done, click Save.**

   The Page Layout Assignment page reappears, displaying your changes.

Changing search layouts

If you've ever seen some search results and wished they showed a few more column headers, you're in for a treat. Search layouts allow you to determine which standard or custom fields appear as headers in three types of search features for your organization:

✔ Search results from the sidebar or advanced search

✔ Lookup dialog boxes that pop up a window when you click the Lookup magnifying glass next to a field

✔ Recent Records lists that appear in a tab's home page

Additionally, you can choose to show or hide standard and custom buttons in a list view page.

To change a search layout, follow these steps:

1. **Click any tab heading under the Customize heading on the sidebar.**

   The selected heading expands with a menu of options.

2. **Click the Search Layouts link under the tab heading.**

   The Search Layouts Page for the selected tab appears.

3. **Click the Edit link next to any of the four types of search features you'd like to change.**

The Edit Search Layout page for the chosen search feature appears.

4. **Move fields from the Available Fields column to the Selected Fields column using the Add and Remove arrows, as needed. Uncheck or check any standard or custom buttons that you'd like on your list view.**

5. **Click Save when finished.**

The Search Layouts page for the selected tab reappears.

Managing Multiple Business Processes

Configuring *multiple business processes* is particularly helpful if you have several groups of users who use a common tab (such as Leads) but whose processes are different. (And maybe the group leaders don't want to compromise.) For example, if your company has two sales teams that follow different sales methodologies, such as Miller Heiman or Solution Selling, you can use multiple business processes and keep everyone happy. Multiple business process features are available only in Enterprise and Unlimited Editions and pertain only to lead, opportunity, case, and solution records.

To set up multiple business processes, click the Setup link in the top-right corner of any Salesforce page and follow these steps:

1. **Click the Lead, Opportunity, Case, or Solution headings under the Customize heading on the sidebar.**

The selected tab headings expand.

2. **Click the Fields link under one of the selected tab headings.**

The Fields page for the selected tab appears, displaying a list of standard fields at the top and a list of custom fields at the bottom.

3. **Under the Standard Fields list, click the Edit link next to the Status or Stage field to modify the drop-down list.**

For example, on the Opportunities Fields page, you'd click the Edit link next to the Stage field.

A Picklist Edit page appears for the selected field.

4. **Review the existing values and click the New button to add additional values.**

An Add Picklist Values page appears.

5. **Add one or more values and click Save.**

The Picklist Edit page reappears.

6. **Review the list to verify that you have a complete master list of statuses or stages to support all business processes for that record.**

7. **Click the Reorder button if you want to change the order of the values.**

   The Picklist Edit page appears in Edit mode, and you can reorder the list.

8. **Use the arrow buttons to change the order of the drop-down list and click Save when you're done.**

   The Picklist Edit page reappears.

9. **On the sidebar, click the Processes link under the selected record heading.**

   For example, under the Opportunities heading, you'd click the Sales Processes link.

   The Processes page for the selected record appears.

10. **Click the New button to create a new process.**

    A Process Edit page appears.

11. **Choose the Existing Process, name the new process, and click Save.**

    A Process page appears, and you can select the values for your new business process.

    If you select Master as the Existing Process, you're able to choose from the master list generated from the Status or Stage field of the record.

12. **Highlight values and use the arrow buttons to modify your Selected Values list.**

    For example, if your company has a sales team that handles boat orders, you could create a simple sales process, as shown in the example in Figure 20-2.

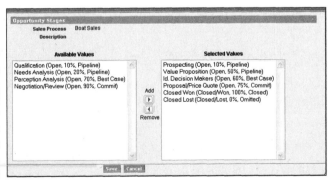

Figure 20-2:
Selecting
a subset of
values for
a custom
business
process.

13. **Choose a Default Value from the drop-down list and, when you're done, click Save.**

    The Default Value drop-down list appears for lead, case, and solution processes but not for sales processes. The Processes page for your selected record reappears.

Managing Record Types

If you're using Enterprise or Unlimited Edition, you can use record types to make subsets of drop-down lists and custom business processes available to specific sets of users. For example, if you have two sales teams, one that sells into financial services and another that sells into retail verticals, both teams might share common fields on an account record but with very different values. With record types, you can customize accounts so that the same Industry field displays retail sectors for one group and financial services verticals for the other. By providing record types to your users, the big benefit is that you make common drop-down lists easier to fill out and more relevant.

You can build record types to support all of the major records in Salesforce, including leads, accounts, opportunities, and so on. But before users can take advantage of the record type feature, you need to first create the record types and then assign them to profiles. The good news is that with Salesforce's Record Type Wizard, you can perform both actions in a series of guided steps.

 Before creating your record types, check to make sure that you've added all values to a master picklist field (drop-down list). (See the section "Viewing and updating fields," earlier in this chapter, for details on editing drop-down lists.)

To create a record type, click the Setup link in the top-right corner of any Salesforce page and follow these steps:

1. **Click any tab heading under the Customize heading on the sidebar.**

    The selected tab heading expands.

2. **Click the Record Types link under the tab heading.**

    The Record Type page for the selected tab appears.

3. **Click the New button.**

    Step 1 of the New Record Type Wizard appears.

4. **Complete the fields at the top of the page.**

   Most are obvious, but here are three important pointers:

   - Use the Existing Record Type drop-down list to clone from another record type. The new record type will inherit all the drop-down list values from the existing record type. You can then modify later.

     If you choose not to clone, the record type automatically includes the master drop-down list values for both custom and standard fields. That's okay; you can edit the drop-down lists later.

   - On a lead, opportunity, case, or solution record type, select the business process from the drop-down list. See the preceding section for details.

   - Select the Active check box if you want to make the record type active.

5. **Select the check boxes in the table to make the new record type available to different profiles.**

   If you ever need to modify the assignment of record types to profiles, you can do this from the Record Type Settings section of a profile page. Simply click the Edit link next to a record type and follow the easy steps on the page that appears. (See Chapter 19 for details on updating profile settings.)

6. **When you're done, click Next.**

   Step 2 of the wizard appears.

7. **Use the drop-down lists to select the page layout that different profiles will see for records of this record type.**

   You can apply one layout to all profiles or assign different layouts to different profiles.

8. **When you're done, click Save.**

   The new Record Type page appears with a list of the drop-down lists on the record type.

9. **Click the Edit link next to a drop-down list to modify the values.**

   A Record Type Edit page appears.

10. **Highlight values in the Available Values or Selected Values list box and use the arrow buttons to build the Selected Values list as you want it.**

11. **Select a value from the Default drop-down list, if necessary, and then click Save.**

    The Record Type page reappears.

If a user will need to make use of multiple record types, remember to add the Record Type field manually to a page layout. For example, if a sales rep sells both cars and boats (and opportunity record types exist for both), providing the Record Type field on a layout allows the rep to switch a car opportunity to a boat opportunity, if needed. See the section "Customizing Page and Search Layouts," earlier in this chapter, for details.

Creating Dependent Picklists

If you find your picklist values building up and affecting the user's experience, you should consider using dependent picklists to show values in one list based on what's selected in another list. For example, you could create a custom picklist field called Reason for your opportunity record and offer two sets of reasons, depending on whether the opportunity was won or lost.

First, your two fields must exist (see the "Adding fields" section, earlier in this chapter, to learn how to add fields). Think about which fields will dictate the drop-down list for what other fields. The field that determines another field's values is called the *controlling field* and can be a standard or custom picklist, or a check box. The field that's dependent on the controlling field to determine its displayed values is the *dependent field*.

Second, you must tell Salesforce about these two fields and their roles in this relationship. To define field dependencies, follow these steps:

1. **Expand the Customize menu until you see the Fields links under the appropriate tab (under the Activities heading, refer to Activity Custom Fields).**

   The Fields page appears.

2. **Click Field Dependencies on the Custom Fields & Relationships related list.**

   The Field Dependencies page for your record appears.

3. **Click New.**

   The New Field Dependency page appears in Edit mode.

4. **Select your controlling and dependent fields. Click Continue to determine what gets filtered.**

   A field can be dependent to just one controlling field. However, that dependent field may also act as a controlling field to daisy-chain together several dependencies.

5. **At the Edit Field Dependency page, select which dependent list items are visible for which controlling field values, and then click Include Values.**

   If your controlling field has several items in its drop-down list, you might have to hit the Next link to see additional columns. You can also select multiple values at once by using Shift+click to select a range of adjacent cells or Ctrl+click to select cells that aren't adjacent.

6. **Optionally, click the Preview button to see a pop-up window demo your dependent picklist.**

7. **Click Save when finished.**

   The Field Dependencies page returns with your new dependent picklist listed.

Record types allow certain people to see the same subset of picklist values every time. Dependent picklists allow a user to see different subsets of picklist values based on what they choose in the controlling field.

Managing Workflow & Approvals

How many times have you lost business because someone forgot to do something in your sales process? With the workflow feature in Salesforce, you can create a rule and associate it to tasks and alerts that can be assigned to different users. Enterprise and Unlimited Edition users can use workflow to automate certain standard processes to make sure important balls don't get dropped. For example, if your sales reps create opportunities that sometimes require special pricing paperwork, you can use a workflow rule to automatically send e-mail alerts and tasks to finance and sales managers, and you can set these alerts and tasks to go out a set number of hours later.

Before creating a workflow process, take a moment to understand some basic workflow concepts:

- ✔ *Workflow rules* are the criteria you set that, when triggered, tell Salesforce to assign tasks or send e-mails.

- ✔ *Workflow field updates* specify what field is updated on an object when a workflow rule is triggered.

- ✔ *Workflow tasks* are the tasks that a workflow rule assigns to users when triggered.

- ✔ *Workflow alerts* are the e-mail templates that a workflow rule sends to specific recipients. (Before creating a workflow alert, make sure you've created the e-mail template that you'll be sending out.)

- ✔ Workflow tasks and alerts may be re-used for different workflow rules.

To create a workflow process, first make sure you can fill in the blanks in this sentence: *When X happens, I want A, B, and C to happen.* Your X will be your workflow rule, and the A, B, and C actions are the field updates, tasks, and e-mail alerts. Choose Setup⇨Create⇨Workflow & Approvals to begin.

Creating workflow rules

To create a workflow rule, follow these steps:

1. **Click the Workflow Rules link under the Workflow & Approvals heading on the sidebar.**

   If this is your first time, the Understanding Workflow page appears.

2. **Click Continue after reading the overview.**

   The All Workflow Rules page appears.

3. **Click the New Rule button to create a new rule.**

   Step 1 of the Workflow Rule Wizard appears for your new rule.

4. **Select the type of object to which the workflow rule should apply.**

5. **Click Next to continue.**

   Step 2 of the Workflow Rule Wizard appears. To configure your rule, review the following steps:

   • Enter a Rule Name and optional description.

   • Decide when the rule will be evaluated by Salesforce: just when a new record is created, when the record is created or it's been edited and didn't previously meet the triggering criteria, or every time the record is created or edited.

   • Use the rule criteria to determine what conditions must be met to trigger the rule. (Use the Advanced Options for more complex AND/OR scenarios.)

6. **Click Save & Next.**

   The Specify Workflow Actions screen appears. Here, you identify what happens when the workflow criteria is met. Either an action can happen immediately, or it can happen a specific number of hours or days before or after certain criteria is met. You can create new actions (see the following section for more information) or use existing ones associated with immediate or time-based workflow triggers.

Approval processes

Approval processes are a more advanced type of workflow that notifies users when an action is triggered; requires the user to review, then approve or reject the action; and then sets off additional actions, as a result. For example, an expense report may follow one route of approvals if it's for $250 or less, and another process if it's for an amount over $10,000. Before setting forth with activating this feature for a certain record, make sure you think through the following questions:

✔ Do all records of this type absolutely require approval, or just certain ones?

✔ Who's allowed to submit records for approval?

✔ Should a record be automatically approved or rejected in certain circumstances?

✔ Should any actions take place on the record as it moves through the approval chain?

✔ Who should be able to edit records that are in the process of being approved?

✔ Who should approve or reject items? Can that person delegate that privilege to someone else, in his or her absence?

✔ What should happen when a record has received all necessary approvals?

✔ What should happen when a record has been rejected?

Although it may be nice to automatically shepherd an approval process through to the right people, make sure your business process is fairly rock solid. For example, are the bottlenecks you face today in your approval process going to disappear, be reduced, or remain if the process is automated? If Philip is the busy executive who needs to approve all the expense reports, and he doesn't manage his e-mail inbox well, you'll have to carefully set expectations about what efficiency gains you'll get with automated approvals.

If you think you have the answers and expectations set and are familiar with creating basic e-mail templates, take some baby steps by using the Jump Start Wizard for an easy practice approval process. You can get there by choosing Setup➪App Setup➪Create➪Workflow & Approvals➪Approval Processes. Select a record for which you want to create an approval process, and then from the Create New Approval Process button, select the Use Jump Start Wizard option.

Assigning workflow tasks

To create a new workflow task, first go to the workflow rule that you want to associate with this task:

1. **Go to Setup➪App Setup➪Create➪Workflow & Approvals➪Workflow Rules and click the Rule Name of the appropriate rule.**

   The Workflow Rule page for the rule appears.

2. **Click New Task from the Workflow Tasks related list.**

The Workflow Task Wizard appears. Configure the Task as you would a regular task, but note the Due Date field.

3. **Complete the Due Date field so the created Task has a due date that's a number of days relative to a base date you select in the drop-down list.**

4. **Click Save when finished.**

The Workflow Task page for this task appears. Note that the Rules Using This Workflow Task related list shows the associated workflow rule.

You can go to Setup⇨App Setup⇨ Create⇨ Workflow & Approvals⇨ Field Updates to choose what field on what object changes when a workflow rule is triggered.

Using workflow alerts

To create a new workflow alert, first go to the workflow rule that you want to associate with this task:

1. **Go to Setup⇨App Setup⇨Create⇨Workflow & Approvals⇨ Workflow Rules and click the Rule Name of the appropriate rule.**

The Workflow Rule page for the rule appears.

2. **Click New Alert from the Workflow Alerts related list.**

The Workflow Alert page appears in Edit mode. Complete the fields to associate an e-mail template with a set of recipients. Note that the recipients may be Salesforce users or not.

3. **Click Save when finished.**

The Workflow Alert page for this alert appears. Note that the Rules Using This Workflow Alert related list shows the associated workflow rule.

Chapter 21

Extending Salesforce Beyond CRM

*W*hat if you could modify your business applications in minutes to match the unique ways you manage your customer relationships? How much more productive could you be if you spent less time fighting your technology — and more time with your customers?

Force.com is Salesforce's platform for customizing and creating your on-demand applications by simply pointing-and-clicking your mouse on easy-to-use Web pages. In fact, with Force.com, you can not only customize your existing Salesforce applications, but also now build entirely new applications to fit the way you do business. If you need a little inspiration, you can also install a pre-existing solution from the AppExchange directory.

In this chapter, we demystify the Force.com platform and define some basic terms to give you a glimpse of the awesome power of creating custom apps. Then you see how you can share your creation on the AppExchange (www. appexchange.com). Finally, we offer simple and critical tips for preparing your deployment game plan.

Understanding the Force.com Platform

Force.com is salesforce.com's on-demand platform, a suite of development tools for customizing, building, integrating, and installing business applications — and you don't need to build or maintain any infrastructure yourself.

Force.com is both a platform of tools and an underlying infrastructure.

Briefly, here's some key terms to know:

- ✔ *Force.com Builder* enables you to customize existing applications or build entirely new ones.

- ✔ *Apex code* is Salesforce's procedural scripting language that allows users to create integrations between Salesforce and other systems. If you're technical, you now have the ability to create triggers, classes, and all that techno-speak stuff.

- ✔ *Visualforce* is another powerful technical capability that Salesforce provides so that you can customize the actual page design and components of your custom application. You're no longer limited to Salesforce's colors and tab layouts.

- ✔ The *AppExchange* is a directory that lets you quickly browse, try, download, and install apps that can instantly run alongside your existing Salesforce applications. Unless you're a developer (or a glutton for punishment), you don't need to know the technical ins and outs. What you do need to know is that Force.com enables Salesforce administrators to easily customize and extend their existing on-demand applications without requiring IT involvement. For building applications, which can take months with traditional software, you can point and click to quickly develop new applications in hours or days, completely integrated with your existing Salesforce CRM system.

To see all options available to you with the Force.com platform, log in to Salesforce and follow these steps:

1. **Click Setup⇨App Setup.**

   The App Setup page appears. This page highlights all the features and functionality available to help you customize, build, share, and integrate your CRM.

2. **On the sidebar menu, notice the menu items below the App Setup header.**

   This chapter focuses on the tools listed under the Create header. We cover the Customize header in Chapter 20. We've left out Develop because that's a more technical discussion, and we promised you "no code required."

Preparing Your Force.com Strategy

Force.com places so much potential at your fingertips that, like a kid in a candy store, you may have the urge to just jump in and start building custom objects and tabs — a baptism by fire. Although that method is appetizing, in theory, it's a quick way to get a stomachache. Resist that impulse until you review these simple steps for planning your strategy for on-demand applications:

1. **Define and prioritize objectives.**

   Your wish list doesn't need to be very involved, but it should spell out the who, what, when, why, and how.

2. **Build a plan.**

   With agreed-on objectives, take your project down another level and lay out a plan to address the most pressing objectives.

3. **Determine the most suitable approach.**

   You have many different ways to tackle a business issue with Force.com — some better than others.

   Here are some tips for selecting the best approach:

   • Use the community boards at the Successforce Web site (www. successforce.com) to check existing or upcoming functionality. You may not need to build a unique solution.

   • Browse the AppExchange and see whether any of the available prebuilt applications meet your general requirements.

4. **Keep it simple.**

   Don't sacrifice your objectives at the expense of simplicity — although at the beginning, simple is often better.

5. **Start with the end in mind.**

   If a custom app seems like the right strategy, figure out what it is that you want to measure.

 A great way to design your application so that it takes full advantage of relationships is to simply draw it out on a piece of paper or a whiteboard. Your design doesn't have to be fancy or complicated, but it should define the standard and custom objects you need and how they should be linked.

Creating Custom Apps with Force.com Builder

After you've sketched out the basic requirements for your new application, you're ready to begin building. A good place to start is to simply create the custom app, much like a container, before you add your objects and tabs.

Underneath the App Setup⇨ Create option in the Setup menu lies a powerful set of customization tools that can empower your business faster than the status quo of traditional software solutions.

Setting up the custom app

Many companies want internal branding for their business applications. You have to first add the logo to a public folder on the Documents tab.

To add the custom app, choose Setup⇨App Setup⇨Create and follow these steps:

1. **Click the Apps link from the sidebar.**

   The Apps page appears. You see a list of both your standard Salesforce apps, plus any custom apps you've created.

2. **Click the New button above the Apps list.**

   The first step of the New Custom App Wizard appears.

3. **In Step 1 of the wizard, enter a name and description for your app.**

   The name you type in the label field will appear on the AppExchange pull-down menu.

4. **Click Next to continue. In Step 2 of the wizard, insert a logo from your Documents tab to brand the app, if you want.**

   The logo will appear as the header whenever a user selects the custom app from the AppExchange app menu. If you don't want to brand the app, you can leave the current Salesforce-provided image.

5. **Click Next to continue. In Step 3 of the wizard, select the tabs that will make up your app.**

   You do this step by simply clicking tabs from the Available Tabs box and using the arrow buttons to create your list of Selected Tabs.

   If you haven't created all your custom tabs yet, don't worry. As you create custom tabs, you can associate them with your custom or standard apps. (For all the details, see the section "Creating custom tabs," later in this chapter.)

6. **Click Next to continue. In Step 4 of the wizard, check the boxes to assign the app to different user profiles.**

   You want to make sure that the right apps are available to the right people in your organization.

7. **When you're done, click Save.**

   The Apps page reappears, and your new custom app now appears on the list.

Building your custom objects

For a rule of thumb, you create a custom object to house a discrete set of information, different from what's contained in other standard objects. For example, an Opportunity object contains opportunity information. A Custom Expense object contains information about expenses that's unique from the typical purpose of other standard objects.

If you want to build a home, you have to add the basic building blocks first. The same analogy applies to custom apps and objects. For example, if you want to build a recruiting application, you may decide that you could use the Contacts object for applicants and need to build custom objects for Job Postings and Interview Feedback because they're distinct blocks of data.

To set up a new object, follow these steps:

1. **Choose Setup⇨App Setup⇨Create⇨Objects.**

   The Custom Objects page appears. This page, your starting point for creating an object, is where all your custom objects are displayed.

2. **Click the New Custom Object button.**

   The New Custom Object page appears.

3. **In the Custom Object Information section, type the basic details for your object.**

   You usually just need to fill out the Label and Plural Label fields. This will then automatically populate the Object Name field.

4. **Complete the Enter Record Name Label and Format fields.**

   The record name appears on page layouts, related lists, lookups, and search results. This is what you use to differentiate one record of this object from another. Depending on the type of object you're creating, you may want to switch the data type from Text to Auto Number.

   How do you know when to use text versus auto numbers?

   • If the name has some intrinsic value, stick with text.

   • If you're creating an object that will relate to other standard objects in a fundamental way, it's often better to use auto numbers.

   Auto Numbers are useful for sequenced business documents, such as invoices, purchase orders, IT tickets, and timecards.

5. **Select the custom object's optional features.**

With simple pointing-and-clicking on your part, Force.com Builder allows you to select your custom object's features that are identical to many of the features found on standard objects, such as tracking activities, allowing reporting, or allowing notes and attachments to be added.

6. **Leave the Deployment Status as In Development so only you can see it, instead of all the other Salesforce users within your company.**

It's best to make sure you can explain the business process around using the new object, before deploying it, to help guide correct adoption.

Select the Deployed button if you're ready for your users to begin using it.

7. **When you're done, check the Launch New Custom Tab Wizard box and then click Save.**

This launches the New Custom Object Tab Wizard. See the section "Adding a tab to a custom object," later in this chapter, for the how-tos on building a new tab.

If you've already mapped out the custom objects that will be part of your app, create all the objects first before modifying them. This action is especially helpful if you're building relationships between them.

Modifying custom objects

Designing your custom object is as simple as modifying a contact record or adding to a contact record's related lists. If you need to change the basic settings, simply click the Edit button at the top of the Custom Object page for the object, and the New Custom Object Wizard reappears.

If you want to customize your new object, you can point-and-click through the related lists on the page.

Keep in mind that certain Setup features — including custom profiles, multiple page layouts, record types, workflow, and field level security — are available only in Enterprise and Unlimited Editions.

Building relationships

One primary reason for building applications with Force.com Builder is to create a single, integrated, one-stop shopping experience for your users.

The key to those linkages is building custom relationships between objects. For example, if your company wants to manage account planning in

Salesforce, you want to create a relationship between the standard Account object and a custom object for the Account Plan.

To build a relationship, follow these steps:

1. **Choose Setup➪App Setup➪Create➪Objects.**

   The All Custom Objects page appears.

2. **Click the desired custom object under the Label column.**

   The Custom Object page appears.

3. **Click the New button on the Custom Fields & Relationships related list (see Figure 21-1).**

   The New Custom Field page appears.

Custom Fields & Relationships	New	Field Dependencies			Custom Fields & Relationships Help
Action	**Field Label**	**Data Type**	**Controlling Field**	**Modified By**	
Edit | Del	Account	Lookup(Account)		Liz Kao, 3/27/2008 7:07 PM	
Edit | Del	Contact	Lookup(Contact)		Liz Kao, 3/27/2008 7:07 PM	
Edit | Del	Days Remaining	Formula (Number)		Liz Kao, 3/27/2008 7:07 PM	
Edit | Del	Opportunity	Lookup(Opportunity)		Liz Kao, 3/27/2008 7:07 PM	
Edit | Del	Project Duration	Formula (Number)		Liz Kao, 3/27/2008 7:07 PM	
Edit | Del	Project End Date	Date		Liz Kao, 3/27/2008 7:07 PM	
Edit | Del	Project Manager	Lookup(User)		Liz Kao, 3/27/2008 7:07 PM	
Edit | Del	Project Name	Text(80)		Liz Kao, 3/27/2008 7:07 PM	
Edit | Del | Replace	Project Stage	Picklist		Liz Kao, 3/27/2008 7:07 PM	
Edit | Del	Project Start Date	Date		Liz Kao, 3/27/2008 7:07 PM	
Edit | Del | Replace	Project Status	Picklist		Liz Kao, 3/27/2008 7:07 PM	
Edit | Del	Status Description	Text Area(255)		Liz Kao, 3/27/2008 7:07 PM	

Figure 21-1: Creating a new custom field or relationship.

4. **In Step 1 of the wizard, choose the type of relationship with another object.**

   AppExchange supports two types of custom relationships: Master-Detail and Lookup. They're both one-to-many relationships.

   The two relationships look the same in the user interface — as a lookup field with a magnifying glass on the record side and as a related list on the related object.

   But here are two big differences:

   - Master-Detail relationships cause the cascade deletion of child records to occur when the parent record is deleted. For example, if you delete an account, all related records are also deleted.

   - In a Master-Detail relationship, the detail record inherits the Owner and sharing rules of the master record. Detail objects are dependent on their masters. In Lookup relationships, they don't transfer sharing rules — they're completely independent.

   When you're in doubt, start with the Lookup option.

5. **Click Next to continue. In Step 2 of the wizard, select the other object that you want to relate your object to.**

   You can create as many as five Lookup relationships with a custom object.

6. **Click Next to continue. In Step 3 of the wizard, enter the label for the lookup field.**

   As a default, Force.com Builder pre-fills the fields with the name of the object you selected, although you can change it.

7. **Click Next to continue. If you have Enterprise or Unlimited Edition, set the field level security in Step 4 of the wizard.**

   If you chose the Master-Detail option, the security is set for you because it's locked to the profile. If you chose the simple Lookup option, simply select the appropriate check boxes to control visibility and edit rights to the field.

8. **Click Next to continue. If you have Enterprise or Unlimited Edition, in Step 5 of the wizard, select the page layouts in which you want to display the field.**

   Suppose that you're creating an expense application. You may want the rep's layout to be different from the manager's layout.

9. **Click Next to continue. In Step 6 of the wizard, uncheck the boxes if you don't want the custom object to appear on the related list of the selected object.**

   For example, if you're linking expenses with accounts, you may not want a long list of expenses showing up on an account record.

10. **When you're done, click Save.**

    The Custom Object page reappears, and your custom relationship is displayed on the Custom Fields & Relationships related list.

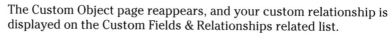 Build your relationships before loading any actual data.

Remember that between two objects, you can have only one object that allows the Master-Detail relationship, so the other object has to be a Lookup relationship.

Creating fields

With Force.com Builder, you can quickly add fields to your custom object, much like you can with a standard object, such as an account or a contact. See Chapter 20 for more information on creating custom fields.

Adding custom links

Adding custom links to an object can be a powerful way to extend your solution to a business issue. You can build custom links for custom objects, too. See Chapter 20 for more information on creating custom links.

Changing layouts

After or as you build out fields, feel free to start rearranging the page layout for the object record. Often, that's one of the easiest ways to get a pulse on what's missing from your record. See Chapter 20 for more information on editing page layouts.

Customizing related lists

After you've added your Lookup relationships and custom fields, you're ready to start customizing your related lists! Force.com Builder allows you to modify the columns that are displayed on a related list.

Don't forget this step — without customizing this section, your users don't see much on a related list. But if you add the right columns, the related list becomes a powerful tool for your users. By customizing the columns displayed on a related list, users can quickly see a summary of relevant information from a record's detail page. See Chapter 20 for more information on customizing related lists.

Creating custom tabs

With Force.com Builder, you can create two types of custom tabs: custom object tabs and Web tabs. They look just like the standard tabs your users already use, and you can build the tabs in less than a minute — piece o' cake.

Adding a tab to a custom object

If you read through the section "Building your custom objects," earlier in this chapter, you've probably already built a custom tab. Sometimes, however, you build a custom object and decide later to add the tab.

Don't over-tab your application if it's not necessary. Ask yourself: "Will my users need all the object's data available from a central area?" If the answer is yes, you may need a custom tab.

To build a custom tab, follow these steps:

1. **Choose Setup➪App Setup➪Create➪Tabs.**

   The Custom Tabs page appears.

2. **Click New on the Custom Objects Tab related list.**

Step 1 of the New Custom Object Tab Wizard appears.

3. **In Step 1 of the wizard, select the object from the picklist, and then use the Lookup icon to choose a tab style.**

The tab style affects both the color of the tab and the icon associated with a custom object record under Recent Items.

4. **In Step 2 of the wizard, select the desired tab visibility for your user profiles.**

With the radio button feature, you can control tab visibility to your profiles.

5. **In Step 3 of the wizard, select the apps to which the new custom tab will be available.**

This step makes it simple to associate custom tabs with just the right apps for your users.

6. **When you're done, click Save.**

The Custom Tabs page reappears with your new custom tab listed.

Building a Web tab

In the normal course of a day, your users frequent other Web sites as part of their jobs. Here are just a few examples:

✔ Access the intranet

✔ Arrange travel plans

✔ Use an internal Web-based application

The list goes on. Why not make it easier for users to get to your business-related sites? With Force.com, you can build Web tabs that access Web applications and S-controls.

We don't go into the details of S-controls because they require coding, but imagine that you have a particular form to which your teams are emotionally attached (a client profile form with four columns, for example). With an S-control and the help of an experienced developer, you can display your data in Salesforce in unique formats (and keep everyone happy). To manage S-controls, choose Setup⇨App Setup⇨Develop⇨S-Controls.

To create a simple Web tab, follow these steps:

1. **Choose Setup⇨App Setup⇨Create⇨Tabs.**

The Custom Tabs page appears.

2. **Click the New button on the Web Tabs related list.**

Step 1 of the New Web Tab Wizard appears.

3. **In Step 1 of the wizard, click a button to select a layout.**

4. **In Step 2, define the content and properties.**

   In this example, we show you how to create a URL-based Web tab for news labeled Company News.

5. **In Step 3 of the wizard, enter a URL and add any additional merge fields.**

   Embedding merge fields is easy, after you get the hang of it. For example, this URL is the standard search results URL from Yahoo News:

```
http://search.news.yahoo.com/search/
        news/?p=salesforce&c=
```

   We copied and pasted the URL in the box. Then we used the merge field tool for `{!Org_Name}` and put that in place of `salesforce` in the URL.

6. **In Step 4, click the drop-down lists to control which user profiles can access the tab and then click Save.**

Sharing Apps on the AppExchange

As customers, employees, and partners began building custom applications (or *apps*), some bright person came up with an idea: Wouldn't it be great if other customers like you could simply try out, download, and install these custom apps without having to build them on their own? iTunes uses the Web to distribute music — why shouldn't enterprise applications work the same way?

Enter the AppExchange, a Web site owned and operated by salesforce.com, where you can try out, download, and install in minutes applications that can extend the value of Salesforce to meet your unique needs. And you can not only install with the AppExchange, but also use the AppExchange to share your custom apps.

Of course, the biggest benefit beyond how much easier your life will be is the impact on your users. The AppExchange directory isn't just about easy sharing — it's about your employees using integrated business apps with all your information in one place.

Customers, partners, and salesforce.com personnel can all provide the AppExchange with applications. Many of them, particularly the ones published by salesforce.com employees, are free to install and use. Others, such as the ones provided by partners, may have a fee associated with them.

Browsing the AppExchange

Downloading music from the Web seemed revolutionary just a few years ago, and now we take it for granted. But downloading enterprise apps? Wow, that seems like a whole 'nother animal.

Yet, when you get down to it, the AppExchange is still about the exchange of a package of goods from one party to another. As with many innovations, getting the most out of a new system usually amounts to understanding some basic terms and knowing your limits before jumping in.

Here are five key things you should know before you get started:

- ✔ *Installation* is the process by which you download, install, and deploy a custom app from the AppExchange.

- ✔ *Sharing* is the process by which you package a portion of your customizations and make them available, either publicly or privately, on the AppExchange.

- ✔ Although anyone can try out the AppExchange, to install and share apps, you must have a Salesforce instance and have administrative rights to that instance. (Did I just hear a sigh of relief?)

- ✔ You can exchange many types of AppExchange components, not just custom apps, on the AppExchange. You can exchange custom links, dashboards, S-controls, and more.

- ✔ Some apps are self-contained, or *native,* in Salesforce. They were built with Force.com Builder and don't depend on other external applications. Other custom apps are *composite.* Such apps may look and feel like Salesforce apps but connect with other services not owned by salesforce.com. *Caveat emptor* (let the buyer beware).

You should familiarize yourself with the AppExchange at www.salesforce.com/appexchange first, and then try out some apps before you decide whether you want to use them.

Installing AppExchange apps

If you want to install a custom prebuilt app, you can do it in a matter of simple clicks. This process amounts to first downloading the package, installing the app into your instance of Salesforce, and deploying it to all or a portion of your users.

A *package* in the AppExchange refers to all the components that comprise the custom app. A package may include custom tabs and objects and also custom links, custom profiles, reports, dashboards, documents, and more.

To install an AppExchange app, follow these steps:

1. **Click the Get It Now button on the app's detail page in AppExchange.**

   The Install page for the custom app appears, requesting your Salesforce login. This is the first step in the Install Wizard.

2. **In Step 1 of the wizard, enter your user name and password for the Salesforce instance in which the app should be installed, check the box after reviewing the terms, and then click Continue.**

   The Examine Package Contents page appears.

   If you're experimenting with the AppExchange for the first time, you may want to consider using the Sandbox Edition or a free Developer Edition instance to install, customize, and test the custom app.

3. **In Step 2 of the wizard, examine the package contents, then click Next.**

   This page summarizes the custom app's details, including objects, tabs, reports, and dashboards.

   Make sure that you examine the contents of a package thoroughly before proceeding.

4. **In Step 3 of the wizard, select a radio button to choose the security settings and click Next to continue.**

   As with other download wizards (for example, AOL and RealMedia), this AppExchange wizard allows you to choose either standard or custom security settings to meet your comfort level. We recommend you choose the Select Security Settings option to start.

5. **After choosing the Select Security Settings option, a Customize Security page appears, in which you can specify the level of access for each profile.**

   The access levels here determine the layout assignments, field-level security, and other fun stuff such as editing permissions for the custom objects in the package. Access levels set here don't affect those of any existing objects you have.

   Any standard profiles will have full access to custom objects in this package since permissions aren't editable for them. The only exception is the Read-Only profile, which will still maintain (duh) read-only permissions.

6. **Click Next to continue. In the last step of the wizard, click the Install button on the Install Package page.**

   A progress page appears as installation begins. An Install Complete page appears after the installation finishes. Bet your traditional software can't create a whole new app that fast!

7. **Click the OK button.**

At this point, you can choose to deploy the app immediately to users or further customize it first. We suggest you click the OK button to confirm the download and begin prepping some dummy data before you deploy this to users.

The AppExchange download page for your newly downloaded custom app appears. It shows the package contents. If you check out the upper-right corner, you'll notice that the AppExchange app menu now contains a listing for your new app.

Now that you've installed the app, you can use Force.com Builder to modify its tabs, objects, and other customizations, just as though you had built the custom app yourself. Remember that even though you've installed the app, it's not available to non-administrators until it's deployed.

Chapter 22

Migrating and Maintaining Your Data

*I*f you're a system administrator, often your greatest headache isn't configuring or customizing the system, but getting your data in and maintaining it so that it's useful. Nothing hurts a rollout more than complaints from users that their customer data isn't in Salesforce, that information is duplicated in several records, or that the information is wrong. And your end user adoption suffers if you don't maintain your records after the rollout. If you're not diligent, you can find yourself in the same mess that drove you to Salesforce in the first place.

If data maintenance is giving you nightmares, use the data management tools in Salesforce to easily import leads, accounts, and contacts. If you have in-house expertise or engage Salesforce's professional services, you can migrate other critical data (such as opportunities, cases, and activities) by using proven third-party tools. And when your data is stored in Salesforce, you can rely on a variety of tools to help you manage and maintain your database.

In this chapter, we first discuss your options for data import. Then we show you how to use Salesforce tools to manage your data (including mass-transferring, deleting, and reassigning data). Finally, we touch on some advanced concepts. Complex data migration and updates of data between your data sources and Salesforce is beyond the scope of this book, but we make sure to point you in the right direction.

Understanding Your Options for Data Migration

Salesforce has easy-to-use wizards that step you through importing your campaign updates, leads, accounts, and contacts. If you're a system administrator or have the right profile permissions, you can perform these tasks for your users. For other legacy data that you want in Salesforce, such as opportunities, cases, and activities, you have to enter information manually or use the Data Loader, an included ETL (extract, transform, and load) tool for Enterprise and Unlimited Edition administrators to automatically migrate desired data into Salesforce. Professional and Team Edition users can enlist the help of salesforce.com professional services.

Using import wizards

Import wizards for leads, accounts, contacts, solutions, and custom objects are conveniently located under the Data Management heading in the Administration Setup section of Setup. If you're an administrator, you also see links to the import wizards in the Tools section of certain tab home pages. For example, if you want to import your company's leads, click the Leads tab, and then click the Import Leads link in the Tools section. Steps and tips for each of the import wizards are detailed in relevant chapters of this book, as follows:

- ✔ To **import leads,** see Chapter 8. Only a user with the Import Leads permission can perform this operation.

- ✔ To **import contacts and accounts,** see Chapter 4 and Chapter 5. Salesforce provides you one wizard that can take you through importing contacts and/or accounts. Individual users also have the ability to import their personal contacts and accounts.

- ✔ To **import campaign leads** or **update contacts or leads linked to a campaign,** see Chapter 12.

Investigating the Data Loader

Data migration is a tricky matter. The Data Loader is a small client application that helps bulk import or export data in comma-separated value (.csv) format. You access this tool from Setup⇨Administrative Setup⇨Data Management⇨Data Loader. Now, with this tool, you can move data into and out of any type of record in Salesforce, including opportunities and custom objects. The Data Loader supports inserting, updating, deleting, and extracting Salesforce records.

Several vendors also provide proven ETL or integration tools that enable you to migrate records to (or from) Salesforce and append those records where appropriate.

Without getting too technical, the experts link data by using something called the Force.com API (application program interface) to enable your technical resource to access data programmatically. Force.com (`www.salesforce.com/developer`) is the platform used to customize or integrate Salesforce to do even snazzier things than what you can do with it out of the box. What's a platform? Think of it as a collection of rules and commands that programmers can use to tell Salesforce to do certain things. To access the Force.com API, you must have Enterprise or Unlimited Edition.

Migrating Your Legacy Data

During the preparation phase of your implementation, you need to have a well thought out and documented plan for your data migration strategy. That plan needs to include details on objectives, resources, contingencies, and timelines based on the different steps in your plan. In the following sections, we discuss some of the steps that you should consider.

Determining your data sources

The average companies we've worked with typically have some type of existing contact management tool, a variety of spreadsheets with other customer data, and often contact information living in users' Microsoft Outlook applications. (Not to mention Word documents and sticky notes.) As you go through your preparation, assess what and how much information needs to be in Salesforce. Here are some tips for this step:

- ✔ Garbage in, garbage out. When you move into a new home, you usually look through your old home's closets and decide what to haul with you and what to throw away. Moving data requires the same type of evaluation.

- ✔ Catalog the different data sources, what types of records, what range, and how many.

- ✔ Work with your customer relationship management (CRM) project team to determine where different information should go and why.

✔ Think about the timing and the sequence of the import. For example, many companies create user records first, then import accounts and contacts, and finally migrate and append opportunities.

✔ Keep it simple, if possible. The more complicated you make the migration, the greater the impact on your timeline. Assess the level of effort versus the potential value of the effort.

Preparing your data

Clean it now or clean it later. Some project teams like to scrub data before importing it into Salesforce. Others prefer to bring all the records in and then utilize Salesforce's data management tools to clean it up later. Regardless of when you do it, cleaning data is not glamorous work, but it's gotta be done.

Here are a few tips as you prepare your data:

✔ Oftentimes, it's easiest to export data to tools such as Microsoft Access or Excel, which let you delete columns, sort rows, and make global changes.

✔ Strive for standard naming conventions. For example, if different data sources refer to accounts by different names (IBM versus International Business Machines), now is a good time to standardize naming.

✔ Edit or add fields in Salesforce to support the migration. For instance, if your pipeline reports track margin per opportunity, you need to build a custom Opportunity field to support margin data.

✔ If your existing data source has unique record IDs, migrate those IDs to a custom field. You can always delete or hide the field at a later stage. Not only can this help you verify the accuracy of your migration, but those IDs might come in handy for integration (especially if you don't plan to shut down the other data source).

✔ Map your data columns to field names in Salesforce. For example, the Company field in Microsoft Outlook typically maps to the Account field in Salesforce. Some system administrators even rename the column headers in migration files so that they exactly match field names in Salesforce. Doing this minimizes the migration madness.

✔ Conform your data to fit Salesforce standards (or the other way around). Each field in Salesforce has certain properties that might include size limitations, decimal points, date formats, and so on.

✔ Add a Data Source column to your import file and map it to a custom field in Salesforce. By doing this, you can defend where data came from.

✔ Wherever possible, assign the correct owners to records. If you don't have all records assigned, the owner defaults to whichever administrator is executing the migration.

✔ Gain acceptance from stakeholders of the files you've prepared. At least, if you offer them the chance to review, you avoid surprises.

Testing the import

Test before you execute the final migration. Often, you discover things that you missed or could improve. Here are a couple of tips:

✔ Select a small sample of significant records. The more high-profile the records, the better — especially when reviewed by a stakeholder.

✔ Consider adjusting the page layouts to make validating the data import easier.

Analyzing the test data results

When your test data is in Salesforce, compare it carefully with your test file to ensure accuracy and completeness. Here are a few tips on how to productively analyze the test data results:

✔ **Build:** Build a custom report that lets you look at the record data collectively.

✔ **Compare:** Open a record, if necessary, and compare it against the import file. Confirm that the record's fields show what you think they should show.

✔ **View:** Build a custom view from a relevant tab home page to see your imported data laid out in columns on a list page. Users could go to a report, but a view keeps them focused.

✔ **Validate:** Validate the data with selected stakeholders to get their feedback and support that the test data results look correct. It's not enough that you think the test import was accurate. Your end users are the ultimate test.

✔ **Tweak:** Adjust your process, or make changes to the import file or Salesforce, based on the results of the test import. For example, maybe you forgot to map a field, or the data didn't import correctly because of a field's properties.

Migrating your final data

After you successfully analyze the test data results, you're ready to import your file or files. (Yes, that's a simplification of what could be a complicated set of tasks, but the overall process is tried and true.)

Here are a few suggestions for this step:

- ✔ Communicate expectations with your users. If you're cutting over from one system to another, you might have a lapse in which data must be updated prior to going live.

- ✔ If you have significant data, consider running the migration during non-working hours. Especially if the system is live for some groups of users already, this might avoid confusion.

- ✔ Build yourself some cushion for error. Don't try to execute the migration the day before sales training. You never know whether something unanticipated might happen that prevents successful completion.

Validating your data

Similar to analyzing results of the test data (see the section "Analyzing the test data results," earlier in this chapter), when the data has been loaded, run reports to validate a cross-sampling of records to ensure accuracy and completeness. Strive for perfectly imported data, but expect less than that, too.

Augmenting your data

Prior to rolling out Salesforce, take the extra step of manually or automatically updating some records to wow users and drive more success.

Managing Your Salesforce Database

After you implement Salesforce, you need to make sure that you create processes for periodically updating and backing up your data. If you don't, human error can lead to frustration and heartache. Duplicate records, dead leads, records that need to be transferred when a user leaves the company — these are just a few examples of data that needs to be updated.

Most of the data maintenance tools are accessible from the Data Management heading located under the Administrative Setup heading on the sidebar of Setup. (See Chapters 4, 5, and 8 for details on de-duplicating accounts, contacts, and leads.)

Backing up your data

If you have Unlimited, Enterprise, or Professional Edition, Salesforce offers a weekly export service of all your data.

To export your data, follow these steps:

1. **Go to Setup⇨Administration Setup⇨Data Management⇨and then click the Data Export link.**

   The Weekly Export Service: Schedule Export page appears.

2. **Select the appropriate export file encoding from the Export File Encoding drop-down list and select the check boxes if you want to include attachments and replace carriage returns with spaces.**

   If you live in the United States or Western Europe, you don't have to change the Export File Encoding selection.

3. **When you're done, click the Data Export button.**

   The Weekly Export Service: Export Requested page appears. You'll receive an e-mail from Salesforce with a link to a page where you can retrieve zipped `.csv` files of all your data. You have 48 hours to download your data, after which time the data files are deleted.

4. **When you receive the e-mail entitled Your Organization Data Export Has Been Completed, click the title to open the e-mail.**

   The e-mail appears with a link to the page in which you can retrieve your data export.

5. **Click the link and log in to Salesforce, if required.**

   The Weekly Export Service page appears, as shown in Figure 22-1. You can also access the Weekly Export Service page through Setup⇨ Application Setup⇨Data Management⇨Data Export.

6. **Click the Click Here to Download This File link.**

   A dialog box appears, allowing you to open or save your Zip file to a location accessible from your computer.

Weekly Export Service Data Export File Delivery	Help for this Page [?]

Data Export

Scheduled By	Admin User
Schedule Date	8/22/2006 12:33 PM
Export File Encoding	ISO-8859-1 (General US & Western European, ISO-LATIN-1)

File Name	WE_00Dx00000001JhPEAU_1.ZIP
File Size	30 KB
	Click here to download this file

Figure 22-1:
Accessing
your data
export file.

Mass-transferring records

A sales rep leaves. Sales territories get readjusted. You imported a file but forgot to assign records to the right owners in advance. These are just a few examples of when you might have to transfer records. Salesforce allows you to mass-transfer lead or account records, and the two processes are very similar.

When transferring leads or accounts, Salesforce automatically transfers certain linked records on the detail page. For both leads and accounts, all open activities transfer to the new owner. For accounts, all notes, contacts, and open opportunities owned by the existing owner transfer to the new owner.

To mass-transfer lead or account records, follow these steps:

1. **Click Setup⇨Application Setup⇨Data Management⇨Mass Transfer Records.**

   A Mass Transfer Records page appears.

2. **Click the Transfer link for the appropriate type of record, depending on your needs.**

   A Mass Transfer page appears with a set of filtering tools to help you search for records.

3. **In the Transfer From and Transfer To fields, use the Lookup icons to find the appropriate users.**

   Note that with leads, you can also transfer to or from queues. See Chapter 8 for details on lead queues.

4. **If you're mass-transferring accounts, select the check boxes to specify whether you want to transfer types of opportunities, cases, and teams.**

5. **Define additional criteria to filter your search by using the drop-down lists and fields provided.**

   You do this by selecting a field in the first drop-down list, selecting an operator in the second drop-down list, and typing a value in the field. For example, if you want to transfer all of one sales rep's New York City accounts to a new rep, your criteria would be City Equals New York.

6. **When you're satisfied with your settings and filters, click the Find button.**

   The Mass Transfer page reappears with a list of results.

7. **Use the check boxes to select the records that you want to transfer.**

8. **When you're done, click the Transfer button.**

   The Mass Transfer page reappears when the transfer is complete.

Mass-deleting records

If you're the administrator, on various occasions, you might want or need to mass-delete records. A couple of typical examples include deleting dead leads and eliminating accounts that haven't had any activity. Salesforce allows you to mass-delete leads, accounts, contacts, activities, and products, and the processes are very similar.

To mass-delete records, follow these steps:

1. **Click Setup⇨Administration Setup⇨Data Management⇨Mass Delete Records.**

   The Mass Delete Records page appears.

2. **Click one of the Mass Delete links, depending on the type of standard record you wish to mass-delete.**

   The Mass Delete Records page appears with a three- to five-step wizard for mass-deleting. The three-step wizard is shown in Figure 22-2. Mass Delete Accounts has two extra steps based on opportunities that are closed/won or that aren't owned by you. Mass Delete Products has one extra step to archive products with line items on opportunities.

3. **Review the Salesforce warnings in Step 1 of the wizard.**

4. **Back up relevant data by generating a report and exporting it to Excel as part of Step 2 of the wizard.**

   See Chapter 17 for details on building and exporting reports.

5. **Use the filters in Step 3 of the wizard to define criteria for the search.**

   You do this by selecting a field in the first drop-down list, selecting an operator in the second drop-down list, and typing a value in the field.

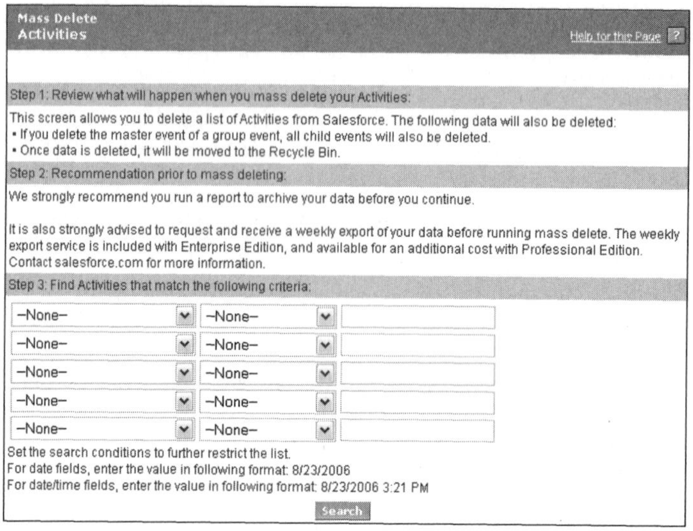

Figure 22-2:
Selecting
records
for mass-
deletion.

Mass Delete
Activities   Help for this Page ?

Step 1: Review what will happen when you mass delete your Activities:

This screen allows you to delete a list of Activities from Salesforce. The following data will also be deleted:
• If you delete the master event of a group event, all child events will also be deleted.
• Once data is deleted, it will be moved to the Recycle Bin.

Step 2: Recommendation prior to mass deleting:

We strongly recommend you run a report to archive your data before you continue.

It is also strongly advised to request and receive a weekly export of your data before running mass delete. The weekly export service is included with Enterprise Edition, and available for an additional cost with Professional Edition. Contact salesforce.com for more information.

Step 3: Find Activities that match the following criteria:

–None–   –None–
–None–   –None–
–None–   –None–
–None–   –None–
–None–   –None–

Set the search conditions to further restrict the list.
For date fields, enter the value in following format: 8/23/2006
For date/time fields, enter the value in following format: 8/23/2006 3:21 PM

Search

6. **Click the Search button.**

   The Mass Delete page reappears with a list of possible records at the bottom of the page. Do the following:

   • If you're mass-deleting accounts, select the check box in Step 4 of the wizard if you want to delete accounts that have Closed/Won opportunities.

   • If you're mass-deleting accounts, select the check box to delete accounts with another owner's opportunities.

   • If you're mass-deleting products, select the check box if you want to archive products with line items on opportunities.

7. **Use the Action column to select records to be deleted.**

8. **When you're satisfied, click the Delete button.**

   A dialog box appears to confirm the deletion.

9. **Click OK.**

   The Mass Delete page reappears, minus the records that you deleted.

Getting Help with Complex Data Tasks

This chapter shows you some of the basic operations that you can perform to import and manage your data in Salesforce. For many companies that have complex data needs, this might be an oversimplification. If you need help with your data, here are some resources you can turn to:

✔ Talk with your Customer Success Manager or account rep. They can help define your needs and point you to the appropriate solution or resource.

✔ If you're looking for some outside help, contact salesforce.com's professional services team. Your Customer Success Manager or account rep can put you in touch.

✔ Check out offerings by partners on the AppExchange. Go to www. appexchange.com and choose the Data Cleansing subcategory under either the Sales or Marketing categories.

✔ On the AppExchange Developer Network, www.salesforce.com/ developer, click the Discussion Boards tab to talk to a community of developers who have wrestled or are familiar with your data challenges. These boards are of a technical nature, but if this is what you're looking for, you might find it here.

Part VIII
The Part of Tens

The 5th Wave   By Rich Tennant

"It's your wife Mr. Dinker. Shall I have her take a seat in the closet, or do you want to schedule a meeting in the kitchen for later this afternoon?"

In this part . . .

The Part of Tens is a standard for all *For Dummies* books. We use this part to highlight certain lists that deserve a special place.

Anyone can have a tough time keeping up to speed with all the feature releases from salesforce.com. That's the aspect of an on demand application that keeps us authors on our toes. In the first list, we discuss ten great productivity tools worth their weight in gold. In the second list, we detail ten keys to a successful implementation. If you're an administrator, this is a must see.

Chapter 23

Ten Ways to Drive More Productivity

In This Chapter

▶ Resources for users and administrators

▶ Tools that you shouldn't overlook

Salesforce.com drives much of their feature updates based on their existing roadmap and requests from customers just like you. A few times a year, salesforce.com comes out with a new release of their award-winning service. Unlike traditional software upgrades, these releases are immediately available to all customers depending, of course, on which edition they use.

Keeping track of all the cool new updates that salesforce.com releases can get a little overwhelming. The speed with which they're able to roll out releases is often barely faster than our ability to write all about it and get it in print to you! On the flip side, perhaps you do keep track of the newest features but have been struggling with an apparent feature limitation or would like more advice on how to best implement a particular feature.

Fortunately for us, both salesforce.com and its community of users strongly believe in helping each other out in order to make every customer success-ful. Through a variety of channels, the salesforce.com community shares best practices and offers suggestions and workarounds for even the toughest, head-scratcher questions.

In this chapter, we summarize five essential resources that every user in your organization should know about. Then we cover five great productivity tools that you might have overlooked.

Finding the Top Five Resources

Salesforce.com realizes that first you have to have healthy business processes before applying any type of CRM solution to them. Combine that with providing information at its customers' fingertips, and you have several resources available to you when you want to talk about all things Salesforce. In addition to providing "how do I do this?" answers, salesforce.com also focuses on topics covering your business processes to address the "why would I want to do this?" question. Here, we highlight five resources that can make a big difference in informing you and your organization about the hows and whys of Salesforce features:

- ✔ **Successforce Best Practices Web site (http://success.salesforce.com):** Whether you're an administrator or end user, bookmark this Web site now. Here you'll find a wealth of best practices information contributed by product experts. Look under the Guides tab to learn more about implementing Salesforce, as well as more information about certain existing and upcoming features.

- ✔ **Salesforce IdeaExchange (http://ideas.salesforce.com):** The IdeaExchange is a forum in which you can recommend new product ideas, see what other users are requesting, and vote for the ideas most important to you. Not only do you get to see what the masses are clamoring for, but you also get to see salesforce.com employees, partners, and customers providing feedback in the IdeaExchange's forums. Then, even more satisfying, salesforce.com's product managers listen to everyone who posts and mark which features have been rolled into new releases.

- ✔ **Salesforce.com local user groups:** One of the best ways to learn about upcoming features, network with your peers, and provide product feedback is to join a local user group. You'll get to learn from and share tips with fellow customers in your vicinity. From Successforce, click the Community tab. Look on the sidebar for the Local User Groups section and drill down to see the participating cities. If you don't see your city, think about starting one!

- ✔ **Salesforce.com knowledge base:** Chances are that if you have a quick question about how to do something in Salesforce, someone else has asked it, too. For access to concise answers, search salesforce.com's own knowledge base for solutions. Click the Help & Training link in the upper-right corner after you've logged in to Salesforce. Once a pop-up window appears, type some keywords relevant to your question into the search box. You'll see suggested solutions and related help topics for your question.

✔ **Salesforce.com Online Help topics:** Finally, if you're working in Salesforce and get stuck with a question, look for a Help for This Page link on that page. Clicking that link opens up a new help window that's context sensitive.

Revisiting Five Great Productivity Tools

Few companies make use of every feature when they first deploy Salesforce to their employees. It would be overwhelming to absorb, and you know that success is a function of end user adoption. So if you're like other CRM project teams, you tend to focus on addressing the core business objectives that often include lead, account, and opportunity management.

If this sounds like you, the following list includes five tools that we'd like to remind you about. Give yourself time to set these up — you can substantially boost adoption and productivity, depending on your objectives:

✔ **The AppExchange (www.salesforce.com/appexchange):** "If only we could use Salesforce to do this . . . " Sound familiar? Well, your business pain may be someone else's, as well. Someone may have already built a solution for it. Head on over to the AppExchange directory to see if a custom app or component already exists that can help you out.

✔ **Outlook Edition:** Corporate e-mail and calendaring systems aren't going away anytime soon. Everyone in your company uses them, while oftentimes, only a subset of your employees are using Salesforce. With Outlook Edition, your Salesforce users who live in both applications can reduce their administrative time by synchronizing information between them.

✔ **Online lead or case forms:** This is a classic feature in Salesforce that every customer should roll out. Capturing lead or case information via a form helps maintain consistency of your data, which will help you increase the accuracy of your reporting. Whether you roll this out in the first phase of your implementation is up to you, but it should be high on your list. See Chapter 12 for Web-to-Lead or Chapter 16 for Web-to-Case details.

✔ **Self-Service Portal:** Help your customers help themselves. This is one tried and true method of delivering great service and managing the workload in your support center. But how do you build a secure customer portal and quickly tie it in with your CRM application? With the Self-Service Portal, you can do this in hours, rather than weeks. To launch a Self-Service Portal, see Chapter 16 for more information.

✔ **E-mail templates:** This is a simple feature that can save your reps and marketing staff a ton of time. You no longer have to dig up an old e-mail, copy and paste it into a message, and scour the text for places where you should replace the old customer's name. E-mail templates are easy to set up and help you send out professional-looking HTML or text e-mails that are personalized to your contacts. We cover this in the Bonus Chapter on the Web site, and you should create a few so your reps can begin using them on day one.

Chapter 24

Ten Keys to a Successful Implementation

Several companies have rolled out customer relationship management (CRM) applications with the mistaken notion that you can buy the licenses, turn on the switch, and use the application as soon as you take it out of the box. Then these same companies look back months later and wonder why they're not experiencing the results they envisioned.

Nine out of ten times, the root cause is poor planning. No matter what size your implementation, building a strong plan and then executing the plan will substantially improve your chance of success.

Salesforce provides you the tools and a platform to enhance your business effectiveness and productivity. If you're involved in the rollout of Salesforce, this chapter gives you ten tips to help you do it successfully. Check out the Guides section of the Successforce Best Practices Web site (`http://success.salesforce.com`) for more tips on leading a successful rollout.

Identifying Your Executive Sponsor

Rolling out or replacing a CRM solution is a big deal. For some managers and reps, this initiative can cause concerns for a variety of reasons: People get set in their ways, they think it's Big Brother, they assume it's going to take a lot of their time, and so on. Or other top priorities at work begin creeping in, and the importance of the CRM implementation falls along the wayside.

Every project needs a champion to help drive the CRM initiative in your company. That person is there to rally support, break logjams, and ensure that your team has the resources to get things done. It's important that you identify an executive sponsor on day one and work with him or her so that person can communicate what's in it for the implementation team and set expectations for what's needed from all participants. This will go a long way in calming fears, gaining support and commitment, and nudging towards a decision when the team is at an impasse.

Building Your Project Team

As you might have already figured out, CRM is less about technology and more about people, human processes, and your business. For your company to get the most out of Salesforce, you need to develop a team made up of critical stakeholders, project resources, and a cross-section of end users. If you're implementing Salesforce for sales and marketing, that might mean that the team includes managers from sales, sales operations, IT, some respected sales reps, and hopefully a member of your executive team. This doesn't have to be a huge team, nor should members expect to be involved in this project full time. But you must have people who can speak for the business and sufficient resources to get the job done. Get every stakeholder to understand the team's objectives and buy in from the first meeting.

Evaluating Your Processes

How can you build something if you don't know what to build and why? Conduct business process reviews as key elements to your planning process. Those meetings should include a key stakeholder (or stakeholders) who can speak for his or her business and to the CRM project team (for example, a channel sales session with the head of channel sales). By doing this, you gain further agreement to your plan and ensure that you're building a solution that meets existing or desired processes of managers and their teams.

Gathering Requirements

Why are you implementing Salesforce? Is it to increase sales, improve productivity, encourage collaboration, or all three? It's nearly impossible to implement anything correctly unless you know your goal. Make your objectives measurable by applying specific success metrics to an objective. (A *success metric* is a numerical goal that you want to achieve, ideally within a specified time frame.) For example, it's one thing to say you want to reduce customer service response time. It's quite another to define that you want to reduce response time by 20 percent by the end of the year.

Defining Your Scope and Prioritizing Initiatives

You can do a lot with Salesforce, but the more complex it is, the longer the implementation will likely take and the greater the chance you'll hit a snag. As you collect the requirements of key stakeholders, prioritize initiatives and determine what's in scope and out of scope for the initial implementation. Consider keeping the implementation limited by focusing on the major priorities. Then you can extend your initiatives by building on prior success.

Modeling Salesforce to Your Business

Once you've evaluated your company's business processes, and gathered and scoped requirements from your steering committee, you next want to model Salesforce to your business. However, we realize that you're probably new to Salesforce and may have some questions as to what information should go where. For your company, what are leads, accounts, contacts, and opportunities? Make sure you check out the various process maps on the Successforce Best Practices Web site (http://success.salesforce.com) before you get started customizing things in Salesforce. If you still have some questions, make sure you ask your peers on the community forums or contact your Customer Success Manager for guidance.

Customizing for User Relevance

When designing records and layouts, keeping it simple isn't always appropriate. Some businesses do have complex needs. But be aware that long, complicated records can affect end user adoption. So don't build a field unless you think end users will use it and focus your customization on relevancy to your users. Standardize information as often as possible, using picklists rather than free text fields, which will help with more accurate reporting. For fields that have to be text fields (such as the Opportunity Name), work out a simple standard naming convention.

As you accomplish major milestones (such as customization of different records or layouts), validate your work with representative of the end users. By doing this, you can make sure at key points that you're building a solution that works for your internal customer.

Importing Clean Data

Identify your data sources that you want to bring over to Salesforce. List out where the information's coming from, what format it will be in, and how clean it'll be.

Armed with this information, you can discuss with your team the scope of your migration. Moving into Salesforce means it's time for some spring cleaning. Work with your team to identify which data sources are the most valuable and whether your end users will benefit from all that information coming over. Remember, data that doesn't make it to Salesforce doesn't necessarily disappear. You can always archive it or keep it in the legacy system.

Once you've decided on what data is going into Salesforce, you have to clean it. Scrubbing data isn't glamorous, but it has to be done. If you don't have the resources to do this, check out the AppExchange (www.salesforce.com/appexchange) for partners that help with data cleansing.

Building a Comprehensive Training Plan

As early as you can in the implementation process, start building a training plan. Don't assume that users will know what to do. And don't just rely on the generic sales training offered by Salesforce; it might not be relevant enough to your customization. Blend prerequisite classes, custom sales training, and reinforcement training in your plan. The key is to make sure that enough relevant training is provided so that people effectively and correctly use the Salesforce application. Also, be sure that your end users have personal copies of *Salesforce.com For Dummies*. Just in case.

Connecting with Peers

Now that your teams are up and running with Salesforce, you should constantly be gathering feedback and tracking how adoption is faring. Also, get out there and meet your peers — others that have rolled out Salesforce and have advice and stories to share. Through online community discussion boards, local user group meetings, and Dreamforce (salesforce.com's annual user conference), you have several channels where you can ask questions, seek guidance, and share information that can help you take your Salesforce implementation to the next level.

Index

• T •

Notes

Notes

Notes

Notes

Notes

Notes

Notes

Notes

Notes

Notes

BUSINESS, CAREERS & PERSONAL FINANCE

Fundraising For Dummies
0-7645-9847-3

Investing For Dummies
0-7645-2431-3

Also available:
- Business Plans Kit For Dummies
  0-7645-9794-9
- Economics For Dummies
  0-7645-5726-2
- Grant Writing For Dummies
  0-7645-8416-2
- Home Buying For Dummies
  0-7645-5331-3
- Managing For Dummies
  0-7645-1771-6
- Marketing For Dummies
  0-7645-5600-2
- Personal Finance For Dummies
  0-7645-2590-5*
- Resumes For Dummies
  0-7645-5471-9
- Selling For Dummies
  0-7645-5363-1
- Six Sigma For Dummies
  0-7645-6798-5
- Small Business Kit For Dummies
  0-7645-5984-2
- Starting an eBay Business For Dummies
  0-7645-6924-4
- Your Dream Career For Dummies
  0-7645-9795-7

HOME & BUSINESS COMPUTER BASICS

Laptops For Dummies
0-470-05432-8

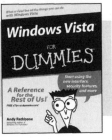

Windows Vista For Dummies
0-471-75421-8

Also available:
- Cleaning Windows Vista For Dummies
  0-471-78293-9
- Excel 2007 For Dummies
  0-470-03737-7
- Mac OS X Tiger For Dummies
  0-7645-7675-5
- MacBook For Dummies
  0-470-04859-X
- Macs For Dummies
  0-470-04849-2
- Office 2007 For Dummies
  0-470-00923-3
- Outlook 2007 For Dummies
  0-470-03830-6
- PCs For Dummies
  0-7645-8958-X
- Salesforce.com For Dummies
  0-470-04893-X
- Upgrading & Fixing Laptops For Dummies
  0-7645-8959-8
- Word 2007 For Dummies
  0-470-03658-3
- Quicken 2007 For Dummies
  0-470-04600-7

FOOD, HOME, GARDEN, HOBBIES, MUSIC & PETS

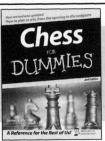

Chess For Dummies
0-7645-8404-9

Guitar For Dummies
0-7645-9904-6

Also available:
- Candy Making For Dummies
  0-7645-9734-5
- Card Games For Dummies
  0-7645-9910-0
- Crocheting For Dummies
  0-7645-4151-X
- Dog Training For Dummies
  0-7645-8418-9
- Healthy Carb Cookbook For Dummies
  0-7645-8476-6
- Home Maintenance For Dummies
  0-7645-5215-5
- Horses For Dummies
  0-7645-9797-3
- Jewelry Making & Beading For Dummies
  0-7645-2571-9
- Orchids For Dummies
  0-7645-6759-4
- Puppies For Dummies
  0-7645-5255-4
- Rock Guitar For Dummies
  0-7645-5356-9
- Sewing For Dummies
  0-7645-6847-7
- Singing For Dummies
  0-7645-2475-5

INTERNET & DIGITAL MEDIA

eBay For Dummies
0-470-04529-9

iPod & iTunes For Dummies
0-470-04894-8

Also available:
- Blogging For Dummies
  0-471-77084-1
- Digital Photography For Dummies
  0-7645-9802-3
- Digital Photography All-in-One Desk Reference For Dummies
  0-470-03743-1
- Digital SLR Cameras and Photography For Dummies
  0-7645-9803-1
- eBay Business All-in-One Desk Reference For Dummies
  0-7645-8438-3
- HDTV For Dummies
  0-470-09673-X
- Home Entertainment PCs For Dummies
  0-470-05523-5
- MySpace For Dummies
  0-470-09529-6
- Search Engine Optimization For Dummies
  0-471-97998-8
- Skype For Dummies
  0-470-04891-3
- The Internet For Dummies
  0-7645-8996-2
- Wiring Your Digital Home For Dummies
  0-471-91830-X

* Separate Canadian edition also available
† Separate U.K. edition also available

Available wherever books are sold. For more information or to order direct: U.S. customers visit www.dummies.com or call 1-877-762-2974.
U.K. customers visit www.wileyeurope.com or call 0800 243407. Canadian customers visit www.wiley.ca or call 1-800-567-4797.

SPORTS, FITNESS, PARENTING, RELIGION & SPIRITUALITY

0-471-76871-5   0-7645-7841-3

Also available:
- Catholicism For Dummies
  0-7645-5391-7
- Exercise Balls For Dummies
  0-7645-5623-1
- Fitness For Dummies
  0-7645-7851-0
- Football For Dummies
  0-7645-3936-1
- Judaism For Dummies
  0-7645-5299-6
- Potty Training For Dummies
  0-7645-5417-4
- Buddhism For Dummies
  0-7645-5359-3

- Pregnancy For Dummies
  0-7645-4483-7 †
- Ten Minute Tone-Ups For Dummies
  0-7645-7207-5
- NASCAR For Dummies
  0-7645-7681-X
- Religion For Dummies
  0-7645-5264-3
- Soccer For Dummies
  0-7645-5229-5
- Women in the Bible For Dummies
  0-7645-8475-8

TRAVEL

0-7645-7749-2   0-7645-6945-7

Also available:
- Alaska For Dummies
  0-7645-7746-8
- Cruise Vacations For Dummies
  0-7645-6941-4
- England For Dummies
  0-7645-4276-1
- Europe For Dummies
  0-7645-7529-5
- Germany For Dummies
  0-7645-7823-5
- Hawaii For Dummies
  0-7645-7402-7

- Italy For Dummies
  0-7645-7386-1
- Las Vegas For Dummies
  0-7645-7382-9
- London For Dummies
  0-7645-4277-X
- Paris For Dummies
  0-7645-7630-5
- RV Vacations For Dummies
  0-7645-4442-X
- Walt Disney World & Orlando
  For Dummies
  0-7645-9660-8

GRAPHICS, DESIGN & WEB DEVELOPMENT

0-7645-8815-X   0-7645-9571-7

Also available:
- 3D Game Animation For Dummies
  0-7645-8789-7
- AutoCAD 2006 For Dummies
  0-7645-8925-3
- Building a Web Site For Dummies
  0-7645-7144-3
- Creating Web Pages For Dummies
  0-470-08030-2
- Creating Web Pages All-in-One Desk
  Reference For Dummies
  0-7645-4345-8
- Dreamweaver 8 For Dummies
  0-7645-9649-7

- InDesign CS2 For Dummies
  0-7645-9572-5
- Macromedia Flash 8 For Dummies
  0-7645-9691-8
- Photoshop CS2 and Digital
  Photography For Dummies
  0-7645-9580-6
- Photoshop Elements 4 For Dummies
  0-471-77483-9
- Syndicating Web Sites with RSS Feeds
  For Dummies
  0-7645-8848-6
- Yahoo! SiteBuilder For Dummies
  0-7645-9800-7

NETWORKING, SECURITY, PROGRAMMING & DATABASES

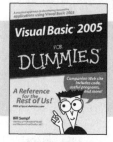 

0-7645-7728-X   0-471-74940-0

Also available:
- Access 2007 For Dummies
  0-470-04612-0
- ASP.NET 2 For Dummies
  0-7645-7907-X
- C# 2005 For Dummies
  0-7645-9704-3
- Hacking For Dummies
  0-470-05235-X
- Hacking Wireless Networks
  For Dummies
  0-7645-9730-2
- Java For Dummies
  0-470-08716-1

- Microsoft SQL Server 2005 For Dummies
  0-7645-7755-7
- Networking All-in-One Desk Reference
  For Dummies
  0-7645-9939-9
- Preventing Identity Theft For Dummies
  0-7645-7336-5
- Telecom For Dummies
  0-471-77085-X
- Visual Studio 2005 All-in-One Desk
  Reference For Dummies
  0-7645-9775-2
- XML For Dummies
  0-7645-8845-1

EALTH & SELF-HELP

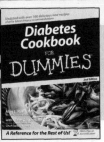

0-7645-8450-2

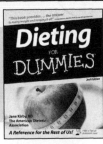

0-7645-4149-8

Also available:

Bipolar Disorder For Dummies
0-7645-8451-0

Chemotherapy and Radiation
For Dummies
0-7645-7832-4

Controlling Cholesterol For Dummies
0-7645-5440-9

Diabetes For Dummies
0-7645-6820-5* †

Divorce For Dummies
0-7645-8417-0 †

Fibromyalgia For Dummies
0-7645-5441-7

Low-Calorie Dieting For Dummies
0-7645-9905-4

Meditation For Dummies
0-471-77774-9

Osteoporosis For Dummies
0-7645-7621-6

Overcoming Anxiety For Dummies
0-7645-5447-6

Reiki For Dummies
0-7645-9907-0

Stress Management For Dummies
0-7645-5144-2

DUCATION, HISTORY, REFERENCE & TEST PREPARATION

0-7645-8381-6

0-7645-9554-7

Also available:

The ACT For Dummies
0-7645-9652-7

Algebra For Dummies
0-7645-5325-9

Algebra Workbook For Dummies
0-7645-8467-7

Astronomy For Dummies
0-7645-8465-0

Calculus For Dummies
0-7645-2498-4

Chemistry For Dummies
0-7645-5430-1

Forensics For Dummies
0-7645-5580-4

Freemasons For Dummies
0-7645-9796-5

French For Dummies
0-7645-5193-0

Geometry For Dummies
0-7645-5324-0

Organic Chemistry I For Dummies
0-7645-6902-3

The SAT I For Dummies
0-7645-7193-1

Spanish For Dummies
0-7645-5194-9

Statistics For Dummies
0-7645-5423-9

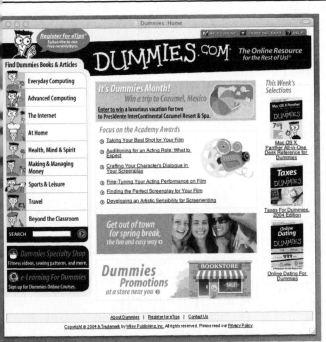

Get smart @ dummies.com®

- **Find a full list of Dummies titles**
- **Look into loads of FREE on-site articles**
- **Sign up for FREE eTips e-mailed to you weekly**
- **See what other products carry the Dummies name**
- **Shop directly from the Dummies bookstore**
- **Enter to win new prizes every month!**

Separate Canadian edition also available
Separate U.K. edition also available

Available wherever books are sold. For more information or to order direct: U.S. customers visit www.dummies.com or call 1-877-762-2974.
U.K. customers visit www.wileyeurope.com or call 0800 243407. Canadian customers visit www.wiley.ca or call 1-800-567-4797.